The Hiker's Guide
to COLORADO

Caryn and Peter Boddie

FALCON PRESS

Recreation Guides from Falcon Press

The Angler's Guide to Montana
The Beartooth Fishing Guide
The Hiker's Guide to Idaho
The Floater's Guide to Colorado
The Hiker's Guide to Utah
The Hiker's Guide to New Mexico
The Hiker's Guide to Arizona
The Hiker's Guide to Washington
The Hiker's Guide to California
The Hiker's Guide to Nevada
The Hunter's Guide to Montana
The Rockhound's Guide to Montana
The Hiker's Guide to Montana's Continental Divide Trail
The Hiker's Guide to Hot Springs in the Pacific Northwest
Recreation Guide to California's National Forests

Falcon Press is continually expanding its list of recreational guidebooks using the same general format as this book. All books include detailed descriptions, accurate maps, and all information necessary for enjoyable trips. You can order extra copies of this book and get information and prices for the books listed above by writing Falcon Press, P.O. Box 1718, Helena, MT 59624. Also, please ask for a free copy of our current catalog listing all Falcon Press books.

Library of Congress Catalog Card Number: 91-072793
ISBN: 1-56044-085-6

Manufactured in the United States of America.

Falcon Press Publishing Co., Inc.
P.O. Box 1718, Helena, MT 59624

All text, maps, and photos by the authors except as noted.
Cover Photo: by J.C. Leacock of Maroon Bells Snowmass Wilderness

ACKNOWLEDGMENTS

We had many people to thank when our book was first published in 1984. We're still grateful.

We'd like to thank everyone again, and acknowledge for the first time those of you who have helped us on this first revision of *The Hiker's Guide to Colorado.*

First and foremost, thanks again to Falcon Press Publishing, Inc. for publishing and marketing our book.

Next, special thanks to all the writers and photographers—too numerous to mention here individually—who contributed either to the initial version of the book or to this edition—and, in some cases, to both. Their names are listed after their respective hike descriptions and/or special sections on topics of interest to hikers, and beneath their photos throughout the book.

Thanks also to the employees of the U.S. Forest Service, National Park Service, and Bureau of Land Management; the Colorado Division of Parks and Recreation and the Division of Wildlife; and the Parks and Recreation departments in several cities along the Front Range.

Thank you to Colorado Mountain Club members who have long promoted hiking in the state, and to members of the various conservation organizations active in Colorado (Appendix I). We appreciate your fight to protect our wild lands and hope all hikers will join with you in the future.

Finally, thanks go again to the families in which we were raised for introducing us to our wilderness heritage, and to hiking. Because of you we are inspired to pass on a love of wilderness, natural history, and hiking to our own family, the rest of their generation, and to generations to come.— *Caryn and Peter Boddie*

Dedicated

to

Crystal Rose

and

Robin Jordan

CONTENTS

The Mountains 83

MAP OF COLORADO

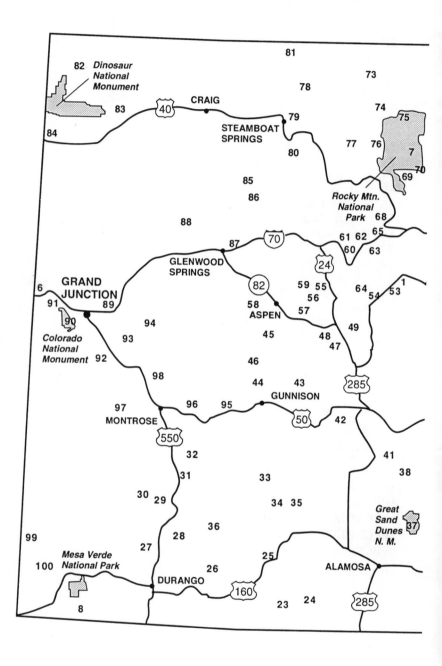

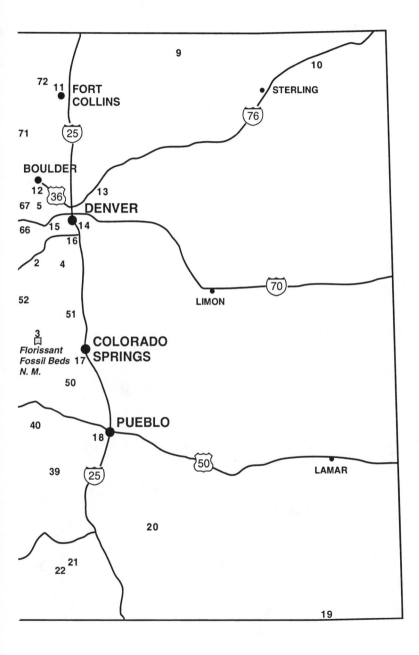

Aspen grove.

HIKING IN COLORADO, AN INTRODUCTION

There's no experience quite like that of heading off on a new hiking adventure; nothing like discovering the beauty and character of country you've never seen before. That's what *The Hiker's Guide to Colorado* is all about.

In Colorado, the opportunities for opening your eyes on new country are unlimited—the regions and terrain of this state are that diverse. You may have climbed a fourteener or fished a high lake, but never watched a sunrise from the plains, taken advantage of the trail systems that run near and through our Front Range cities, or hiked along the bottom of a sandstone canyon. The purpose of this book is to aid you in discovering ALL of Colorado.

Of course, we weren't able to cover every trail in the state. So, we've described 100 hikes representative of Colorado's various regions and terrain. If you fall in love with one area in particular, you can then turn to one of the many good regional outdoor guides available (See Appendix IV) for a more in-depth look—or simply go out and explore on your own.

We've also tried to include hikes to suit the veteran hiker and beginner, backpacker and day hiker, and hope that our descriptions will provide a variety of information on flora, fauna, geology and history—whatever a particular writer found of interest on his or her trip through the area.

The Hiker's Guide to Colorado is also dedicated to helping all kinds of people discover our state, including families with children of all ages, and people who are physically challenged whether that be because they can only walk a short distance due to their age, or because they must travel by wheelchair, or because they are visually impaired. We have included two new sections in this revision of *The Hiker's Guide* entitled "Hiking as a Family" and "Trails and Facilities for Hikers With Special Needs" in order to help everyone get out and have fun.

In addition to helping many different people discover a variety of places in Colorado, it is also our goal to impart the importance of responsible use of those places, and to give hikers information about how they can help protect out wildlands.

We must all practice minimum impact hiking and camping. We've worked with federal and state agencies in selecting many of the trails included in this guide, not wanting to publicize those that are overused nor adversely affect delicate areas. No trail can sustain careless use, however. You will find information herein to help you touch the land lightly; to enjoy but not harm it.

Our "Afterword" will explain why we must protect our wildlands and provide you with a plan of action that you may take to help. We've also included a new section entitled "Volunteering in the Outdoors," which will inform you about how you can help support hiking and wilderness preservation in Colorado.

In reading these preliminary sections you will also find information to help you organize your trips and make them safe. And, our resource section will direct you to hiking and conservation organizations, to books of interest to

Early hikers. Colorado Historical Society photo.

hikers, to sources of maps, and to the agencies that care for our trails and wild lands.

It's our hope that this book will help you discover and appreciate Colorado through hiking. Have fun!

Plains, Mountains and Plateaus: A Variety of Wild Places

From the eastern plains to the mountain ranges of central Colorado and on to the plateau and canyon country, the intricate workings of natural forces have combined to paint a landscape nearly infinite in its variety. An understanding of these workings and their resulting landforms and life zones will serve to enhance any hiker's enjoyment and appreciation of Colorado's wild places.

The following information is meant as a sort of primer to the natural history of Colorado with brief discussions of geology and ecology. Further information can be obtained through numerous field guides (birds, mammals, wildflowers, trees, geology, etc.). Additional information resources are available through libraries and museums. Many local conservation groups and government land agencies conduct guided hikes and have meetings where speakers may discuss a variety of natural history topics. The last section of this book, "Resources," will direct you to many of these additional sources of information.

Geology

Colorado occupies portions of three major physiographic provinces: the Great Plains, the Southern Rocky Mountains and the Colorado Plateaus. The landforms included in these large-scale divisions govern not only the topography of Colorado, but have largely determined the patterns of weather, plant and animal life, and human settlement in the state.

The Great Plains occupy approximately the eastern two-fifths of Colorado. They rise gently from about 3,500 feet at the eastern border of the state to about 5,000 feet at the foothills. The eastern plains are underlaid by nearly flat-lying sedimentary rocks which rise gently towards the west and are steeply upturned along the line of contact with the mountains. Most of the rocks exposed at the surface are young geologically, and contain many mammal fossils including those of ancestors of the horse and camel. The landscape of the Great Plains varies from featureless prairie to rolling hills over most of its area. In some sections, however, differential erosion of the sedimentary rocks has produced spectacular erosional remnants such as the Pawnee Buttes and deep canyons such as that of the Apishapa River.

The Rocky Mountains, for which Colorado is most well known, occupy the central and west central portions of the state. This lofty backbone of the continent, with numerous peaks reaching to more than 14,000 feet in elevation, is the source of four major rivers: the Colorado, the Rio Grande, the Arkansas, and the Platte.

The Colorado Rockies are composed of several (primarily north-south

Butterfly on Rabbitbrush.

trending) ranges interrupted by broad open basins or "parks." The mountain ranges and parks are the result of complex folding and faulting which occurred as the entire region uplifted. This complexity, combined with variations in the composition of the exposed rocks, makes each of Colorado's ranges unique. For example, the San Juan Mountains in the southwest are composed largely of volcanic breccias and lavas, while the Mosquito and Sangre de Cristo ranges are composed primarily of Paleozoic sedimentary rocks. In contrast, along most of the Front Range sedimentary rocks have been removed by erosion, exposing the ancient metamorphic and igneous rocks of the mountain core. Acting upon this complex of geologic structure and composition, the forces of erosion have sculpted the mountains of Colorado into the myriad forms we see today. Most notable of these forces has been glaciation, which has been responsible for the impressive peaks and ridges, wide U-shaped valleys and numerous lakes which characterize the higher ranges of the state.

The Colorado Plateaus occupy the western portion of Colorado. This area is characterized by a series of uplifted plateaus and moderately dipping anticlines, synclines and monoclines. These structures are dissected by many canyons and broad valleys formed by tributaries to the Colorado River. The exposed rocks are predominately sedimentary, ranging in age from recent river deposits back to the Cambrian age. In a few places, such as the Black Canyon of the Gunnison, the underlying ancient Precambrian metamorphic rocks are exposed. This incredible range in the character of rock formations over western Colorado has provided an infinitely varied source of material upon which the forces of erosion have acted. These erosional forces have stripped away the less resistant rocks leaving the resistant layers to form alternating flat mesas and cliffs. Dissecting these uplands are numerous deep canyons and broad valleys. The result is a spectacular variation in scenery providing both far-reaching vistas and intricate erosional features throughout western Colorado.

Ecology

Spread out across the framework of Colorado's landforms is an equally varied pattern of plant and animal life. Colorado displays ecological life zones ranging from the desert to the arctic, often over the space of only a few miles. These life zones are determined primarily by climatic factors, which in turn are governed largely by Colorado's topography. Two factors are dominant in this climatic-topographic relationship: elevation and the orientation to mountain barriers. Elevation of the land surface in Colorado varies by more than two miles from about 3,500 feet on the state's eastern boundary to more than 14,000 feet at the summits of several mountain peaks. The effects on temperature of this elevation range are similar to those associated with traveling a distance north from southern Colorado to above the Arctic Circle.

The relationship between precipitation and elevation is just the opposite— precipitation increases with elevation. The orientation of the mountains affects this pattern by creating a rain shadow on the leeward side. Because storm systems move predominantly from west to east across Colorado, the western slopes of the mountains generally receive greater precipitation than the eastern sides. This pattern may be observed for the length of the Continental Divide and, more locally, at individual ranges and high plateaus. In addition, there is a difference between north and south-facing slopes, with the latter receiving greater solar radiation, and being consequently drier.

In general, the types of plant and animal communities found in Colorado closely follow these large- and small-scale climatic patterns. Biologists and ecologists have categorized the plant and animal life of Colorado into several characteristic life zones. They are briefly described below, but you can obtain a far wider knowledge of them by visiting the Walter C. Mead Ecological Hall at the Denver Museum of Natural History (see Appendix IV). Beginning at the eastern border of Colorado, we find the upper Sonoran Life Zone (the Colorado plains) from 3,500 to 5,500 feet in elevation. Characterized by short grass prairie, warm canyons, prairie ponds, marshes, sand hills and bluffs, this life zone features many species of grasses, as well as cactus, yucca, pinyon and juniper. It is home to many species of birds, including three of herons and Colorado's state bird, the lark bunting.

To the west at 5,500 to 8,000 feet is the Transition-Upper Sonoran Zone, the Foothills, where ponderosa pine, Douglas fir, and Rocky Mountain juniper grow on rolling hills. Blue spruce, alder, narrow-leaf cottonwood, birch and willows grow along the streams. Animal and plant life here ranges from that of the plains to that of the higher coniferous forests—a true transition zone.

Further to the west and above the Transition Zone is the Boreal Region and within it three distinct life zones: the Canadian (8,000 to 11,000 feet), the Hudsonian (timberline-11,000 to 11,500 feet) and the Arctic-Alpine above timberline. These are the mountains of Colorado.

The Canadian Zone includes, at lower elevations lodgepole pine, aspen, Douglas fir, and ponderosa. At higher elevations you will recognize Engelmann spruce, subalpine fir, white fir, and limber pine. A plethora of wildflowers bloom in this zone during the spring and summer, including Indian paintbrush, columbine, golden banner, fairy slipper, wild iris and many, many more species.

The Hudsonian Zone at timberline is a narrow zone, characterized by bristlecone pine, Englemann spruce, and subalpine fir, twisted into odd shapes by high winds and heavy snows.

The Arctic-Alpine Zone is like the life zones of the Far North: a delicate, yet harsh ecosystem of treeless alpine tundra and sparse vegetation, but with beautiful displays of wildflowers. Here small mammals and birds make their homes in the alpine meadows and boulder fields.

Beyond the mountains and on to the western border of Colorado is another transition zone dominated by sagebrush in the intermountain valleys and basins in the west-central and northwest areas of the state and by gambel oak and ponderosa pine along the mountain margins in the southwest. Below the transition zone is the classic Upper Sonoran Zone or "pygmy forest" dominated by pinyon pine, juniper or "cedar," and rabbitbrush. Soils are rocky and well-drained. The understory of this "pinyon-juniper woodland" is sparse and includes currant, yucca, mountain mahogany, big sage, and snowberry. Grasses and herbs common to this zone are blue grama grass, western wheatgrass, Indian ricegrass, yarrow, and aster.

Denizens of the Transition-Upper Sonoran Zone are deer, elk, pronghorn antelope, coyote, bobcat, fox, mountain lion, cottontail rabbits, mice, and rattlesnakes. Birds include pinon jay, mourning dove, mountain bluebird, kestrel, red-tail hawk, green-tailed towhee, and horned lark. Bald eagles and prairie falcons are sometimes seen here as well.

Study of these life zones and the plant and animal life within them could last a lifetime. The average hiker just needs to know generally of their existence. If you find these subjects interesting, carry along field guides on some of your hikes, learn to know the names (scientific and common) of trees, birds, flowers and animals, as well as the geology of the areas you travel through. It's a lot of fun and is a good way to add to your knowledge of the State of Colorado.

Our Archaeological Resources

Colorado is a state rich not only for natural history, but in human history as well. The earliest people arrived on the eastern plains some 12,000 years ago as small hunting and gathering bands, probably migrating across the land bridge from Asia. These people hunted many now extinct large mammals in a boreal forest much cooler and moister than today's. Evidence of their lifestyle includes flakes of chert (remnants of the manufacturing of weapons and butchering tools) and fire hearths in old terrace arroyo walls, in sand dunes, and along the margins of ancient playa lakes.

Studies of soil and plant pollen indicate that the climate of Colorado gradually moderated until about 6,000 years ago. Archaeological evidence from caves and river terraces along the west slope indicates that the people responded to this climatic change by adjusting to more local ecological settings with a greater emphasis on gathering and collecting. The drier climate during this period was conducive to the preservation of more perishable materials such as sandals, wooden dart throwers and bone sewing implements. These types of artifacts have been found at habitation sites along the Gunnison, Colorado, and White Rivers.

By 2,000 years ago and until about A.D. 1300, the people inhabiting southwestern Colorado developed remarkably efficient capabilities for using regionally available resources. Agriculture and village life appeared on the highland plateau west of the San Juan and south of the LaPlata Mountains. Dwellings ranging from single-room structures to multiple-room pueblos have been identified at sites from Chimney Rock to Mancos Canyon, including the well known ruins at Mesa Verde. Evidence of irrigation, basket and pottery manufacturing, use of the bow and arrow and marked reliance on ceremonialism testify to the cultural sophistication achieved during this period.

Other areas of Colorado have provided a wide variety of natural resources to all prehistoric inhabitants, as well. Middle and South Parks were quarried for chert well prior to 6,000 years ago. Various mountain passes and subalpine pastures were seasonally exploited for game and edible plants. The San Luis Valley provided an opportunity for hunting waterfowl until modern agricultural needs affected the closed-basin water table.

The value of the archaeological evidence left by these peoples is enormous. Correct interpretation of the diverse Indian heritage of Colorado is dependent on evaluating remaining artifacts in their Plains, Great Basin, Plateau, and Intermontane contexts. Casual removal of this evidence by interested hikers and other backcountry visitors reduces the historic value of each site and gradually destroys a fragile cultural resource that is not renewable.

When you are hiking, remember that you are an essential part of a team including federal and state land management personnel working to conserve archaeological sites in Colorado. The Archaeological Resources Protection Act and State Antiquities Act encourage reporting of discovered sites to professional land managers. If you discover any prehistoric or historic sites on federal lands, report them to the appropriate land management personnel. Archaeological sites on land under state jurisdiction should be reported to the state archaeologist in Denver. Leave the "souvenirs" for those who'll come

Vandalized pictographs in southeastern Colorado.

after you to see and enjoy the intriguing archaeology of Colorado.

If you would like to learn more about Colorado archaeology, *The Archaeology of Colorado* by E. Steve Cassells (Johnson Books) provides a good overview. A visit to the Denver Museum of Natural History and University of Colorado Museum would be of interest as well. In southwestern Colorado, the Anasazi Heritage Center near Dolores, the Crow Canyon Archaeological Center near Cortez, Mesa Verde National Park, Hovenweep National Monument, and the Ute Mountain Tribal Park offer a unique combination of educational opportunities ranging from extensive museum exhibits to participation in research excavations and backcountry tours of remote ruins accompanied by an Indian guide.—*Emerson Pearson*

HIKING TECHNIQUES AND EQUIPMENT

Touching the Land Lightly

It's a special feeling to hike through pristine wilderness, imagining you're the first human being who's ever been there. It's also very disheartening to come upon evidence of other humans, unless that evidence is historic or prehistoric.

Colorado's backcountry has the capacity to handle the ever increasing number of users it will see in the coming years, but only if those users abandon the outdated ethics of past generations of hikers who left fire rings, dug trenches around tents, and set up camp near lakes and streams. As the size of our wilderness shrinks and the number of backcountry users multiplies, we must follow a new code of backcountry ethics based on one phrase: leave a minimum impact on any area you visit. The following tips will help you to develop good backcountry manners based on that idea.

When on the trail:

• Stay on the trail. Cutting switchbacks and walking alongside trails causes erosion. On the tundra and in the desert, proceed with care to protect these fragile environments.
• Leave "souvenirs" for the next hiker to see, whether they be wildflowers or Indian artifacts.
• Watch wildlife from a distance.
• If hiking with a dog, keep it under control at all times.
• Be considerate of other hikers when you meet them on the trail; be careful not to disturb the solitude and wilderness experience they may be seeking.

While camping:

• Choose a site well away from trails and lakes (at least 200 feet). This practice will both protect the water quality of high country lakes and streams, and give you and others seclusion, increasing everyone's enjoyment of the area.
• Try to camp below timberline. Alpine areas are delicate and require special care. Often, it's only a short hike to a good campsite below timberline.
• Do not build any structures at your campsite.
• Use a gas stove for cooking, if possible. But, if you do have a fire, keep it small. Dig out the native vegetation and topsoil and set it aside. Don't build a fire ring with rocks. When breaking camp, douse the fire thoroughly, scattering or burying the cold ashes. Replace with native soil and vegetation.
• Be careful with all waste. Bury human wastes at least six inches deep, 200 feet from water. Pack out all trash.
• Waste water from boiling foods should be poured around the perimeter of the fire: this keeps the fire from spreading and protects the natural vegetation as well. Wash dishes and clothing well away from streams and lakes and carefully discard dish water, perhaps in a sump hole to be covered with soil later. If you use soap, carry water at least 200 feet from a water source and wash there. Strictly follow the pack-in, pack-out rule and leave your camp-

sites and the backcountry, in general, as you found it. You will then be doing your part to protect wilderness for those who'll follow.

Dress and Equipment for Backcountry Travel

Nothing ruins a hiking or backpacking trip faster than improper clothing and equipment. What follows are some time-tested ideas on proper clothing and equipment for backcountry travel.

The most important thing to keep in mind is to dress in layers. Three layers of clothing, at least, will allow you to adapt to weather conditions as they change. The first layer, next to your skin, should provide some ventilation, the next—of wool or down—should insulate. The third should be wind and waterproof. How much money you spend on dressing for the outdoors is really up to you. You can buy the most expensive gear from your local sports store, or make do with military surplus. Just make sure the clothes you take with you will keep you comfortable, warm, and dry in any kind of weather.

Another essential item of clothing is a wool hat—if you'll be hiking in the high country. It is well known that a large percentage of body heat is lost during cold weather when a hat isn't worn, so take one with you (and some mittens or gloves). It's good protection against hypothermia.

Probably the most important equipment you'll wear are your boots; pick them carefully. Be prepared to spend a few extra dollars. The old adage that you get what you pay for definitely applies. Spending extra time picking out your boots will pay off in the long run.

Shop in a reputable store and take the time to ask the sales people some questions. Ask about the "welt" of the boot; the manner in which the leather upper part of the boot is attached to the sole. Norwegian welting lends itself to a heavier boot; Littleway to a lighter boot (these are your best bets). Ask about seams, making sure your boots won't be causing pressure points on your feet. Look for quality boots made in one piece, with only one side or back seam. Look also for boots with a firm heel counter, box toe and arch for good support and protection and make sure you'll have proper ankle support for the kind of hiking you'll be doing. Inspect the backstay, which covers the seam on the back of the boot. It should be narrow. Finally, consider whether the boots are too heavy or too light for the type of hiking you plan to be doing and wear them around a bit. There are many lightweight boots that have evolved from running shoes. They are moderately priced and feature new materials that keep feet dry but still let feet breath. Make sure the fit is right.

After you've chosen your boots, take good care of them! Ask your sales person how.

Now that you're clothed and booted, let's take a look at the other equipment you'll want to take with you. If you're day hiking, you won't need too much. The essentials are a daypack for carrying your gear, a water bottle with water, sunglasses, and sunscreen for protection from Colorado's high altitude ultraviolet radiation, a map and compass, and your emergency gear: matches and a small candle, a pocket knife, high energy food such as hard candy, dried fruits or nuts, a first aid kit and survival kit (see "Backcountry Safety").

If you are backpacking, you'll need to take all these things plus some others. To begin with you'll need a good sleeping bag—again take care to select the bag that best fits your needs. Most backpackers prefer a bag that will take them through three seasons—all but winter—with a high loft and a shell of ripstop nylon, which is durable and also "breathes" well. Check the stitching on the sleeping bag you plan to buy: stitches should be even and there should not be less than ten of them to an inch. Next, you'll want a lightweight tent. There are so many new shapes and sizes of tents on the market these days that it shouldn't be hard for you to find one to suit your needs. Just decide whether you'll be using the tent in humid or arid environments—humid and you'll need room to store gear when it rains and good ventilation; arid and you'll need less room, but still want good ventilation. In any case, you'll want good mosquito netting and a tent that will withstand occasional downpours and heavy winds. Again, you have a wide variety of price ranges to choose from, and, once more, you get what you pay for. Just remember, when it's raining or blowing out there, you'll want a tent that will keep you dry and won't fall down in the middle of the night.

Packs are another item for backpackers. Once more, take the time to find one that fits and suits your anticipated needs. There are many types of packs on the market today with internal or external frames and a variety of pockets, straps, and other features. Get a good sales person to help you find the pack for you. Then wear it around for awhile with some weight in it, and make sure it's what you need.

One of the best ways to find the equipment you like best is to rent for an outing or two. You may save quite a bit of money by not buying before you

Proper clothing is important for comfortable hiking. Colorado Historical Society photo.

All hikers should know how to use a topographic map.

really know what you want. Beyond the clothing and equipment listed above, what you take on your hiking and backpacking outings is up to you. Just keep in mind your own comfort and safety in the wilderness and consult the checklist in Appendix VI before you go to make sure you have everything you need and want to take.

About the Maps

The maps that accompany each of the hikes have been prepared from United States Geological Survey (USGS) or United States Forest Service (USFS) maps. Each map is accompanied by a small map of Colorado indicating the location of the hike in the state. There is also a north-south directional indicator and a scale. A general legend for all the maps is on page 12.

While these maps are up-to-date, you should also take along the appropriate USGS topographic map(s) on more difficult hikes, or the appropriate Trails Illustrated maps—excellent maps based on USGS maps. (See Appendix V for outlets around the state.) The USFS maps are also helpful, offering an excellent overview of an entire national forest. The appropriate maps for each hike are listed in the introductory information prior to each hike description.

If you are not used to reading maps and not familiar with topographic maps, we would suggest that you set out on one of the easier hikes with a national forest map, topo map, compass and the book map and learn how to use all of them. Then when you really need a map you'll know how to use it. We also suggest consulting with the appropriate land management agency before your hike if you must drive to the trailhead on a low-grade road, particularly after bad weather.

MAP LEGEND

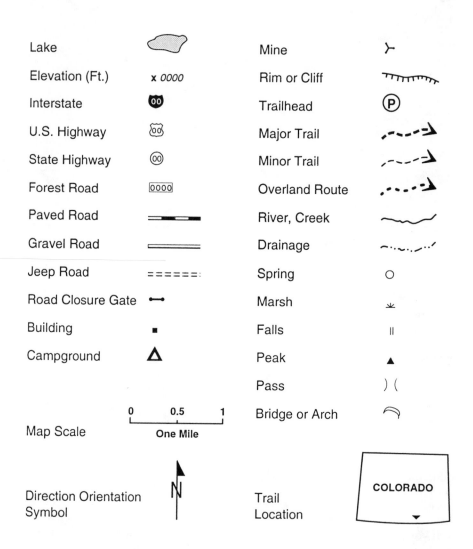

Lake		Mine	
Elevation (Ft.)	x *0000*	Rim or Cliff	
Interstate		Trailhead	
U.S. Highway		Major Trail	
State Highway		Minor Trail	
Forest Road	0000	Overland Route	
Paved Road		River, Creek	
Gravel Road		Drainage	
Jeep Road	======:	Spring	O
Road Closure Gate		Marsh	
Building	■	Falls	||
Campground	△	Peak	▲
		Pass	) (

0   0.5   1

Map Scale   **One Mile**

Bridge or Arch

N

Direction Orientation
Symbol

Trail
Location

COLORADO

MAKING IT A SAFE TRIP

Backcountry Safety

The history books are full of stories of men who ventured into the wilds of Colorado unprepared and overconfident only to meet with a less than pleasant end or, if they were lucky, to be rescued by wiser travelers. Safety advice can be never ending—we won't overdo it—but to make your hiking trips safe and enjoyable, follow these tips. It's been said often enough, but it bears repeating—be prepared:

• Travel with the proper equipment to suit the climate, altitude and any weather you might encounter.

• Dress in layers you can put on and take off with changes in the weather.

• Carry a first aid kit, topo map, and compass on more difficult hikes—and know how to use them. Also, take along matches and some high energy food. A space blanket is also a good thing to have in case of emergency (see checklist).

Be smart:

• Don't underestimate the power of nature. Know how to read and interpret the weather and watch it carefully. You don't want to find yourself atop an exposed ridge in the middle of an electrical storm, in a gully during a flash flood, or at a high altitude during a snow storm.

• Know how to react to emergency situations. Take a first-aid course.

• Listen to your body. Learn the symptoms of hypothermia (see "Hypothermia and Other Hazards") and guard against fatigue.

Be cautious:

• In general, don't take unnecessary risks by glissading down steep snowfields with cliffs or boulders below, climbing rock faces without ropes, exploring abandoned mines, jumping ravines or canyons, or wading across swift mountain streams.

• Always file a "flight plan" with someone before you leave, telling them where you're going and when you'll return.

• Do not drink the water unless you are positive it is safe to do so. Boil or chemically treat it. Become familiar with *Giardia* and the illness it causes, giardiasis (see "Water: To Drink or Not to Drink").

• Avoid hiking alone.

• When hiking in a group, gear your pace to the slowest member and don't push on to a destination if a group member is really not up to it. Don't split up.

• Follow your topo map from the beginning of your hike and there is little chance you'll become lost.

• If you do become lost, don't panic. Sit down and relax; consult your map and compass. Thousands of hikers have spent unplanned nights in the wilderness and if you followed the rules and left word with someone of your whereabouts and expected return, they'll soon be searching for you. In the meantime, find shelter for yourself and stay put. (Children are taught these days to "hug a tree"—good advice for adults, too.)

View from near the summit of Saint Vrain Mountain of Long's Peak and Pagoda Mountain.
Norm Nielsen photo.

Survival kit

Compass, whistle, matches in waterproof container, candle, surgical tubing, emergency fishing gear, sixty feet of six-pound line, six hooks, six lead shots, and six trout flies, safety pins, copper wire, signal mirror, fire starter, aluminum foil, water purification tablets, space blanket and flare.

First aid kit

Sewing needle, snake bite kit, twelve aspirin or acetametaphin, antibacterial ointment, two antiseptic swabs, two butterfly bandages, adhesive tape, four adhesive strips, four gauze pads, two triangular bandages, twelve codeine tablets, two inflatable splints, moleskin, one roll of three-inch gauze and lightweight first-aid instructions.

Hypothermia and Other Hazards

Be aware of the danger of hypothermia—subnormal temperature of the body. Lowering of internal temperature leads to mental and physical collapse.

Hypothermia is caused by exposure to cold, and it is aggravated by wetness, wind, and exhaustion. It is the number one killer of outdoor recreationists.

The first step is exposure and exhaustion. The moment you start to lose heat faster than your body produces it, you are undergoing exposure. Two things happen: You exercise to stay warm and your body makes involuntary adjustments to preserve normal temperature in the vital organs. Both responses drain your energy reserves. The only way to stop the drain is to reduce the degree of exposure.

The second step is hypothermia. If exposure continues until your energy reserves are exhausted, cold reaches the brain, depriving you of judgment and

and reasoning power. You will not be aware that this is happening. You will lose control of your hands. This is hypothermia. Your internal temperature is sliding downward. Without treatment, this slide leads to stupor, collapse, and death.

To defend against hypothermia, stay dry. When clothes get wet, they lose about ninety percent of their insulating value. Wool loses heat; cotton, down and some synthetics lose more.

Choose rainclothes that cover the head, neck, body and legs, and provide good protection against wind-driven rain.

Understand cold. Most hypothermia cases develop in air temperature between thirty and fifty degrees Fahrenheit.

If your party is exposed to wind, cold, and wet, think hypothermia. Watch yourself and others for these symptoms: uncontrollable fits of shivering; vague, slow, slurred speech; memory lapses; incoherence; immobile, fumbling hands; frequent stumbling, lurching gait; drowsiness (to sleep is to die); apparent exhaustion; and inability to get up after a rest.

When a member of your party has hypothermia, he/she may deny any problem. Believe the symptoms, not the victim. Even mild symptoms demand treatment.

- Get the victim out of the wind and rain.
- Strip off all wet clothes.
- If the victim is only mildly impaired, give warm drinks. Get the person into warm clothes and a warm sleeping bag. Well-wrapped, warm (not hot) rocks or canteens will help.
- If the victim is badly impaired, attempt to keep him/her awake. Put the victim in a sleeping bag with another person—both stripped. If you have a double bag, put the victim between two warm people.
- Build a fire to warm the camp.—*U.S. Forest Service*

Water: To Drink or Not to Drink?

There are few backpacking pleasures that can top a cool drink from a high country lake or stream. Whether on a day hike close to a large metropolitan area or miles into the backcountry, the refreshing sip along the trail is a tradition.

Unfortunately, that cool sip of water from a cold mountain stream may be hazardous to your health.

The most common problem is a waterborne parasite called *Giardia lamblia*, an invisible protozoan which, when ingested, can have results far from inconsequential. *Giardia* is now reported as being in epidemic proportions in Colorado.

The illness (called giardiasis, "beaver fever," or "backpacker's diarrhea") is caused by the ingestion of the dormant cyst form of the protozoan. These cysts can survive in cold (40°F) streams for up to three months and can be spread by the droppings of dogs, cats, horses, cattle, beavers, rabbits, marmots, ground squirrels, elk, and especially people.

The cysts are activated in the small intestine of the host, changing into the reproductive trophozoite stage, which attaches to the wall of the intestine. Symptoms may appear from within several days to three weeks after ingestion of the cysts and are characterized by severe diarrhea, weight loss, "rotten egg" belches, fatigue, and cramps. Apparently, some people are "carriers" of giardiasis and may have only very mild symptoms of the disease.

If you suspect you have the disease, see your doctor immediately. Giardiasis must be treated by a doctor. Quinacrine and metonidazole (Flagl) are most often used in treatment. Both have unpleasant side effects.

The only thing worse than coming down with giardiasis after a trip into the backcountry is coming down with it during a trip in the backcountry. There is little you can do, except try to get to a physician as best you can. You probably won't feel like eating anything, but you should avoid foods such as dairy products (milk, cheese, etc.) which may only worsen your discomfort. It is

River bottom flora.

important to drink plenty of fluids, in order to lessen the dehydrating effects of the illness. Also, stomach coating medicines such as Pepto-Bismol and Milk of Magnesia may calm (but not cure) the intestinal cramps and allow you to hike out to civilization.

How can you prevent the spread of this nasty protozoan? By practicing good sanitary habits in the wilderness. Studies done in Colorado indicate that backpackers may be the most common cause of the spread of *Giardia* because of improper human waste disposal. Bury feces at least 200 feet away from any waterway and cover them with six inches of organic soil to aid in decomposition. If you travel with dogs or horses, keep them out of streams and lakes as much as possible.

The difficulty of controlling the organism stems in part from its extremely small size and its resistance to chemical treatments, and in part to the cold mountain waters. Because of the cold water temperatures, chlorine, halazone, and iodine treatments may be required in greater concentration or for longer treatment times than is either safe or convenient. Any chemical treatment kit should include thorough instructions for use in varying temperatures and water chemistry and state its effectiveness against *Giardia*.

Even the time-honored method of boiling water is not always 100 percent effective. This is due to Colorado's high elevations. As you go up in elevation, the decreasing air pressure causes water to boil at a lower temperature, and the one-minute boiling time which is effective against *Giardia* and other organisms at sea level, might barely phase the critters at your timberline campsite. To be safe, you should boil water for a minimum of five minutes anywhere in Colorado and increase that for very high elevations or whenever the water is cloudy or muddy. Extreme conditions may require boiling for up to thirty minutes.

Fortunately, there is an easier solution. Recent mechanical filters have become available which will remove *Giardia* and other microscopic organisms. Two of these, First Need and Katadan, are designed specifically for backcountry use and are tested effective against *Giardia*. A caution is in order, however: no filter device is effective unless properly used and maintained. Be sure to follow instructions.

Before purchasing any filter for backcountry use, be sure that it has a five micron or smaller pore size (smaller than a *Giardia* cyst), or that it specifically states "effective against *Giardia*." Before you buy the filter, also make sure that you understand how to take care of it.

Proper treatment of water in the backcountry will keep you from being infected with *Giardia*, and proper sanitary practices in the backcountry will help keep others from being infected.

Altitude or Mountain Sickness

It takes two to three days to acclimate to Colorado's high altitudes, particularly if you are coming from sea level. You may experience what is called altitude or mountain sickness while hiking if you do not allow time for acclimation. This condition is caused by a lack of oxygen at high altitude, resulting in a general "sick all over" feeling.

You may notice that you or someone in your party is experiencing nausea, dizziness, headache, and loss of appetite.

• Stop and rest.
• Go slower.

- Have the victim drink plenty of water (making sure he/she is also getting enough sodium, either in food or tablets).
- Have the victim eat high energy foods.

If these treatments don't help after a period of time, the only option is to go to a lower elevation where there is more oxygen.

VOLUNTEERING IN THE OUTDOORS

How would you like to enjoy exerting yourself in the outdoors, meet some great people, see new country, and do something good for our state? You can do it all by volunteering in the outdoors. Colorado needs volunteers of all ages and interests.

There are exciting jobs in beautiful parts of our state. You won't earn money doing them, but many expenses related to volunteer jobs are tax deductible, you may receive free lodging or a parking site for a recreation vehicle, and sometimes there is subsistence pay. You'll also gain valuable experience. The jobs range from operating computers to maintaining wilderness trails to greeting tourists in Colorado's eleven national forests. You can also help people who have special needs get out into Colorado's outdoors by building trails for folks who are wheelchair bound, by guiding someone who is visually impaired—there are any number of ways you can help. Many children would love to explore the outdoors but have no one to take them. There are organizations that would love to have you share your love of nature with a child, among them: Big Brothers/Sisters of America and of Canada, 4-H Clubs of America, Boys and Girls Clubs of America, Camp Fire, Salvation Army, and YMCA's all over the country. Your help is needed by these organizations, but they will check your qualifications (and intentions) very carefully. Check your local phone book for their numbers.

If you are a pragmatic sort and you need a concrete reason to volunteer, consider this: you have a real stake in keeping up our outdoors: our trails, wildlife habitat, trout streams, historic cabins or sod houses, trees, and wilderness. As a Coloradan, you own a large percentage of the state from parks and county open space to state recreation areas, national forests, wildlife refuges, and Bureau of Land Management lands. These lands not only provide you with beauty and recreation to enjoy, but also protect our state's economy by encouraging tourism. You can help to protect your piece, and all of Colorado.

If you are a visitor to Colorado, you are encouraged to return to our state and join us in volunteering in the outdoors, too. It really is a wonderful way to get to know parts of the state and the people who live here. Families, clubs, youth groups, teenagers, retirees, college students: all can contribute.

One of the best ways to volunteer is to choose an area of the state that you particularly enjoy, or that interests you, then look up the district office of the appropriate land management agency in that area in Appendix II or III of this book and contact them directly. Tell them you are interested in volunteering and ask what needs they have, also let them know what your special interests are. Or, call the regional office listed at the end of this section and ask where they need help.

You may also want to join Volunteers for Outdoor Colorado (VOC). VOC is a non-profit organization that increases Coloradans' sense of responsibility for their public lands, and helps to maintain and improve those public lands through p73 volunteer efforts. Members receive the VOC quarterly newsletter and updates describing volunteer opportunities and outdoor excursions. Discounts for outdoor-related products and services are some of the "perks" that also come from belonging to VOC. Their address is listed at the end of this section.

The American Hiking Society (AHS) also publishes a directory entitled *Helping Out in the Outdoors: A Directory of Volunteer Jobs & Internships in Parks and Forests*. A two year, four issue subscription is $12. A single copy of the current issue is $3. Make checks payable to: "AHS Helping Out." Their address is: American Hiking Society, 1015 31st Street, N.W., Washington, DC 20007.

Not every volunteer job will be listed in either the VOC newsletter or the AHS directory. You may want to check any special columns on volunteering in your local newspaper, look in your local phone book in the white business pages under "volunteer," and, again, contact the land management agencies directly. Here are some Colorado organizations that could use your help:

Bureau of Land Management
Colorado State Office
2850 Youngfield St.
Lakewood, CO 80215

Colorado Division of Parks and
    Outdoor Recreation
1313 Sherman St., Room 618
Denver, CO 80203
(303) 866-3437

Colorado Division of Wildlife
6060 Broadway
Denver, CO 80216
(303) 291-7239

Colorado Mountain Club
2530 W. Alameda Ave.
Denver, CO 80219
(303) 922-8315

National Park Service VIP
    (Volunteers in the Parks)
    Coordinator
Rocky Mountain Regional Office
655 Parfet St., P.O. Box 25287
Lakewood, CO 80225
(303) 236-8650

Sierra Club
Rocky Mountain Chapter
2239 E. Colfax Ave.
Denver, CO 80206
(303) 321-8292

The Colorado Outdoor Education
    Center for the Handicapped
P.O. Box 697
Breckenridge, CO 80424
(303) 453-6422

U.S. Forest Service
11177 W. Eighth Ave.,
P.O. Box 25127
Lakewood, CO 80225
(303) 236-9628 ·

Volunteers for Outdoor Colorado
1410 Grant St., Suite B-105
Denver, CO 80203
(303) 830-7792

Wilderness on Wheels Foundation
7125 W. Jefferson Ave #455
Lakewood, CO 80235
(303) 936-8100

Any volunteering you can do in Colorado's outdoors will be appreciated by all of us. Thanks for your efforts.

THE HIKES

Trails and Facilities for Hikers With Special Needs

Happily, in this second edition of the Hiker's Guide to Colorado, we are able to include information on Colorado trails and facilities that suit hikers who have special needs. Now the whole family can go hiking—and camping—from babies in strollers and newly walking toddlers to elderly family members and people of all ages with various disabilities.

Thanks go to Roger West, founder of the Wilderness on Wheels Foundation (WOW), and Sharon Harms for providing us with a list of US Forest Service and Colorado Division of Parks facilities in Colorado through their newspaper Rollin' On Times. We have augmented this list with more hikes and facilities throughout Colorado. Thanks also to Roger for providing us with a hike description of his innovative and excellent facility at the foot of Kenosha Pass in central Colorado. (The description is at the end of this section.)

We hope you and your family enjoy some—or all—of the trails and facilities listed below and that you may want to spend some time volunteering to help make more such places a reality. Your help is needed! (See "Volunteering in the Outdoors" for information.)

Because we realize people have different types and varying degrees of disabilities and special needs we recommend that you be sure to call the appropriate land management agency to check the conditions and accessibility of trails and facilities and to make reservations, if they are required, before you go.

The hikes in our book that are accessible or accessible with assistance are the following:

Mesa Trail
Barr Lake State Park Trail
Highline Canal
Poudre River Trail
Monument Valley Trail
Roxborough Park

Arkansas River Trail
Florrisant Fossil Beds National Monument
Parts of the Dillon Pinnacles and Crystal Creek trails
Wilderness on Wheels

Please see the Table of Contents for the pages on which these descriptions begin.

Colorado Division of Parks and Outdoor Recreation

There are thirty-three state parks, all of which have different levels of accessibility for people with special needs. General information is available at (303) 866-3437.

The parks that feature hiking as accessible or as accessible with assistance are:
Barr Lake State Park (303) 659-6005
Boyd Lake State Recreation Area (303) 669-1739
Chatfield State Recreation Area (303) 791-7275
Castlewood Canyon State Park (303) 688-5242

Cherry Creek State Recreation Area (303) 699-3860
Island Acres State Recreation Area (303) 464-0548
Pueblo State Recreation Area (719) 561-9320
Ridgeway State Recreation Area (303) 249-7812
Stagecoach State Recreation Area (303) 879-3922
Vega State Recreation Area (303) 487-3407.

Many of these also feature camping, fishing, picnic areas, and even hunting and fishing, and have visitor's centers. All but three state parks (Mancos, Navajo, and Sweitzer Lake state recreation areas) have restrooms that are accessible or accessible with assistance.

US Forest Service Trails and Facilities

Forest Service sites featuring trails that are accessible or accessible with assistance are listed here. Phone numbers and addresses for USFS Ranger District offices are listed under "Resources" at the end of *The Hiker's Guide.*

Arapaho National Forest, Middle Park Ranger District: Williams Fork Boardwalk, southeast of Ute Pass off of Grand County Road 30: a 1,600-foot boardwalk, campground, and natural surfaces.

Arapaho National Forest, Sulphur Ranger District: One-mile trail, north of Granby: hard-pack gravel between Shadow Mountain and Pine Beach picnic areas.

Pike National Forest, Pikes Peak Ranger District: BPW Nature Trail at Rampart Reservoir, twenty miles west of Colorado Springs: 2,100-foot packed-gravel trail, Braille information, restroom.

Pike National Forest, South Platte Ranger District: Buffalo Creek fishing trail, fifty miles southwest of Denver (take US 285 to Pine Jct., go south on Colorado Hwy. 126 for ten miles): one-fourth mile treated hard-surface trail, picnic area, campsites, restroom. Waterton Canyon Recreation Area, south of Chatfield Reservoir on Wadsworth Blvd: hard-surface trail, restrooms.

Roosevelt National Forest, Boulder District: Camp Dick, five miles north of Ward: 300-foot paved fishing trail along the bank of Middle St. Vrain Creek.

Roosevelt National Forest, Estes/Poudre District: Big Thompson Fishing Access, (west of Loveland) 2.5 miles west of Drake: boardwalk to sixty-foot fishing platform on Big Thompson River.

Routt National Forest, Hahns Peak District: Fish Creek Falls, four miles northeast of Steamboat Springs: 2,200-foot asphalt trail.

San Isabel National Forest, San Carlos District: Lake Isabel, forty-five miles southwest of Pueblo at San Isabel: 1,500-foot asphalt trail, 2,500-square-foot fishing pier, picnic sites, restroom.

San Juan National Forest, Animas District: Animas Overlook, eleven miles west of Durango: seven-tenths of a mile of nature trail, natural surface, and vista points.

San Juan National Forest, Pagosa District: Chimney Rock Archaeological Area, east of Durango: 1,500-foot natural surface trail, restroom.

Uncompahgre National Forest, Norwood District: Lizard Head Pass Overlook, twelve miles south of Telluride: trail to overlook, picnic sites, gravel surfaces, restroom.

White River National Forest, Aspen District: Maroon Lake Overlook, eleven miles southwest of Aspen: paved parking area and restroom. Braille Trail, twenty miles east of Aspen: .25 mile gravel-surface trail with braille interpretive signs and restroom.

White River National Forest, Holy Cross District: Camp Hale Picnic Area, fifteen miles south of Minturn: 3,000-foot paved trail, picnic table, restrooms.

In addition, many USFS campgrounds and day use areas are accessible or accessible with assistance. Contact the appropriate ranger districts for more information before you head off for a camping and hiking adventure.

National Parks

Of the nine national parks and monuments in Colorado, all are listed as having some degree of accessibility to people with special needs. Some have hiking trails that are wheelchair accessible while others offer opportunities for fishing and picnicking. Call for more information.

National Parks in Colorado: Bent's Old Fort: accessible restrooms, tours given (719) 384-2596; Black Canyon of the Gunnison National Monument: accessible restrooms at Gunnison Point Visitor's Center; Tomichi Point Overlook accessible (303) 249-7036; Colorado National Monument: accessible trails, picnic grounds, restrooms, visitor's center, and overlooks of desert canyons (303) 858-3617; Curecanti National Recreation Area: accessible trails, camping, fishing, picnicking, and restrooms (303) 641-2337; Dinosaur National Monument: restrooms, overlooks, and dinosaur quarry accessible (303) 374-2216; Florissant Fossil Beds National Monument (see description on page 34): accessible trails, restrooms, visitor's center(719) 748-3253; Great Sand Dunes National Monument: campground and restrooms accessible, but there is no trail into dunes (719) 378-2312; Mesa Verde National Park: campgrounds and visitor's center accessible, cliff houses not (303) 529-4461. Rocky Mountain National Park: many accessible trails and braille guides; Handicamp at Sprague Lake: 660-foot hard-packed trail following the shoreline and leading to campsites, picnic tables and restrooms. Reservations required (303) 586-2371.

Other Accessible Trails and Facilities:

Anasazi Heritage Center, two miles west of Dolores on C-184, (303) 882-4811. Trail to overlook ruins and reservoir, museum with Indian artifacts, restrooms.

Breckenridge/Vail Bike Path, follows C-9 and I-70. Paved bike path winds through mountain valleys and over a pass.

Cortez/Centennial City Parks, in town of Cortez, (303) 565-3414. Trails, restrooms and swimming.

Easter Seals Handicamp, ten miles west of Idaho Springs off I-70, (303) 892-6063. Organized outdoor activities.

Keystone Village, six miles east of Dillon on US 6, (303) 534-7712. Walkways and bike paths around the village at the base of the ski area.

McPhee Reservoir Recreation Center, eight miles west of Dolores on C-184, (303) 882-7296. Campgrounds, marina, restrooms, trail to overlook of reservoir.

Rifle Falls & Rifle Gap State Park, north of Rifle on C-325, (303) 866-3437. Trail to falls, stream and lake fishing, restrooms, camping, swim beach.

Rio Grande Trail, downtown Aspen, (303) 925-1940. Two miles of paved trail along an old railroad grade.

Silver Jack Recreation Area, thirty miles southeast of Montrose, (303) 249-3711. Paved campsites, picnic area and trail to overlook.

Two Rivers Park, downtown Glenwood Springs, (303) 945-6589. Trails, picnicking, restrooms at the confluence of the Colorado and Roaring Fork rivers.

Walden Pond Wildlife Habitat, four miles NE of Boulder, (303) 441-3950. Dirt trail, stocked trout pond.

Winter Park Ski Area, twenty miles N of I-70 on US 40, (303)892-0961 (v/TDD*). Trails and picnic area at the base of the ski area.

Resources

Colorado Outdoor Education Center for the Handicapped
P.O. Box 697
Breckenridge, CO 80424
(303) 453-6422

Denver Commission on the Disabled
303 W. Colfax Ave.
Denver, CO 80204
(303) 575-3056 (vTDD*), 575-3840 (TDD**)

Denver Parks and Recreation
Special Needs Coordinator
1805 Bryant
Denver, CO 80204
(303) 575-2757 (v/TDD*)

Wilderness on Wheels Foundation
7125 W. Jefferson Ave. Suite 455
Lakewood, CO 80235
(303) 988-2212

*voice or telecommunication device for the deaf
**telecommunications device for the deaf

HIKE 1 *WILDERNESS ON WHEELS*

General description: An accessible eight-foot-wide boardwalk beginning along the bank of Kenosha Creek and continuing up the side of North Twin Cone Peak.

General location: Fifty-four miles southwest of Denver.

Degree: Easy.

Length: 3,000 feet.

Elevation: 9,100 to 9,250 feet.

Special attractions: Easily accessible from the Denver Metro area; designed for wheelchair use, the boardwalk rises no more than one foot for each twelve feet of length.

Best season: Open between mid-April and mid-October by reservation.

For more information: Wilderness On Wheels Foundation, 7125 West Jefferson Ave., #455, Denver, CO 80235, (303) 988-2212 (reservations can be made at this number).

The hike: On the edge of the Continental Divide, Wilderness On Wheels

Hikers enjoy the Wilderness on Wheels facility near Denver. Photo by Rae Jean Matlack.

(WOW) is a model wilderness-access facility being developed to stimulate people to provide access for disabled persons to natural wilderness environments.

While the non-profit goal is to build a seven-mile boardwalk to the top of North Twin Cone Peak, one mile of the boardwalk is currently available for the enjoyment of persons with disabilities and their able-bodied friends and families.

To reach WOW, take US Highway 285 west from Denver through the towns of Conifer, Bailey, and Grant. Exactly 3.8 miles west of Grant turn left or south into the WOW entrance, marked with a large sign.

The boardwalk follows the bank of Kenosha Creek for about 1,000 feet. Lively brook trout dart from deep pool to underwater cavern. A small pond is stocked with rainbows. Turning into the mountain, the trail begins to climb through a veritable garden—one of Colorado's lush forests—where wildflowers dazzle the senses. Majestic evergreens flank the level wooden path that scales ever upward along the steep side of a rocky mountain. Following the contour of the land, the trail curves into a deep gulch. Huge moss-covered rock outcroppings sing their melody of color. A gentle breeze sets aspen leaves into motion. It's the music of wilderness, and one can enjoy it on wheels.

All manner of wildlife live here. Elk, deer, bear, cougar, owl, eagle, raven, rabbit, raccoon, grouse, porcupine, weasel, fox, coyote, and more.

In addition to the trail, accessible sites for camping have been prepared. Tent decks elevated to the height of the seat of a wheelchair are complemented by elevated cooking grills. Picnic tables are present. Accessible restrooms are also available, but, as in any wilderness environment, hikers or campers must pack out their own trash.

Please note: hikers are not encouraged to bring dogs, but if they are along they MUST be kept on a short leash. Reservations are necessary at WOW. There is no charge for using the facility. However, because the foundation is not funded by any government source, donations are requested. Volunteer labor and donated materials are always welcome, as well—*Roger West*

HIKING AS A FAMILY

Hiking as a family is especially challenging—and rewarding! The challenges: buying and carrying gear for people with differing needs; motivating children; lowering expectations to match the abilities of the slowest or youngest person in your family; and handling crises. The rewards: fun and time to be together apart from everyday distractions; time to share adventures, accomplishments, discoveries, and create memories that will last a lifetime.

Additionally, you have the opportunity to give a bit of sanity to your children by introducing them to wilderness through hiking. "I cannot imagine a sane life without wilderness. . .Wilderness is essential in the lives of my children," wrote Edward Abbey. Even in small doses, getting out and exploring our national forests, parks, mountain parks, and wilderness areas gives our children the sense that they have a home on the earth, and that they have a stake in taking care of it. That kind of "grounding" is very valuable now when people are so often insulated and isolated from the steady, peaceful (though changeable) natural world.

Also, you have the chance to see the natural world through the eyes of a child again. Children may not hike as far with you as you'd like, but they will take you further in imagination and insight than you've allowed yourself to go in some time. They'll help you to see again—and listen, and smell, and feel.

Our goal in this section of *The Hiker's Guide to Colorado* is to help you get out there with your family, successfully! The information that follows is meant to help you prepare for your trips; know what you need to take along; understand how to hike with children so everyone has fun; and use helpful resources. We will also introduce you to seven easy to moderate hikes that are especially good for families. Of course, many of the hikes throughout this book are appropriate for families, but this is a starting point, and some of these first hikes feature added attractions that will be of interest to children.

Fortunately, our hiking resources in Colorado can meet the needs of all of the family: youngsters and oldsters, handicapped and able-bodied. So when you think of hiking with family, think all of the family. Our section on resources for hikers with special needs will introduce you to some hikes that are appropriate for oldsters who may not be able to walk too far, as well as handicapped individuals. The whole family can have fun in Colorado's outdoors. And, don't feel that you have to be a "traditional" family to get out hiking together. Whatever family is to you, hiking with family can be fun.

We hope the rest of this section of *The Hiker's Guide to Colorado* will help you go hiking as a family.

Preparation

Preparation is so important. Prepare well for your family hikes and you will have the freedom to be flexible, laugh at the mishaps you encounter, and be spontaneous. You'll be able to enjoy the serendipitous discoveries, pleasures, and adventures that arise when you're hiking with your family.

To begin with, involve all members of the family in the preparations. Choose your hikes together, with the youngest, or slowest, or least able-bodied person in mind and be as realistic as possible about what every member of your family can do. You may want to take several walks around your neighborhood as a family to get an idea of how fast or how slow everyone will go. Gather information on the hike and buy the maps you'll need. Talk about how long it will take to get to your destination, how far the hike will be and what children can expect to see and do.

How far can kids go? The key principle in hiking as a family—and this can't be overemphasized—is to set your pace and the distance you plan to hike by the abilities of the slowest member of your family. Children should set the pace for the adults, not the other way around. Consider the age and activity level of your children when you're choosing a hike. Veteran hikers often take small babies on long hikes because they can be carried and sleep most of the way. Toddlers can be carried some of the way, but need variations in activities and easy footing; they can only walk a mile or so. Young children from five to seven can go three or four miles, but also need variation in activities and smooth trails. Older children from eight to nine can go about six or seven miles with an easy pace and tend to push themselves. Adolescents can work up to twelve miles by the time they're eighteen. During different times as they grow, kids have growth spurts when their endurance may be less and their balance shaky. Keep these factors in mind as you choose where and how far to hike. With small children it's also a good idea to stay within a reasonable distance of civilization in case medical care is needed, particularly if you're backpacking.

After choosing your hikes, make your own checklist and check the items off as you pack for your trip. You may want to create a main list for the whole family and then make small lists for individual members of the family if their needs are very different. (See our sample checklist in Appendix VI.)

Let the kids pack their own packs. Children used to carrying a pack to school can carry raingear, snacks, a small water bottle, and a sleeping bag without a frame pack. More than that and they need a framepack. When fitting a framepack for your child, fasten the waistbelt just above the hips and check to make sure that the anchor points of the shoulder straps are an inch or two below the shoulder. It must be comfortable or your child will be miserable.

All members of the family should take along layers of clothing, appropriate footwear, and good sleeping gear if you're camping. (See "Dress and Equipment for Backcountry Travel.")

Remember that children must be just as comfortable with their clothing and footwear as the adults in your family if they're going to enjoy hiking. For layering a child might wear a t-shirt, wool sweater, and rain jacket on a mild day; or longjohns, a pile jacket, and rain jacket and rain pants on a cold day. The layers can be taken off and put back on according to how warm or cold he is. Be sure to take a warm cap along on high mountain hikes, so that if the weather turns cold you can conserve the child's heat and guard against hypothermia.

Some additional tips for children's clothing: a wide-brimmed hat is better than sunglasses for young children because sunglasses fall off; it has been reported that blue clothing attracts some insects, so choose another color; buy some mosquito netting and attach it to your baby or child's hat and drape it over his or her face to protect against mosquitoes; have your child wear clothes that he can get dirty—happy hikers are meant to get dirty. Tennis shoes are o.k. for first hikes, but as children hike farther, you'll want to invest in boots. The new lightweight boots that have evolved from running shoes are especially good for children and are moderately priced.

Plan your meals and snacks together so that everyone will have something to eat that they enjoy. Older children can take responsibility for preparing a meal or two; younger children can help put snacks in individual bags. When you're planning food for the trail, take along extra snacks for children. Always take along high energy snacks, such as candy bars or trail mix, oranges, fruit leathers, etcetera. Kids use a lot of energy hiking. Don't give kids hard candies or other snacks that they can choke on when hiking, however.

Be sure to take along lots of water. Children need to drink more often than adults.

Help them pack an "exploring kit," a treasure bag with a hand magnifier, bandana, baby food jars or unbreakable plastic containers with holes poked in the tops, empty cardboard rolls from paper towels or toilet tissue, a small net, and tweezers. For a long trip take a good book to be read aloud and your children may want to take crayons and a small art notebook. You may also want to give your children whistles and a space blanket to pack so that they can use them if they get lost.

Consider how you'll carry the littlest kids in your family. It's great to get babies and toddlers out on hikes, because the outdoors is part of their lives

A young family making tracks in Rocky Mountain National Park.

from early on; "outdoorese" is like a second language to them, and loving wilderness comes naturally. Front pack carriers are excellent for babies up to about six months. After babies can hold their heads up, they and their parents will be more comfortable with a frame carrier. There are many carriers available today ranging from $50 to over $125. You may want to rent one or two different models from a mountaineering store in order to try before you buy. Keep in mind that the carrier is an investment for everyday use, as well as for hiking.

Look for a frame carrier that faces the child forward so he can see and so that the load will be closer to your center of gravity. The child can also snooze with his head on your shoulder this way. Make sure the carrier has a safety belt. A "kick stand" is handy for stops along the trail, but never leave the child alone in the carrier. Many carriers have handy pockets for carrying child-related snacks and gear.

Hiking

You can catch more flies with honey than with vinegar and you can motivate more young hikers with rewards, encouragement, excitement, and fun, than with all the lecturing and prodding in the world.

The operative principles in hiking with children are: make it fun, and be flexible. Let nature and your children lead the way and be ready to forgo the summit ascent or the botany lesson you planned, if appropriate. It really isn't until children are eight or nine that they can be destination oriented and push themselves toward a goal. If you can lower your expectations and hike at their level, your entire family will have more fun hiking.

There are some games with which you can get your children to keep going on the trail with less whining and to help them see, hear, smell, and feel wilderness. Here are a few (keep them up your sleeves until children need some motivating): "Follow-the-Leader" in which everyone takes turns leading the hike and doing goofy things on the trail; "Trust-Me" in which family members take turns being blindfolded and led by other members; "What's This" in which blindfolded hikers try to tell what their leaders have them touch or smell or hear; "Sames and Differents" in which your child collects objects that are the same and then finds "differents;" "Shape Search" in which your child, armed with geometric shapes, hikes and searches for shapes along the trail; "Add-On Stories" in which, as you walk together, you make up a story by adding on to each other's sentences. You may also challenge your children to learn the names of trees, flowers, birds, and animals or search for animal prints. Another favorite game is "Quiet as an Indian" during which you all try to walk as quietly as a native American would walk through the woods. There are many, many games to play. You and your children can make up your own. Be ready to share discoveries and laughter along the way and share your enthusiasm for the natural world. Don't forget to give your children some quiet moments alone, too.

Praise and treats are important tools for getting your children to hike, as well. Positive reinforcement does more than you can imagine. Promise a snack at the next rest stop, or at the destination, and a treat at the end of a trail well-hiked. Tell them what good hikers they are, how proud you are of them, what good outdoorspeople they've become. Let them help set up camp, make fires, cook, and cleanup and praise them heartily. Your children will feel good about themselves and want to hike again and you'll hear a lot less complaining and whining.

A word about safety before we move on to the hikes. Spend time teaching your children how to behave if they get lost—they should stay put (hug a tree) and blow their whistle. Show older children how to read a topo map and use a compass. Always take along a first-aid kit and know how to use it. In addition to the list in our introductory section, "Dress and Equipment for Backcountry Travel," the kit should contain a bar of Fels Naptha soap with which to wash your child should he get into poison ivy, meat tenderizer

When hiking with children it is important to make it fun.

to put on insect bites or stings (1/4 tsp. meat tenderizer to one tsp. water), and children's acetametaphin.

If you prepare well for your hikes, hike at a pace and to a distance determined by the slowest in your group, and make hiking fun and exciting, your hiking as a family will be memorable not because it was miserable, but because it was enjoyable.

Bibliography

Backpacking With Babies And Small Children by Goldie Silverman. Wilderness Press.

Family Camping Made Simple by Beverly Liston. Globe Pequot Press.

Nature for the Very Young by Marcia Bowden. Wiley and Sons.

Sharing Nature With Children by Joseph Cornell. Dawn Publications.

Sharing the Joy of Nature by Joseph Cornell. Dawn Publications.

Listening to Nature by Joseph Cornell. Dawn Publications.

Take 'em Along: Sharing The Wilderness With Your Children by Barbara Euser. Cordillera.

A good cassette tape for young children with some fun songs about hiking on it is *Rocky Mountain Holiday* with John Denver and the Muppets.

HIKE 2 *EAGLE'S VIEW*

General description: A short day hike to the top of a ridge from which hikers have a scenic view of Front Range mountains.

General location: About seven miles southeast of Conifer, forty-five minutes west from Denver.

Maps: Reynolds Park Map (available at the park); USGS Pine quad; Trails Illustrated Rampart Range Map.

Degree of difficulty: Easy for adults; moderate for children six and up; difficult for children under five.

Length: 1.3 miles one way.

Elevations: 7,000 to 8,000 feet.

Special attractions: Great first destination hike for young children; "eagle's" view of Front Range peaks; wildflowers; wildlife; interpretive trail; wide variety of terrain within the park.

Best season: Spring, summer, and fall.

For more information: Jefferson County Open Space Department, 1801 9th St., Golden, CO 80401, (303) 277-8332.

The Hike: A hike to Eagle's View in Jefferson County's Reynold's Park is a great introduction to destination hiking for families. The distance of the hike is not too great to be discouraging for young children, the trail makes for easy walking, and the elevation gain is moderate, while the name beckons children to keep hiking to the top. They wonder, "What does an eagle see? Will we see eagles up there?" The reward for reaching the destination is, indeed, an eagle's view of Front Range mountains.

To reach Reynolds Park take U.S. Highway 285 from Denver to Conifer. After you reach the Safeway shopping center at Conifer continue on another .2 mile. Turn left at the signs for Foxton and Reynolds Open Space Park. You'll be driving through Kennedy Gulch on County Road 97, Foxton Road. Follow the road about 5.1 miles until you come to a big dirt parking lot.

Reynolds Park is named in memory of John A. Reynolds whose family gave a substantial portion of the park to Jefferson County. This area was one of the first settled in Colorado's pioneer era. The Reynolds ranch house (now the park manager's residence) once served as a stop for pack trains traveling between Denver and Leadville and as a way station for the Pony Express. It was also a dude ranch in the first half of the twentieth century.

This hike description is written from the perspective of six-year old Crystal who recorded her impressions with a microcassette tape recorder (a fun activity for kids!).

"You can take a map from the map box at the Reynolds Park sign. It's kind of hard to find the opening to it. The top doesn't open. It's down underneath and there are lots of maps so I don't think you would come and there wouldn't be any maps.

"During the week you won't expect many people so that's a good time for you to come. On the weekend there are lots and lots of people.

"From the outhouse, walk uphill and cross the Elkhorn Trail.

"Well, it's really pretty up here. Some of the trees have their leaves off. There are juniper trees, aspen, and Ponderosa pine and a few flowers. There

View of Front Range peaks, looking south from Eagle's View in Reynolds Park.

butterfies. There are some buttercups, too.

"Now it's pretty hot up here. We've walked just a tiny bit and I'm getting pretty hot. So don't expect it to be cool up here on most days.

"There are lots of moss rocks, lots of pretty rocks, and lots of rocks on the trail, too. There are some pretty little bushes too that have really prickly scales on them. Better watch out for those.

"There's lots of pretty wild roses out here too. There are new baby trees coming in. They're cute. There are really lots of buttercups here. I can't believe how many there are. There are some pretty white flowers and some chiming bells, but the white flowers I don't know what they're called, though. And there's some purple flowers that are pretty too. Well, my mom says there are some black-eyed Susans.

"Keep going straight 'til you get to the sign that says Oxen Draw Trail and follow that to the left.

"Me and my mom just saw some Queen Anne's lace. There's some blue spruce, too, I think. And there are some forget-me-nuts, forget-nots. They're really pretty. There's a few anthills and I think you should bring along a couple of warm things even though it is pretty hot.

"We just saw some more wild roses. You can get some great pictures of the trees and the wild roses. Oops! There are some of our state flowers here, too. Columbines they're called. There's lots of those.

"We saw some flowers that my mom thinks look like honeysuckle, but they're not really, I guess. We're walking just by some Douglas fir; they're

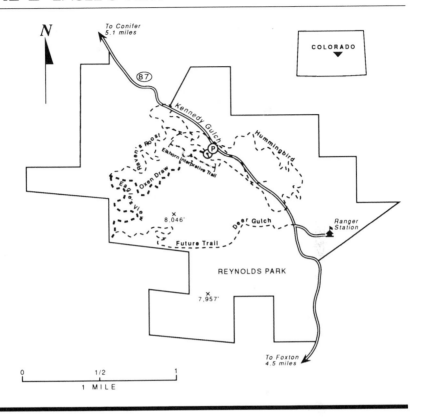

really really tall. And even though it's warm here, the sun isn't shining very much and it's starting to cool off right now. It's kind of cool sometimes and hot.

"The trail starts out gradually and it starts getting kind of steep after that. The trail is kind of rough. Not really, though. Not like other trails. I just passed more wild roses.

"We're following a little brook that's very pretty. It's not very big at all. There's a big stream back more and that's really big. There's lots of carpenter ants here that might sting you so be careful of those. There's a few dandelions. I just saw another of our state flowers. There's some shooting stars here. There's some pretty pink flowers with purple around them, but I don't know what they're called. Sometimes the brook gets bigger and sometimes it gets smaller, kind of like our heart gets bigger and smaller.

"Mom thinks we saw some violets. Right here the brook has gotten bigger and gets bigger down at the bottom and then it gets smaller. You get really tired after you've walked a little ways. It's like half-a-mile, a mile to get to Eagle's View. We're at the Eagle's View Trail and I think there might be some eagles up at the top and you could look at the eagles, I think. I really don't know if there's eagles up at the top. I think there might be a few pieces, but I just saw one piece of iron pyrite. Oh! I see another one right here.

"When you get up at the top it's very, very pretty when you get there. There are mountains way, way in the distance. We have a little bit of the plains in the view. Over to the right there are lots of bumpy, bumpy mountains.

"Well, um, bye!"

Atop Eagle's View the bumpy, bumpy mountains are the pointed Cathedral Spires, Banner Peak, and far, far away to the south Raleigh Peak on the east, Baldy Peak center, and Redskin Mountain to the west, all in the Pike National Forest.

The descent from Eagle's View is easy and fast. You may want to have a picnic following your hike; children will enjoy exploring around the picnic area and feeding the very friendly ground squirrels. Then you may want to walk the short Elkhorn Interpretive Trail.—*Crystal Boddie* (accompanied by Caryn and Robin Boddie)

HIKE 3 *FLORISSANT FOSSIL BEDS NATIONAL MONUMENT*

General description: A variety of day hikes of different lengths along trails that feature fossils, petrified wood, and a homestead, as well as beautiful, spacious views.

General location: About thirty-five miles west of Colorado Springs.

Maps: National Monument maps and brochures available at the monument; USGS Lake George quad; Pike National Forest map.

Degree of difficulty: Easy.

Length: From one-half to four miles.

Elevations: No elevation gain.

Special attractions: Great educational opportunity for families. Interesting geology, fossils, petrified wood, homestead, wide open views, programs put on by staff.

Best season: Spring, summer, fall.

For more information: Florissant Fossil Beds National Monument, P.O. Box 185, Florissant, CO 80816, (303) 748-3253.

The hike: Families will have a wonderful time at Florissant Fossil Beds National Monument. There are numerous hikes of varying lengths so that you can be flexible according to what you and your family wants to do and, at the same time, see fossil beds, petrified wood stumps, and a homestead in good shape, and learn about geology, and flora and fauna.

To reach the monument take U.S. Highway 24 west from Colorado Springs for thirty-five miles to the town of Florissant. At the town center, turn south toward Cripple Creek on the unpaved Teller County Road No. 1. The park is .5 mile from the town of Florissant.

With the exception of special pgrograms the monument is usually open only from 8 to 5 p.m. daily. You should plan to be finished with your hiking by about 4:30, because there is a gate to the park, which is locked every afternoon.

The monument was established by Congress in 1969 and is administered by the National Park Service. The main reason for its being is to protect and preserve fossils and petrified wood that are unique and can never be renewed. The park staff puts on lots of educational activities and they coordinate their efforts with Pike National Forest staff. They do a lot of work with the schools, particularly in Colorado Springs. Natural history talks are given daily every hour on the hour from 10 to 6 p.m. These will give you an introduction to the fossil beds. Wildflower and wildlife talks are given daily from 12:30 to 2 p.m.

There are over ten miles of trails in the monument. Start out behind the Visitor's Center where you'll find a map box. You may want to start by hiking the "Trail through Time," along which two inches equals one million years. This will help you and your children understand time in terms of our planet's history. You will also see petrified sequoia stumps, the part of the valley once occupied by Lake Florissant, an exposure of fossil-bearing shale, a view of Pike's Peak, and a lightning scarred tree. The hike also introduces you to various species of evergreen.

After the short "Trail through Time" hike, you may want to take the Hornbek/Wildlife Loop or one of the other, shorter hikes. The Hornbek/Wildlife Loop follows a meadow to the historic Hornbek Homestead. In 1878 Adaline Hornbek and her three sons came to live in this area. At the homestead site

HIKE 3 *FLORISSANT FOSSIL BEDS NATIONAL MONUMENT*

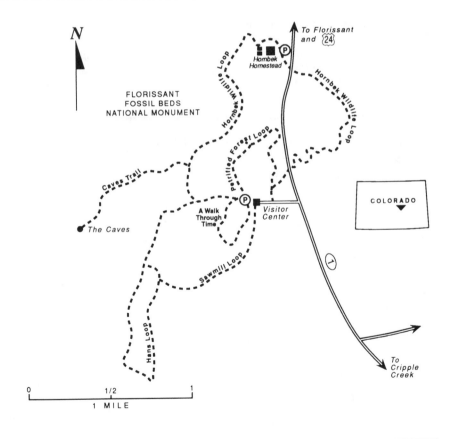

The Hornbeck Homestead at Florissant National Monument.

you'll see buildings and exhibits showing their way of life. Tours of the homestead may be taken anytime during the summer between ten and six p.m. Lake Florissant once filled this valley. The trail crosses Tellers County Road No. 1 and follows it back to the Visitor's Center. Look for sign of elk, deer, coyote and other wildlife on your way back.—*Caryn Boddie*

HIKE 4 *ROXBOROUGH STATE PARK*

General description: A variety of hiking opportunities in an area unique for its geology, its mixture of plains and mountain flora and fauna, and the many learning opportunities found there.

General location: Southwest of Denver where the plains meet the foothills.

Maps: Roxborough State Park Map; USGS Kassler quad; Trails Illustrated Rampart Range map.

Degree of difficulty: Ranges from easy to moderately-difficult depending on which hikes you choose to do.

Length: From one mile to 5.5 miles round trip.

Elevations: 6,000 to 7,200 Feet.

Special attractions: The park is in close proximity to Front Range Cities; a wonderful resource for families; opportunity to see and learn about spectacular geologic structures and a unique mixture of prairie and mountain flora and fauna; warm and knowledgeable park staff sponsors many interesting programs each season.

Best season: Year round.

For more information: Roxborough State Park, 4751 N. Roxborough Drive, Littleton, CO 80125 (303) 973-3959.

The hike: Roxborough State Park is a special treasure every Colorado family should consider their own. Visitors to Colorado will certainly enjoy it as well. The first park within Colorado's state park system to be designated both a Colorado Natural Area and a National Natural Landmark, Roxborough offers opportunities for exploration and discovery, as well as for hiking. Trails include a half-mile (round trip) gentle hike from the Visitor's Center to a 5.5 mile (round trip) hike to the summit of Carpenter Peak, from which you'll have a spectacular view in all directions.

To reach Roxborough State Park, drive south and west to Wadsworth and C470. Take Wadsworth (State Hwy. 121) south through the town of Waterton. Turn left (east) on Waterton Road. Turn right (south) on North Rampart Range Road. Just before the road goes into the Roxborough Park residential area turn left. This is Roxborough Park Road. Then turn right (south) just after the fire station onto the access road leading to the state park. You may also reach the park by driving south from C470 on Santa Fe (State Hwy. 85) to Titan Road. Follow Titan Road west to Roxborough Park Road. Turn left (south) and follow this road around to the access road. Turn left (south) before the fire station.

You'll need to purchase a daily pass for each vehicle on your way into the park, unless you display a current Colorado State Parks Pass on your windshield. Colorado senior citizens (sixty-two and over) are allowed free admission to the park with a free Aspen Leaf Annual Pass. Colorado disabled veterans who display Colorado Disabled Veteran (DV) license plates are also admitted free.

As you drive into Roxborough Park you may notice an old kiln. It represents only one, short-lived chapter in the story of this area when a brick company held a land and mineral lease to manufacture brick there.

Roxborough State Park features spectacular geology and a variety of hiking opportunities.

The first people to inhabit the Roxborough Park area, which was originally called Washington Park after a rock formation that looked like George Washington, were the Arapaho and Ute Indians. The story has been passed down that they were often at war among the red rocks of the park and that when they departed from the area, there were several days of ceremony.

In the late 1800's the Hayden survey party came through the area. One of the members of the party was photographer William Henry Jackson.

Soon settlers came. They were miners, farmers, ranchers, and speculators. They homesteaded and "proved up" their claims—improved their claims— in order to stay. Schools were opened. Settlers realized the importance of the park as a recreational area and planned to build a resort there. Fortunately, that didn't happen, but the area did become well known to many in Denver. It wasn't until 1975, however, that a portion of Roxborough Park was designated Roxborough State Park. The park's rich human history is but a fraction of a second in the geologic history of this park.

The granite of Carpenter Peak is about 190 million years older than that of Pikes Peak. It is a combination of sedimentary rock that was formed 1240 million years ago during the Precambrian era and magma that joined with it to create megmatite. When the magma cooled the granite was formed.

The formation of the spectacular red spires that you see as you approach the Roxborough State Park Visitor's Center began during the Paleozoic era when Colorado was flooded by seas that encroached and then receded.

"About 300 million years ago, at the beginning of the Pennsylvanian period, Colorado was lifted and formed into a series of high mountains and deep basins," according to Cecilia Armbrust, author of "The Geology of Roxborough State Park." "Gradually, the ocean sediments were eroded away until even the ancient Precambrian rocks were exposed and stripped down. The sediments formed by the wearing away of the 'Ancestral Rockies,' as these mountains were called, were deposited in the adjacent deep basins as alluvial fans and stream beds. This accumulation of gravel and sand forms the red rocks known as the Fountain formation." The red color of this formation at Roxborough is due to the effect of oxidation or rusting of iron minerals.

Millions of years later, during the "Laramide Revolution" the Fountain formation was raised when there was strong uplift and mountain building. The Dakota, Lyons, Lytle, and Platte formations, which had been formed of muds, silts, sands, and limestones when seas had returned to Colorado and again receded, were uplifted, as well.

A good place to start exploring Roxborough State Park is in the Visitor's Center. Here you can view a slide show that will introduce you to the wildlife, vegetation, and geology of the park. Children will enjoy trying to match animal names to paw or hoof prints and will be able to touch various bones and antlers. Be sure to sign up on the park mailing list: the staff at Roxborough (many volunteers) put on some excellent programs and are willing to put on special group activities. Many schools take advantage of this excellent opportunity. You might call before you go out to see what is going on.

After you've spent some time at the Visitor's Center get out and explore the park. The Roxborough trails offer a variety of hiking opportunities. If you are hiking with small children, you might enjoy taking them on the short Willow Creek trail, which is a gentle one-mile loop. If you would enjoy more of a destination hike with the promise of beautiful views, a hike to Carpenter

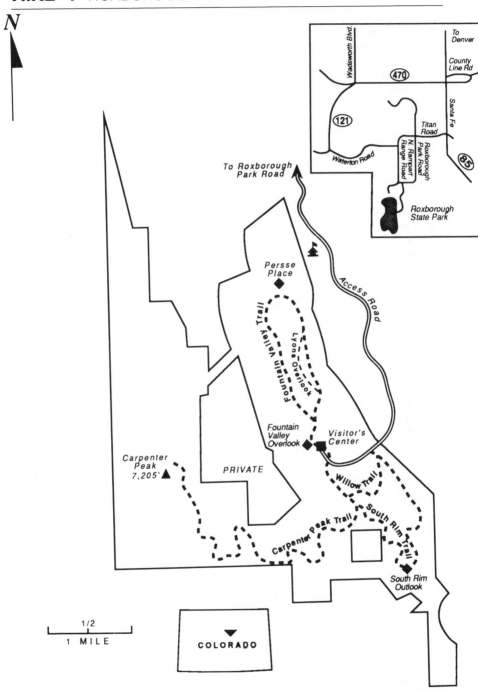

Peak (5.5 miles round trip) might be more to your liking.

As you hike, notice that Roxborough is in a transition zone. Here the plains and the mountains meet and you have the opportunity to see a variety of prairie and mountain vegetation. Also, the geological structure of the park has created conditions in which several distinct plant communities thrive.

You will see oak brush, dry grassland, wet meadows, cottonwoods and box-elders, aspen groves, and along Carpenter Peak you'll see ponderosa pine and Douglas fir.

It is important that hikers stay on the trails at Roxborough, not only to protect the environment, but because there is poison ivy in the park and prairie rattlesnakes hide in the grass. They are shy creatures that will warn people to stay away, but they don't take kindly to being stepped on.

As you enjoy Roxborough, keep an eye open for mule deer, coyotes, mountain lion, bear, and elk; and be sure to look overhead for golden eagles.

We're sure you and your family will enjoy Roxborough State Park over and over again.—*Caryn, Peter, Crystal & Robin Boddie*

HIKE 5 *WHITE RANCH PARK*

General description: An easy to moderate hike through the foothills northwest of Golden. An excellent trail to take for a first family backpacking trip.

General location: About ten miles northwest of Golden, about twenty-five miles southwest of Boulder.

Maps: White Ranch Park map available from the Jefferson County Open Space Department or at the park; USGS Ralston Buttes quad.

Length: From one mile to six miles depending upon which hike you choose to take. There are about eighteen miles of hiking/equestrian trails located in the park.

Degree of difficulty: Easy to moderate.

Elevations: 6,150 to 8,000 feet.

Special attractions: Both gentle and rugged terrain, nice views of the plains and foothills, a good beginning backpack for families.

Best season: Spring, summer, and fall.

For more information: Jefferson County Open Space, 18301 W. 10th Ave., Suite 100, Golden, CO 80401, (303) 278-5925.

The hike: White Ranch Park is another excellent destination for families because there are over eighteen miles of trail at the park, which means you can hike as far as your family can, or wants to go. It is an excellent place to try backpacking with your family because an easy hike of only about one mile takes you to the "Sawmill Hiker Camp."

White Ranch Park is dedicated to the memory of Paul R. White, whose family homesteaded part of the land in the early 1900s. To reach it drive north from Golden or south from Boulder on State Highway 93. To take the short backpack trip, drive west on Jefferson County Road 70 (Golden Gate Canyon Road) for 4.1 miles to Jefferson County Road 57 (Crawford Gulch Road). Drive north for another 4.1 miles, then turn right to enter the park after 1.5 miles. Park in the first parking lot you come to.

There is also an east entrance to the park. You can reach the Sawmill Hiker

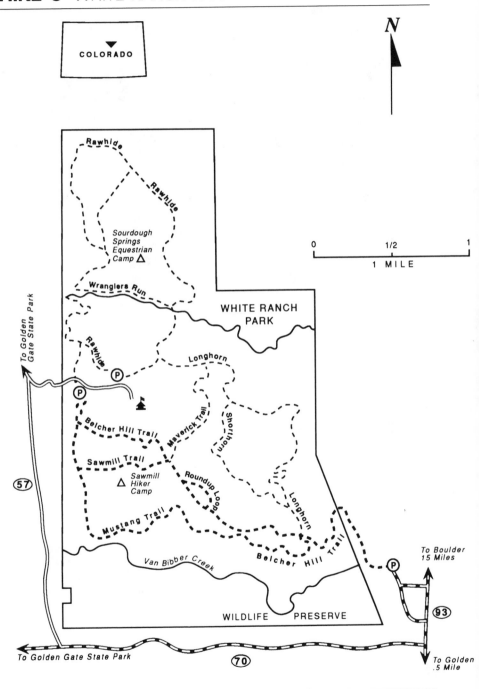

Hiking down the trail through White Ranch Park.

Camp from there, as well, but you will hike about four miles to it. To reach the east parking lot drive north from Golden or south from Boulder to W. 56th Ave. Drive west to the parking lot.

Begin your hike by walking south on the trail from the parking lot. In about one-third mile you'll come to a fork in the trail. To your left is the Belcher Hill Trail. To your right is the Mustang Trail. If you're hiking with small children it will be easiest to walk south on the Mustang Trail for .4 mile until you reach the intersection with the Sawmill Trail. Then head east to the Sawmill Hiker Camp. You can take your time and have fun making camp together, especially because the kids won't be too worn out. Then you can look at your map and explore other trails either the day you arrive or the next day. Perhaps you can all ascend to the highest point in White Ranch Park, Belcher Hill, which is 8,000 feet and only a short hike from camp.

Notice all the deadfall you'll see on the Mustang and Sawmill trails. In the late 1980's many trees were cleared because of insect infestation that killed them. This may be a good spot for children to learn how a forest comes back after fire or disease has destroyed it.

Watch for wildlife at the park. Deer, elk, bear, mountain lion, and wild turkey have been seen there. And enjoy the views of the foothills to the south and west and the plains to the east.—*Caryn, Peter, Crystal and Robin Boddie*

HIKE 6 *TRAIL THROUGH TIME*

General description: A short day hike in the Rabbit Valley Research Natural Area where many dinosaur bones and fossils have been discovered and excavated.
General location: Thirty miles west of Grand Junction.
Maps: Trail Through Time map available at the trailhead.
Degree of difficulty: Easy.
Length: 1.5 miles.
Elevations: No elevation gain.
Special attractions: Dinosaur bones, fossils, imprints of bones that have been excavated.
Best seasons: All seasons.
For more information: Bureau of Land Management, Grand Junction Resource Area, 764 Horizon Drive, Grand Junction, CO 81501 (303) 243-6552; or the Museum of Western Colorado, (303) 243-DINO.

The hike: The "Trail Through Time," also called the Rabbit Valley Interpretive Trail, will take your family through the 280-acre Rabbit Valley Research Natural Area from which dinosaur fossils have been quarried since 1982. Apatosaurus, Camarasaurus, Diplodocus, Allosaurus, Stegosaurus, Goniophois, Iguanadon, two turtles, and sauropod remains have been recovered. You will also see animal and plant fossils there. If you and your children are very interested in dinosaurs, you may want to plan this hike as part of a "dinosaur adventure" in the dinosaur triangle, which extends west from Grand Junction to Price, Utah, north to Vernal, Utah, and southwest again to Grand Junction. Many prehistoric specimens have been discovered in this area. Plan time to visit other field sites and museums, which are listed at the end of this hike description. You may also want to buy the book *Dinosaur Triangle: Land of the "Terrible Lizards"* by James Keener (published by Grand River Publishing), which will inform you about these sites and help you plan your trip.

To reach Rabbit Valley, drive west from Grand Junction on Interstate Highway 70 for thirty miles to the Rabbit Valley exit. Turn right (north) and park southwest of the frontage road.

To begin your hike, walk north on the dirt road to the beginning of the trail. There you will find information posted on a trailhead sign, and brochures for you to take along.

Once upon a time, during the Jurassic Age some 140 million years ago, this desert-like area was a lush, green floodplain. The land was covered with "giant conifer, palm and cycad trees. The weather was warm and humid, the skies were dark with clouds," according to the "Trail Through Time" brochure. There were crocodiles here, turtles and, of course dinosaurs. Reptiles flew over head.

Trapped and buried for millions of years, specimens of some of those plants and animals were preserved and eventually the layers under which they were

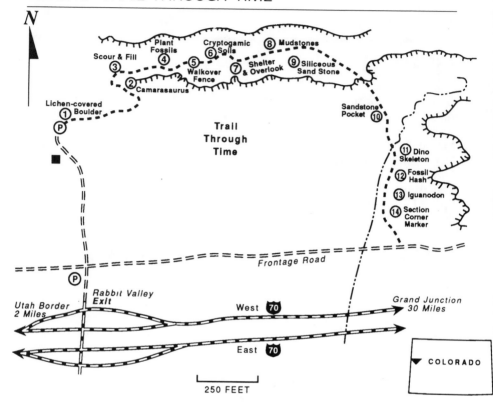

caught were turned to rock and the fossils you see on this hike were created.

As the rock has eroded, the fossils have been uncovered and will continue to appear for years.

Follow the signed hike, using the brochure. Walk past and explore the: lichen-covered boulder, Camarasaurus bones, ancient stream channel, plant fossils, sheep fence, cryptogamic soils, shelter and overlook, bentonitic mudstones, siliceous sandstone, pocketed boulder, articulated skeleton of another plant-eating dinosaur, fossil hash, Iguanadon's resting place, and finally, the section corner marker.

Also watch for hawks and eagles; coyotes, rabbits, bats, squirrels, and mice; whip, garter, and midget faded rattlesnakes; and yellowhead collared lizards. You may also see cactus, yucca, and rabbit brush in this dry part of our state. It's hard to believe there were once palm trees here.

You may also want to visit:

Dinosaur Valley Museum
Main and 4th
Grand Junction, CO
(303) 243-DINO

Cleveland-Lloyd Dinosaur Quarry
Thirty miles south of Price, Utah on Utah Highway 10
College of Eastern Utah Prehistoric Museum
Price, Utah
(801) 637-5060

Dinosaur National Monument
Near Vernal, Utah
(801) 789-2115

Utah Field House of Natural History
Vernal, Utah
(801) 789-3799

—Caryn, Peter, Crystal & Robin Boddie

HIKE 7 *MILLS LAKE TRAIL*

General description: A day hike past beautiful Alberta Falls to Mills Lake, a high mountain lake in Rocky Mountain National Park.
General location: Sixty-five miles northwest from Denver.
Maps: Rocky Mountain National Park Map available at the park. Trails Illustrated map of Rocky Mountain National Park.
Degree of difficulty: Moderate.
Length: Five miles round trip. Families may also hike just to Alberta Falls, which is .6 mile.
Elevations: 9,300 to 10,000 feet.
Special attractions: Beautiful Alberta Falls, Mills Lake surrounded by high mountain peaks, opportunity to learn about glaciers and see what they can do.
For more information: Rocky Mountain National Park, Estes Park, CO 80517.

The hike: If Rocky Mountain National Park is in your family's travel itinerary, a hike to Mills Lake in Glacier Gorge is worth including in your plans. The lower portion of the trail is crowded, but not nearly as crowded as many other trails that radiate from Bear Lake. After you pass Alberta Falls there are fewer and fewer people and the trail becomes less like a highway and more wild. Eventually, you end up in a high mountain valley encircled by peaks, and overlooking a beautiful, windswept mountain lake.

If you have small children in your family you can attempt this five-mile round-trip hike, especially if they can be carried part way. However, if things aren't going so well, you can also opt for hiking just to Alberta Falls.

To reach the Mills Lake Trail, drive to Estes Park, then west on U.S. Highway 36 to the entrance of the park and past the visitor's center. Turn left on the Bear Lake Road and follow it until you see a sign for the Bear Lake Shuttle parking lot on the west side of the road. It's a good idea to park here and take the shuttle to Bear Lake, because the parking lot there is often overcrowded. Besides, children usually get a kick out of riding the bus. The shuttle leaves every ten minutes or so during the summer, but be sure and check the exact times before you board and notice when the last bus comes down from Bear Lake in the afternoon.

You can get off the shuttle bus at the Glacier Gorge bus stop or at Bear Lake. From the Glacier Gorge bus stop you head right up the trail and save some walking distance. You may also take the bus to Bear Lake where there are restrooms and rangers, but also lots of people.

If you're starting from Bear Lake, take your first left and follow the signs to Alberta Falls.

Alberta Falls is a long, beautiful falls. After spending a little time looking and listening, continue straight uphill.

The trail continues to be wide and unmistakable for some time, but then becomes an unimproved trail as you hike around the eastern side of Glacier Knobs and meet the North Longs Peak Trail. Follow the trail to the right for another .4 mile until you meet another trail. A sign points you to either Loch Vale or Andrews Glacier or Mills Lake. Go to your left. You'll cross a brook and then Glacier Creek. Keep a sharp eye out for the cairns that

HIKE 7 *MILLS LAKE TRAIL*

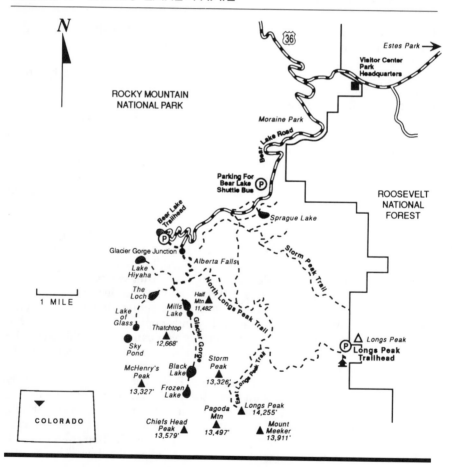

Mills Lake in Rocky Mountain National Park.

lead you over glacier-scraped rock to the lake.

At Mills Lake as you're facing the head of the valley, Thatchtop Mountain is on your right. Up the ridge from Thatchtop is Powell Peak and McHenry's Peak. The big knob on your left is Storm Peak, southeast of which is "The Keyhole" on Long's Peak, and then Long's Peak itself at 14,255 feet. At the head of the valley is Chiefs Head Peak.

If you were to continue up Glacier Gorge, you would come to Black Lake and Frozen Lake.

You may want to spend some time exploring and discovering "glacier sign." Glaciers are massive ice and snow fields that slowly move downhill. They contain not only snow and ice, but rocks that help to carve a glacial signature in a valley over a long period of time. These same materials are dropped from the glacier on its journey, sometimes in bits at a time, sometimes in great piles called moraines. See if your family can discern a signature in Glacier Gorge. And, remember, there are a few glaciers still around. West of Thatchtop Mountain is Andrews Glacier.

After enjoying this exquisite spot, return as you came.—*Caryn Boddie*

HIKE 8 UTE MOUNTAIN TRIBAL PARK

General description: Day hikes or backpacks with a guide to ancient Anasazi ruins in the Ute Mountain Tribal Park on Mesa Verde. Recommended for children over eight and their families.
General location: Twelve miles south of Cortez in the Ute Mountain Indian Reservation.
Maps: Available at the site.
Degree of difficulty: Easy to difficult, depending on hike.
Length: Varies.
Elevations: Varies.
Special attractions: Opportunity to visit Anasazi ruins in an undisturbed condition with a Ute Indian guide giving you a personal perspective on Indian life. Hikes vary from short trips to ruins on half- and full-day tours, to extended backpacking trips to remote ruins and canyons.
Best season: Late spring, summer, and early fall.
For more information: Ute Mountain Tribal Park, Arthur Cuthair, Superintendent, Towaoc, CO 81344; (303) 565-3751, Ext. 282, or (303) 565-4684.

The Hike: Here is an opportunity for you and your family to experience a wilder and rarer Mesa Verde with a guide from the Ute Mountain Tribal Park in the Ute Mountain Indian Reservation. This hike is not meant to take the place of Mesa Verde National Park—by all means visit there, too, for an overview of the area and Anasazi culture—but to give you a more primitive experience of the area.

You will be touring the Ute Mountain Tribal Park, a part of the Ute Mountain Reservation. It includes about 125,000 acres of sandstone cliffs, green plateaus (thus the name Mesa Verde), and wild canyons. The tribal park, which surrounds Mesa Verde National Park on three sides, was established to protect the many Anasazi ruins and cliff dwellings that exist there and to provide access for the public to the area. Because the Anasazi sites may be visited only in the company of a guide, they have been left in a much more primitive condition than the sites in nearby Mesa Verde National Park. While you are in the park you and your family will enjoy the trek most if you use your imaginations, step back in time, and look closely at the intricate work of the Anasazi.

Tours of the Ute Mountain Tribal Park begin at the Ute Mountain Pottery Factory twelve miles south of Cortez on Hwy. 666. You will need to make advance reservations (see above for phone numbers), but it is sometimes possible to make arrangements without too much notice, providing a guide or space on a tour is available. If you want to arrange a guided backpacking trip you should make reservations well in advance: a deposit will be required. Please note: you must have a guide to tour the area—respect this homeland of the Anasazi and Ute by observing this rule.

Day hikes can be taken with guides all over the park. Backpacking trips will take you into remote areas and to ruins not visited by many. Tours can be arranged around your interests, but you will need to provide your own food and equipment.

You may also camp at a primitive site set up by the Utes along the Mancos

Eagles Nest ruin in the Ute Mountain Tribal Park.

River. Contact the Tribal Park office to make arrangements and to obtain a permit.

At the time of this writing the cost per person for the trip up Mancos Canyon to Johnson Canyon (all day) was $25; $20 for a group of twelve or more. Cost per person for a short tour up Mancos Canyon to the campground (half day) was $10. A guided backpacking trip of two-five days with a minimum group of five will be $40 per person, per day. Check on current prices when you make your reservations.

For the full-day trip up Mancos Canyon to Johnson Canyon be sure to bring a lunch, plenty of water, a hat, sunscreen, insect repellent and a rain jacket for each person in your group.

This tour begins with a drive up the Mancos River Canyon, stopping at points of interest. (You will be driving your own vehicle. Be sure to have plenty of gas; the main ruins are about forty miles off the highway.) You then go to the mesa top south of the river to a place where you can view the ruins you'll be visiting across the canyon.

The tour ends with a moderate one-mile hike down into the Lion Canyon arm of Johnson Canyon where there are four sizable Anasazi cliff dwellings. On this hike you will have to negotiate several ladders to reach the ruins. There are no guard rails, but if you take reasonable care, it should not be a problem.

The climax of the hike is the Eagles Nest ruin, a precariously perched cliff dwelling which is reached only by a steep ladder up to a sandstone ledge. Constructed in about 1200 AD, this ruin includes a kiva with painted plaster still on the walls and a room wall with hooks for holding a loom, not to mention an unbelievable view. With grinding stones, corn cobs, pieces of sandals, pottery and other remnants of past occupation still visible throughout this and the other ruins, it is easy to let your mind wander back to the time of the Anasazi.

After this day trip, you may find that you want to arrange another, back-country trip with an Indian guide to explore the more remote canyons in this unique tribal park.—*Peter Boddie*

The Eastern Plains and Front Range Cities

The plains of Colorado are the state's forgotten country: wild and intricate, with a subtle beauty often lost on hikers used to mountain landscapes.

There's a lot to discover east of the Front Range, from wildflowers that bloom in a short, vibrant burst of color each spring to pictographs—Indian history recorded on the land itself—to a feeling of unlimited space the like of which you won't feel in many other places.

Colorado's Front Range cities—Fort Collins, Boulder, Denver, Colorado Springs, and Pueblo—also offer many unique hiking experiences. You won't find wilderness here, but you will discover some getaway places close to, or within, these cities: good trails to take advantage of when you can't get away for the weekend.

We hope the following hikes will help you discover some of these overlooked places.

HIKE 9 *PAWNEE BUTTES*

General description: A short day hike or overnighter in the short-grass prairie to the Pawnee Buttes.

General location: Forty miles northeast of Greeley.

Maps: Grover SE and Pawnee Buttes USGS quads; Pawnee National Grassland Map.

Degree of difficulty: Easy.

Length: Two miles one way.

Elevations: 5,200 to 5,420 feet.

Special attractions: A unique hike accessible year-round; spectacular erosional features; abundant wildflowers in the spring; good bird watching.

Best season: Anytime, but spring is most colorful.

For more information: Contact Pawnee National Grassland, 2017 9th Street, Greeley, CO 80631; (303) 353-5004.

The Hike: The trip to Pawnee Buttes is an easy and popular one and can be hiked during any season, weather permitting. In a short distance (two miles one way), the trail covers a surprising variety of terrains, from sweeping expanses of grassland to intricately dissected badlands. It arrives at the base of the Pawnee Buttes, two imposing landmarks of the plains, made famous as Rattlesnake Buttes in James Michener's novel, *Centennial*.

This land of sun, wind and grass may pique your imagination so that you

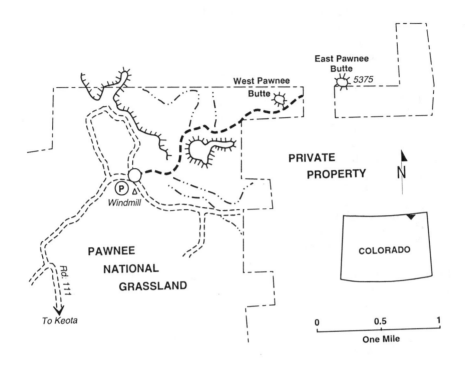

feel the presence of those creatures and humans that have come before: ancient ancestors of the camel and horse now fossilized in the rocks forming the buttes, herds of giant bison and the Paleo-Indians that followed them, and, most recently, the settlers who tried to tame this land with plows.

Depending on the season, you may observe a variety of wildlife, including many species of songbirds, prairie falcons, and other raptors, and the graceful pronghorn antelope. In the spring the prairie turns green in one short, but spectacular burst of growth, and if it is an unusually moist year, you will encounter a display of wildflowers which would rival that of any mountain meadow.

To reach the Pawnee Buttes trail, take State Highway 14 either thirteen miles east from Briggsdale or ten miles west from New Raymer and look for the sign to Keota. Follow the gravel road for approximately five miles until you reach Keota, now nearly a ghost town. From the northeast corner of town, follow County Road 105 for about three miles, go right on County Road 104 another three miles, and then turn left onto County Road 111. Follow 111 north about 4.5 miles until the road makes a sharp bend to the west. Look for a road (Forest Road 685) which heads north from this curve. This access road leads you to the trailhead and on to an overlook.

Follow the gravel road about one mile to a fork. Take the right fork and park near the windmill a short distance ahead. Across from the windmill, there is another road leading northeast and a couple hundred feet along this road you will see the sign for the Pawnee Buttes Trail. From here you have an excellent view of the surrounding landscape with the Pawnee Buttes visible to the northeast.

From the sign, the trail descends a small draw and goes out onto the prairie again. After crossing a wide gully it passes through a gate and arrives at a saddle separating two bluffs. From here it descends into a badlands area where, in places, it becomes indistinct. Watch for it on the flat ground below where it emerges again and crosses a deep gully.

After crossing the gully a second time, the trail climbs onto a gently sloping grassland at the base of the bluff. From here you get your first good view of the western of the two Pawnee Buttes. Following the trail towards the buttes, you will reach a jeep road. Follow this for a short distance until you again see the trail heading left in the direction of the buttes. As you near the first of the two buttes, the trail becomes indistinct, but you should be able to see the trail posts circling the south side of the butte where the trail merges with jeep roads which lead to the second butte. Do not be surprised if you encounter company when you arrive at the Pawnee Buttes, as the jeep roads provide motorized access to the area.

You should allow about 2.5 hours for the roundtrip to the Pawnee Buttes, plus plenty of time for exploring. The buttes themselves are impressive landmarks and a hike around them will reveal a great deal about the geology of these erosional remnants. The chimney on East Pawnee Butte toppled in a wind storm in 1986. Climbing on the buttes is not recommended, however, due to crumbling rock.

You will hear the cries of prairie falcons as you approach the buttes. They nest in the cliffs above and can be seen with the aid of binoculars. Please avoid disturbing any nests you may encounter, as these and many other prairie species are particularly sensitive to intrusion. In fact, Division of Wildlife and Forest Service personnel require hikes to stay on trails and roads from March 1 to June 30 of each year to minimize disturbance.

Because of the openness of the area, you can easily leave the trail to explore on your return trip. You may want to follow one of the gullies into the badlands area where hours can be spent discovering the infinite ways that water has been at work sculpting the land. If you should become disoriented while exploring, the Pawnee Buttes, the fence line, and the windmill near your car are all good landmarks. Camping is permitted anywhere on the National Grassland property, but because of the concentrated use in the immediate vicinity of the Pawnee Buttes, camping here is not recommended. Likewise, you should avoid camping too near the trail and in gully bottoms where there is a danger of flash floods.

As you may have guessed, firewood and water are not in abundance on the prairie, so you should come prepared with plenty of water and a stove if you are going to camp. Any water you encounter while hiking should be considered unfit for drinking.

If you do spend a night out under the stars, you'll find a unique experience; an opportunity to feel what it must have been like to cross this vast prairie by covered wagon. The sense of unlimited space is impressive. The prairie sunrise, with grasses rustling in the wind, and birds singing in accompaniment, is an event not soon to be forgotten.—*Peter Boddie*

The eastern Pawnee Butte.

HIKE 10 . *TAMARACK RANCH*

General description: A day hike in the rolling sand hills prairie of the Tamarack Ranch State Wildlife Area.
General location: Twenty miles northeast of Sterling.
Maps: USGS Tamarack Ranch and Crook Quads; Logan County Sheet 2.
Degree of difficulty: Easy.
Length: Four to eight miles round trip.
Elevations: 3,800 to 4,000 feet.
Special Attractions: This hike affords you the opportunity to experience a native sandsage/bluestem prairie that is in the process of restoration, and to view prairie wildlife. The adjacent riparian habitat of the South Platte River is worth exploring, too.
Best season: Winter, spring, fall.
For more information: Colorado Division of Wildlife, 6060 Broadway, Denver, CO 80203, (303) 297-1192.

The hike: The Tamarack Ranch State Wildlife Area includes two distinct areas separated by Interstate 76: the sand hills prairie to the south and the riparian habitat along the South Platte River to the north of the highway. Both provide opportunities to view wildlife and experience contrasting ecosystems of the Colorado plains.

To reach the ranch, take Interstate Highway 76 northeast from Sterling or southwest from Julesburg. If you want to check in at the wildlife area headquarters, get off at the Crook exit and follow State Highway 55 north .5 mile

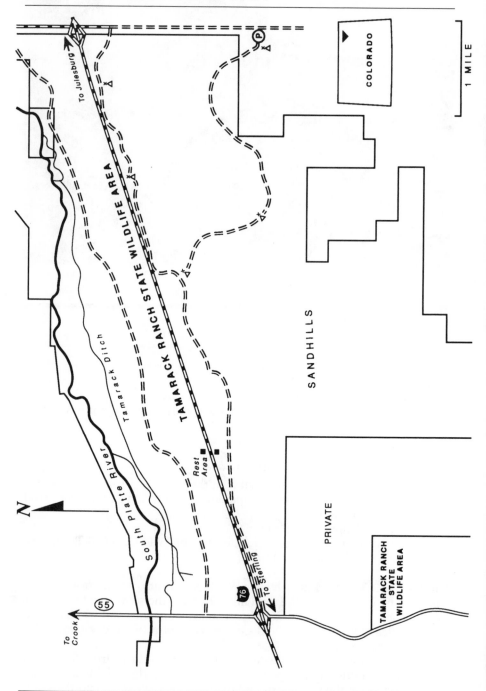

to the wildlife area headquarters on the right. If you would like to go directly to the start of this particular hike, follow I-76 northeast to Exit 155 (Red Lion Road). Turn south and follow the county road 1.8 miles to a gate on the right. Park outside or just inside this gate, taking care to avoid any tall grass which might be ignited by your car exhaust system. Motorized vehicles are not allowed beyond this point in the wildlife area.

The focus of this hike is the mid- and tall-grass prairie of the sand hills of northeastern Colorado, an area not often experienced by hikers. Most of the native prairie in Colorado has been overgrazed or broken up for farming, and, thus, severely altered or destroyed. Within the Tamarack Ranch State Wildlife Area, the Colorado Division of Wildlife is attempting to restore native sandsage/bluestem prairie through the suspension of cattle grazing, controlled wildfires and the reseeding of native plant species. The goal of this project is to provide native grassland capable of sustaining the endangered greater prairie chicken, the threatened lesser prairie chicken, the upland sandpiper, and other prairie wildlife. As part of this project the division has recently reintroduced greater prairie chickens to the sand hills area of the ranch. To support these efforts please follow these hiking restrictions requested by the Colorado Division of Wildlife:

During the "booming" and nesting period for prairie chickens between mid-March and the end of June, you must stay entirely on ranch roads. The "booming" or mating ritual of the greater prairie chicken is so-named because of the hollow booming sound (like blowing across the top of a bottle) made by the male when he inflates the orange air sacs on his neck to attract a hen. Should you come upon a booming display, stay at least 100 yards away and DO NOT DISTURB. Also, please note that no dogs are allowed during this season. For the remainder of the year, dogs on leash are allowed and hikers may explore the sand hills and prairie away from the roads.

To begin your hike, follow the ranch road to the northwest past a windmill and around a large sand hill to the west for approximately .75 mile to a high point. From this vantage point you can see both the interstate to the north and the expansive interior of the sand hills to the south and west. As the trail descends into the first depression between the sand hills, you enter a vast but secluded world, ruled by sky, wind and a sea of grass.

For a short introduction to the sandsage-bluestem prairie, follow the ranch road through a series of sand hills and depressions about two miles to the second windmill. Along the way, you may pass areas where orange-colored switchgrass has been seeded. Other common grasses include big and little bluestem, prairie sandreed, and Indian grass. Sandsage is also native here but may have become more dominant as a result of past overgrazing. By late summer, the prairie grasses may reach chest-high, a condition rarely seen since the introduction of cattle to the west.

The sand hills themselves are ancient sand dunes, which were deposited by winds carrying sand from the channels and floodplain of the South Platte River. As climate change ended the glacial period, and the source of river sand declined, the dunes became stabilized by grasses. There have probably been several periods in which the sea of sand and grass have alternated in this area. Another climate change, "sodbuster" farming, or serious overgrazing could easily tip the delicate balance of the grassland and reactivate the dunes.

From the second windmill there are a number of hiking options. You can head to the northwest over a saddle and drop down to a ranch road that

Sand hills and mid-grass prairie of Tamarack Ranch.

parallels the interstate. This road could be used to loop back to the Red Lion Road. and your starting point, or to continue west to State Highway 55 at the Crook exit if you shuttled a car to that point. It is also possible to head off cross-country (seasonal regulations permitting) or connect with other ranch roads to further explore the interior of the sand hills to the southwest. Please be mindful to stay within the boundaries of the wildlife area.

As an alternative, you may want to explore the north portion of the Tamarack Ranch which includes approximately sixteen miles of riparian habitat along the South Platte River. This area is dominated by cottonwood forest and wet meadows and includes a rich variety of birds and animals— perhaps the richest in the state. Please check with the Division of Wildlife ahead of time, as the riparian area may be closed to hiking during the spring nesting season and during hunting season in the fall.—*Peter Boddie*

HIKE 11 *POUDRE RIVER TRAIL*

General description: An easily accessible day hike in the city of Fort Collins.
General location: The north end of Fort Collins.
Maps: City of Fort Collins Department of Parks and Recreation Map.
Degree of difficulty: Easy.
Length: Seven miles one way.
Elevations: No elevation gain.
Special attractions: An easily accessible hike along the Poudre River in undeveloped portions of Fort Collins; a wide, level and paved trail highly suitable for wheelchair travel, featuring river bottom flora.
Best season: Year round.
For more information: Fort Collins Parks and Recreation Department, 145 E. Mountain, Fort Collins, CO 80521, (303) 484-4220.

HIKE 11 *POUDRE RIVER TRAIL*

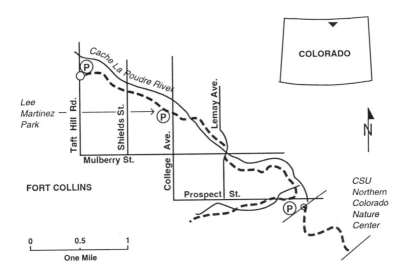

The hike: The Poudre River Trail, located near the northern and northeastern city limits of Fort Collins, is ideally suited for all types of hikers, from the youngest to the eldest members of any family to wheelchair-bound people who enjoy the outdoors. The wide, paved trail paralleling the Cache la Poudre River has multiple purposes, multiple accesses, and is hikeable during any season of the year.

You may reach the trail at four different access points: Taft Hill Road, north of Vine Drive; Lee Martinez Park at College Avenue and Cherry Street; Lemay Avenue and Mulberry Street; or Prospect Avenue east of Timberline Road. A new extension of the Poudre River Trail starts south of East Prospect at Prospect Ponds. There are two trailhead parking areas here, a handicapped fishing access, and sixteen-foot-wide asphalt trail which is wheelchair accessible, extending to the Northern Colorado Nature Center operated by Colorado State University. The two other parking lots for the trail are located at the Taft Hill and Lee Martinez Park access points. To reach the Taft Hill access point, simply drive west on any major road to Taft Hill Road, and go north past Vine Drive to the Cache la Poudre River. The parking lot is just .25 mile south of the river. To reach Lee Martinez Park, drive north on Fort Collins' main drag, College Avenue, to Cherry Street and turn west one block to the trailhead entrance.

The Poudre River Trail is seven miles measured from Taft Hill Road to Prospect Street where it connects to another trail heading southwest, the Spring Creek Trail, five miles long. Beyond that, the trail also connects to Fort Collins' extensive bicycle trail network.

Beginning at Taft Hill Road, you will first travel through the only "open" portion of the trail between your starting point and Shields Street. Here you will have a panoramic view of the foothills to the west. This is a beautiful spot for a stroll during autumn's change of color; a perfect stretch for grandma to take her new grandchild to see the golds, reds and browns of the season. At Shields Street you may exit the trail or continue on via an underpass.

The 1.4-mile stretch of trail between Shields Street and Lee Martinez Park at College Avenue is the most diversified and heavily-used portion of the trail. You're likely to encounter people traveling by every mode of transportation imaginable—except those modes that are motorized. You will also find numerous benches to relax on, or, if you're energetic, the mile-long "Wells Fargo Physical Fitness Trail".

From Lee Martinez Park you'll have to cross College Avenue and then you'll continue over the 1.5-mile section to Lemay Avenue, a section less traveled and without the man-made convenience of the last section, but surrounded by the same lush river-bottom flora.

When you reach Lemay Avenue, follow the trail along the street for .25 mile, across the overpass, then back to the river. It is still quite well marked. This final 3.5-mile stretch is used by fishermen and the occasional jogger and it is here that you are most likely to see birdlife such as herons, kingfishers, ducks and geese.

At Prospect Street you have the option of continuing southwest on the Spring Creek Trail, catching a ride back in whatever way you've arranged, or hiking back the way you came. Whatever you decide to do, I'm sure you'll agree that the Poudre River Trail offers limitless possibilities for relaxation and recreation not far from the busy center of this northern Front Range city.
—*Kevin, Leslie & Jesse Conrad*

HIKE 12 *MESA TRAIL*

General description: An easy, accessible, and scenic day hike along the base of the Flatirons.

General location: West edge of Boulder.

Maps: Boulder and Eldorado Springs USGS quads; Arapaho National Forest Map.

Length: Approximately six miles one way.

Degree of difficulty: Easy.

Elevations: 5,600 to 6,500 feet.

Special attractions: Good views of Boulder, the Flatirons, and the eastern plains; wildflowers and a good example of the contact between the plains and the Rocky Mountains.

Best season: Year round.

For more information: Boulder Mountain Parks, P.O. Box 791, Boulder, CO 80306, (303) 441-3408. Boulder Open Space Department, P.O. Box 791, Boulder, CO 80306 (303) 494-0436. (The Mesa Trail north from Bear Creek is under the jurisdiction of Boulder Mountain Parks.)

The hike: The Mesa Trail offers an easy hike along the base of the Flatirons near Boulder, taking you through forest, meadows and grasslands, and offering

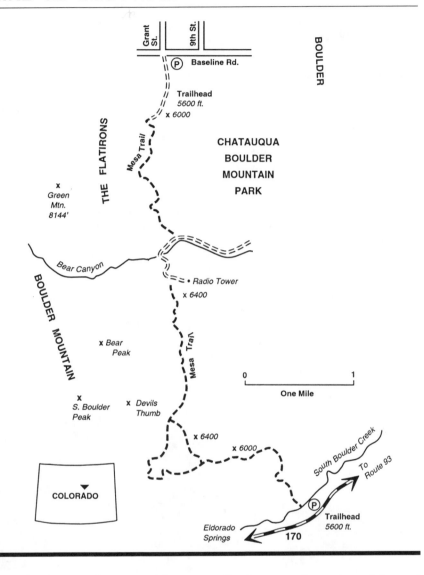

many great views. It traverses the contact line between the eastern plains and
the Rocky Mountains where the underlying Precambrian rocks have been
uplifted and the overlying sedimentary rocks upturned. Nowhere along the
Front Range is this geological phenomenon more spectacular than here in the
Flatirons. Great slabs of Pennsylvanian-age rocks of the Fountain Formation
rise nearly vertically at the western edge of Boulder. Similarly, this area is
the contact point where the grassland vegetation of the eastern plains merges
with the mountain brush and ponderosa pine forests of the foothills. The trail
is about six miles long and takes you from Boulder's Chautauqua Park south

to South Boulder Creek near the town of Eldorado Springs.

To reach the north end of the Mesa trail, take Baseline Road west in Boulder to Chautauqua Park at Baseline and Grant. From there hike south on the paved road near the ranger cottage about .5 mile to where the road begins to switchback at a restroom and look for the Mesa Trail to the left.

To reach the south end of the trail, go south from Boulder on State Highway 93 (Broadway) to State Highway 170 and the sign for Eldorado Springs. Head west on 170 about 1.5 miles and look for the trailhead parking area down and to the right next to South Boulder Creek. If you decide to hike the entire length of the Mesa Trail, you will need to shuttle cars between these two points.

Starting at the north end of the trail, you quickly enter a beautiful forest of ponderosa pines, alternating with many small meadows and offering views of the Flatirons and Boulder to the northeast. At one point, the trail swings around to the base of one of the cliffs, giving you an appreciation of the steepness of the Flatirons. As you hike along, you may notice that other hikers have cut switchbacks. This is a heavily used area and, for that reason, it is important that you not cut switchbacks.

About two miles into your hike, the trail drops down and connects with a road along Bear Canyon. Follow this road upstream to where it crosses the creek and then climbs steeply uphill. Near the top of the hill, and before you reach the radio tower, look for the Mesa Trail taking off to the right. This stretch of the trail, leading through many meadows with spectacular views of the Flatirons, is beautiful and only lightly used.

About two miles farther, you are rewarded by a view of the Devil's Thumb, a spectacular rock outcrop of the Flatirons. Shortly past this point, there is a fork in the trail. The left fork follows an old road for about 1.5 miles to the south trailhead. As you descend, the vegetation changes from ponderosa pine forest to open grassland. The right fork takes you to a beautiful meadow at the base of Shadow Canyon. The last .25 mile is private property with no public access. In Eldorado Springs you can sooth your tired muscles at the hot springs.

The Mesa Trail along the Flatirons.

The Mesa Trail can be hiked during any season and offers access to many side trails along its length. You could easily spend many hours exploring all the hiking possibilities they provide.—*Caryn, Peter and Crystal Boddie*

HIKE 13 *BARR LAKE STATE PARK TRAIL*

General description: A pleasant day hike around a prairie reservoir with excellent opportunities to observe wildlife and birdlife.
General location: Eighteen miles northeast of Denver.
Maps: Park brochure map available at park office.
Degree of difficulty: Easy.
Length: Approximately nine miles one way.
Elevation: Remains at about 5,000 feet.
Special attractions: Easily accessible from Denver Metro area; lots of wildlife and birdlife to observe; a boardwalk takes you out into the lake for a good view of a heron rookery; the trail is accessible to wheelchairs, though parts of it are steep.
Best season: Spring or fall.
For more information: Contact Barr Lake State Park, 13401 Picadilly Rd., Brighton, CO 80601, (303) 659-6005.

The hike: In the middle of the plains east of Denver, Barr Lake State Park, with its towering cottonwoods and accompanying wildlife, is a veritable oasis in a dry and spacious land.

To reach it, take Interstate 76 east to Bromley Lane, continue east on Bromley Lane to Picadilly, and head south on Picadilly to the park entrance. There is a park pass fee for all motorized vehicles.

Barr Lake is an irrigation reservoir surrounded by the old ditchrider's road. You will be hiking a trail which follows this road closely-an easy hike, maintaining a fairly constant elevation of approximately 5,000 feet. Keep in mind that the trail and canal road become quite muddy after a rain.

Begin your hike at the nature center located within view of the parking area. The center, operated by the Division of Wildlife, offers informational displays and a naturalist who will inform you of recent and/or unusual bird sightings.

From the center, cross the bridge over the Denver-Hudson Canal. Immediately to the left of the bridge is the Niedrach Nature Trail, named for Robert Niedrach, an ornithologist who did much fieldwork in the Barr Lake area. This trail includes a boardwalk with a beautiful view of the lake. Here, as you pass under the tall cottonwoods and by the willows that form their understory, you may observe smaller birds that frequent the lakeshore. In the spring, you may see waterfowl such as coots or the elusive western grebe (a species that seems to spend more time under the water than above it).

Barr Lake is an irrigation reservoir and the lake level drops dramatically at the end of the summer. Since visitors are required to stay on designated trails, this usually means that hikers are far away from the shoreline in the fall. However rangers install temporary trail systems leading visitors from the nature trail to the lake where they can get a good view of migrating shore birds.

From the nature trail, you will rejoin the main canal trail, passing a treeless section of the shoreline. When the water level is high in the lake, this area is a

HIKE 13 *BARR LAKE STATE PARK TRAIL*

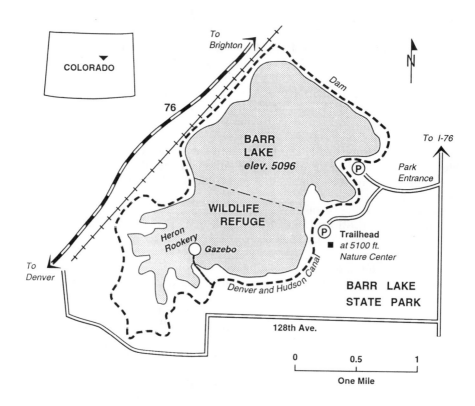

shallow bay where you may see mallards, pintails, and teal.

At about the one-mile marker on the canal trail, you will find a meadow that lies between the canal road and the lakeshore. Here you can remain on the main trail or follow a side trail along the shore under the cottonwoods. This trail leads to a photoblind built along the shore. If you are a photographer, set your camera up here and wait for the white pelicans, grebes, and other waterfowl that may float within range of your camera lens.

Back again on the main canal trail, proceed to the highlight of your hike: the boardwalk which extends about .25 mile out over the lake to a large gazebo from which you can focus your binoculars and spotting scopes—or just your eyes—on an active rookery to observe great blue herons, double-crested cormorants, black-crowned night herons, and snowy egrets. Geese, coots, and grebes will dot the water surrounding you, especially in the spring when the water is highest. This is also the best place to view the bald eagle nest, which

Boardwalk and gazebo at Barr Lake State Park.

is near the other rookery nests. This is the only active eagle's nest along the Front Range. Information and a display on the eagles are featured at the Barr Lake Nature Center.

If you can tear yourself away from the gazebo, you may choose to hike back to the nature center, making a round trip of about three miles. If you choose to proceed around the lake, you will discover some cattail marshes, alive with yellow-headed blackbirds in the spring.

Just beyond the two-mile marker on the trail are the headgates which control the water entering the lake from the South Platte River. At this point, you will leave the park and hike along the gravel road in order to cross the canal. Turn to your right to cross the bridge on the road. Follow the trail marker telling you how to re-enter the park. The southern end of the lake has many shallow bays which become isolated pools as the water recedes during the summer. These are prime feeding areas for great blue herons. In this area you will come upon the old headgates and canal which fed the lake prior to 1906, when the size of the dam was increased. As you continue hiking, notice that the trees in this area form a dense screen along the lake, and be alert for flocks of pelicans, geese, grebes, coots, and other waterfowl. From the south end, the canal trail continues along the west side of the lake. As you pass the middle of the west side, you will be in an open field where a variety of hawks are frequently seen. From here, the trail follows the railroad tracks for a short way. The trail continues to the west end of the dam. A stone house, constructed in 1888, is situated here. Although the house has not been restored, steps have been taken to stabilize its condition for possible future restoration.

At this point, cross the top of the dam, an earthen structure faced with concrete, from which you are offered an expansive view of the nearly 2,000-acre reservoir. Then follow the eastern side of the lake past the boat ramp and back to the nature center. Here you have a last opportunity to observe many small birds, as well as an occasional hawk or owl.

Be sure to take plenty of water with you, to not take pets into the southern end of the park (which is a wildlife refuge), and to enjoy this unique hike.
—*Carol Leasure*

HIKE 14 *HISTORIC DENVER*

General description: A "Walking Tour of Denver Historic," which also highlights other important landmarks and attractions of downtown.
General location: Downtown Denver.
Maps: Denver Historic Self-Guided Walking Tour Map available at the Denver Metro Convention and Visitor's Center (reprinted here). A good road map of Denver.
Degree of difficulty: Easy.
Length: 8.5 miles. Hikers may choose to walk the tour in shorter sections, however.
Elevations: About one mile high consistently.
Special Attractions: This tour really allows you to see downtown Denver. It focuses on the historic architecture of the city, and points out every museum, park, public square, bike path, cultural and culinary attraction, and entertainment and shopping spot.
For more information: Contact the Denver Metro Convention and Visitors Center, 225 W. Colfax Ave., Denver, CO 80202, (303) 892-1505.

The hike: *The following description is reprinted here by permission of Charles A. Hillestad, author of "Denver Historic! A Self-Guided Walking Tour," which is available at the Denver Metro Convention and Visitors Center. A few minor updates and adaptations have been made in the text.*

This walking tour is deliberately designed so that it can be done piecemeal if time is a problem. The text indicates convenient stopping points that will lead the hiker back to his or her car. The hiker may also hike the entire tour at once. Attractions along the tour are indicated by numbers in the text, which correlate with the numbers on the accompanying map.

A nice place to start touring Denver, known as the Queen City of the Plains and Gateway to the Rockies, is Benedict Fountain Park (1). Free parking abounds and from the Carrara marble fountain, which was carved in Italy, there are wonderful views of the skyline, Longs Peak and Denver's oldest surviving residential neighborhood.

From the fountain, walk across the park toward the restored Victorian homes to pick up the tour route. Flagstone sidewalks delineate the Clements Historic District (2) listed on both the federal and city historic registries. Denver currently has twenty-two official historic districts and well over 250 buildings certified as historic.

Heading toward the high rises, you will first pass the historic St. Andrew's

Church (3) and then the Holy Ghost Church (4) home of a Vietnam War Memorial.

The federal complex, site of the customs house (5) the courthouse (6) and the post office (7) lies just ahead. The courthouse contains the U.S. Geologic Survey, a great source of Denver and Front Range maps (great resource for hikers). Across from the post office on 18th Street stands the Ghost Building (8). Originally located six blocks away, it was resurrected on this site stone by stone using a numbering system for identification of each piece.

Around the corner and down the street, catercorner from each other are two of Denver's earliest banking centers (9,10). If you want to do only half the tour at this time, skip ahead to item 35, the Equitable Building.)

The route passes through narrow Skyline Park (11) with its three fountains. The fountain closest to the route represents a high mountain brook.

The next point of interest is the old Cable Car Barn (12) remodeled into a restaurant. Much of the old cable car track and the cobblestone lining it are still in the streets, merely buried under modern blacktop.

Sakura Square (13) with its Buddhist Temple, shops and restaurants, serves the local Japanese community. Each year the Cherry Blossom Festival is held here.

The route next enters Lower Downtown (14), or LoDo, as the locals call it. Union Station (15) the largest structure in this end of town, heads 17th Street. Also in the area is one of the nation's finest assemblage of late 1800s commercial structures, such as the Oxford Hotel(16). Half a block from the route, at 1330 17th Street, are the Historic Denver, Inc. offices (17). Stop by for a map showing all historic properties.

The Tabor Center (18), Writers Square (19) and Larimer Square (20), the latter being one of the most famous restoration projects in the state, offer some of Denver's finest shopping. The same can be said of the Tivoli (21), originally a brewery and now an entertainment and restaurant complex. (Tired of walking? Larimer Square is also the base for several horse-drawn carriage companies that will allow you to continue the tour riding in style.)

The Auraria Campus (22), a common campus for several colleges, occupies the former site of Auraria, a township overtaken when Denver jumped claim on it and St. Charles. The Ninth Street Historic Park (23) is also located on the campus.

Heading back downtown, you'll cross Cherry Creek (24) again. The bike path next to the stream connects with an extensive system reaching into the foothills. The grand staircase on the city side of the creek enters the Denver Arts Center (25) home of several theater, ballet, and opera companies and the Colorado Symphony. The Denver Convention Center (26), which opened in 1990, is to the east, between 12th and 14th Streets.

Skyline Park on Arapahoe Street provides the foreground for the cubistic black offices (27) of the Denver and Rio Grande Railroad Company. (Note the structure's resemblance to a steam locomotive; the entries are wheel wells and the cab is to the left.) Back on 16th Street, you can't miss the Daniels and Fisher Tower (28). Copied from St. Mark's in Italy, it has always been Denver's most famous landmark. Although once attached to a major building (note the contrasting brick on the rear), the tower is now all that remains.

Don't miss the Ticket Bus (29). It is an excellent stopping point to see what entertainment is going on in Denver. By the way, all buses on the mall are free. They stop every block. The terminals on each end of the mall are transfer points for buses circulating to other parts of the city.

The Changing Scene Theater (30) on Champa is part of a delightful row of restored structures. Just down the street is the "Wedding Cake Building." (31) Formerly the Electric Company headquarters, it features hundreds of lights on its facade.

On the way back to the mall, you will see the Denver Post Building (32). The glass wall on the California Street side allows pedestrians to watch the huge printing presses in operation. Next is the Masonic Temple (33) which was once completely gutted by fire.

The Neusteter Building (34) and the Denver Dry Goods Building (35) were originally showpieces of two mercantile empires. Note the fossils embedded in the Neusteter facade. Next on the walk is the Equitable Building (36) Be sure to enter the lobby and see the signed Tiffany glass panels. Its location is "Bank Row" (37) which appeared in the opening of the television show "Dynasty." (If you want to save the capitol/museum leg of the tour for later, simply continue down 17th Street to the Brown Palace, item (52), picking up the route there.)

The Paramount Theater (38) is the only remaining theater out of the "Great White Way" that once existed downtown. The Denver Partnership, a source for free brochures of upcoming Denver events, is located in the Kittridge Building (39) adjoining the Paramount. A large collection of outdoor restaurants graces this block.

The Firefighters Museum (40) is open to the general public as is the Denver Mint (41) located between the old Rocky Mountain News building (42)—the new home of Colorado's oldest newspaper is just to the west—and the City and County Building (43).

All kinds of brochures are available free at the Denver Visitors Center (44). Where to stay. Where to eat. What to visit. Pick up several to use to decide what to do when you return to your car.

The next stretch of the tour could be called Museum Row with the Denver Art Museum (45) the Byers-Evans House (46) the Colorado History Museum (47), and the Western Historic Collection in the Public Library (48), not to mention the State Capitol (49).

Climb the front steps of the capitol to a point exactly one mile high. You can also climb to the top of the rotunda. Its dome is real gold, but more valuable is the rose onyx wainscotting lining the interior walls. The world's entire supply was used in building the capitol. Free tours are available.

In front of the capitol is Civic Center Park. Most of Denver's largest festivals take place here: the Festival of Mountain and Plains, the People's Fair, and others. It is not the only locale for festivities, though. Almost every plaza and park downtown has at least one festival, concert or other free event sometime during the year. Noon hours in the summer are particularly rewarding with all the music put on by various groups in the open spaces.

Back on the path, several historic churches can be seen including the Catholic Church's Basilica (50). Of a more earthy nature is the Chamber of Commerce Building (51). Earthier yet is the Rodin sculpture of "The Thinker," in the Amoco lobby (52). Around the corner is the famous Brown Palace Hotel (53) with its nine-story atrium. Ask for a tour brochure. Facing the Brown is the Museum of Western Art (54). It is inside the Navarre Building, which was once a brothel.

Trinity Methodist Church (55), headquarters of the Denver Chamber Orchestra, is next and last. Step inside to learn more about this beautiful church and to see its peaceful sanctuary.

Finally, stroll on back to the Benedict Fountain Park. If you want to linger in the historic residential area, stop by the Queen Anne Inn at 2147 Tremont for a free brochure detailing each home in the district.

If you get turned around or lost at any time, ask for directions. Almost everyone you see will be glad to assist you. Denver is a friendly town. Unlike many big cities, it is a safe place to be. Enjoy the great weather, incredible views, fine shops, galleries, clubs and restaurants, not to mention our delightful cultural, sports and entertainment activities. Remember, you have only scratched the surface with this tour. There are plenty more "precious stones" to be found if you dig a little deeper.—*Charles Hillestad*

HIKE 15 *GREEN MOUNTAIN*

General description: An easy and easily accessible day hike through a relatively undisturbed foothills ecosystem.

General location: About four miles north of Morrison.

Maps: Jefferson County Open Space Hayden's Green Mountain Park Map.

Degree of difficulty: Easy.

Length: 3.5 miles one way; 7.25 miles round trip.

Elevations: 6,200 to 6,800 feet.

Special attractions: Wonderful example of foothills ecosystem: birds, animals, and wildflowers to be seen. Easily accessible to Metro Denver residents.

For more information: Jefferson County Open Space Department, 18301 W. 10th Ave., Suite 100, Golden, CO 80401, (303) 278-5925.

The hike: Green Mountain offers a number of day hikes in a unique foothills environment that is close to Denver.

To reach Green Mountain, drive west on 6th Avenue past the exit for Interstate 70 and turn left onto U.S. Highway 40. After a short distance, turn left onto Rooney Road. Drive south until you see a parking area on the east side of Rooney Road and a walking bridge over Colorado Highway 470. This is where you'll find the west end of the Green Mountain and Lonesome trails. You may park here and walk over the bridge.

You may also park at the east end of the trails by taking Rooney Road to Alameda Parkway, then driving east to the parking lot near the eastern boundary of the park. It is on the north side of the street.

The Lonesome Trail follows Alameda Parkway for the length of the park and meets the Green Mountain Trail, which climbs the mountain, at east and west ends. You may want to make a loop trip. At the north end of the park is the John Hayden Trail, which was cut short with the construction of C-470.

Green Mountain was donated to Jefferson County by the Hayden family as a memorial to William Frederick Hayden. The Open Space park is called "Hayden's Green Mountain Park."

The hike is especially exciting when days are cool and sunny, mysteriously foggy, or when snow or rain is gently falling. Wild ravines reveal small spring-fed streams and wet areas.

Hiking up the ridges of Green Mountain, you will find the north-facing slopes covered with mountain mahogany, chokecherry, and many other shrubs. Handsome ponderosa pine, and aspen, cottonwood, willows and juniper dot some areas.

Atop Green Mountain you will have a panoramic view: Longs Peak, and the Flat Irons to the northwest; Table Mountain to the north; Mount Evans to the west; Red Rocks, the Dakota Hogback, and Pikes Peak to the south; and the Front Range cities and plains to the east.

Early morning and evening are the best times to see wildlife. There is a resident herd of about fifty mule deer, and foxes, coyotes, rabbits, raccoon, prairie dogs and birds are often sighted.

The bird listings are about 150 plus species, ranging from golden eagle to

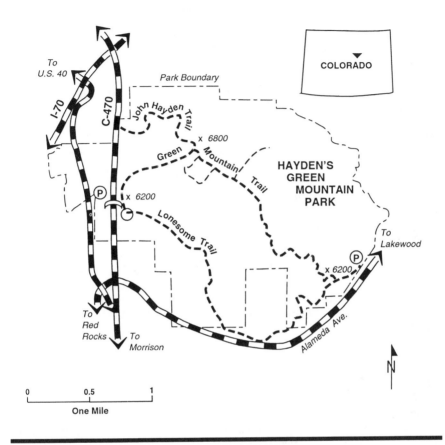

hummingbirds. The rufous-sided towhee will hop over to observe you as you hike by. And March brings the bright blue mountain bluebird during its migration north.

Springtime on Green Mountain is green time. From the thrill of the first Easter daisy in March abundant wildflowers take turns showing off. There are: Indian paintbrush, lupine, larkspur, Mariposa lily, yucca, evening primrose, and wild rose. More than 100 species flourish in this area.

Summer brings sightings of fox pups and fawns.

Fall brings big bucks rounding up their mule deer does. The hillside becomes a riot of reds, rusts, and browns highlighted by the gold of the rabbitbrush.

Winter provides an opportunity for an invigorating experience of breaking trail in new snow, and the chance to see how many animal tracks you can identify.

Every day spent on Green Mountain is a unique experience.—*Nan Brehmer and Mary Dolan*

HIKE 16 *HIGH LINE CANAL*

General description: A day hike in the southern portion of the Denver Metropolitan area.

General location: Beginning one mile southwest of Waterton near Chatfield Reservoir and ending near the Rocky Mountain Arsenal.

Maps: USGS Front Range Corridor Map, Sheet 2 of 3.

Degree of difficulty: Easy.

Length: Can be hiked in easily accessible sections for fifty-eight of its seventy-one total miles.

Elevations: Follows a "high line of gravity," dropping only 300 feet for its entire length.

Special attractions: A beautiful strip of open space winding its way through residential, urban and country settings; used by a variety of people; features lush prairie pond vegetation and wildlife; accessible to the wheelchair-bound; beautiful views of the Front Range.

Best season: Year round.

For more information: The Denver Water Department, Office of Community Affairs, (303) 623-250.

The hike: When James Duff, a hardy Scotsman, introduced the idea of irrigating the dry plains of Colorado back in 1870, he met with the overwhelming skepticism of early Denver residents. But he completed his seventy-one-mile irrigation ditch anyway and opened it in 1883. Little did he realize that, with this "High Line Canal," he was not only providing Denver and the eastern plains with a water source but with a narrow oasis that Denverites of the next century would value more for its recreational opportunities than for its original purpose of irrigation.

The High Line Canal today is used by people on horseback, by joggers, bikers, the wheelchair-bound, roller skaters, mothers with babies in strollers, and by hikers. It is a refreshing strip of nature in the midst of a very busy city. To reach the High Line Canal, which winds its way through the southern portion of the Denver Metro area, take a look at the map portion of the Denver Metro area shown below and find the street nearest to you that meets the canal. Or, if you are ambitious and want to see a variety of country, begin at the canal's southern end near Waterton and Chatfield Reservoir and hike its length in sections.

For the fifty-eight miles that is hikeable (it is unhikeable in Waterton Canyon and near the Arsenal), the canal is paralleled by a twelve-foot-wide road along which you'll be hiking, and which is lined with tall cottonwoods, providing shade in summer and beautiful colors in fall.

As you follow the canal, you will hike through open plains where you will feel far away from the hustle and bustle of the city, through beautiful open areas where you'll have views of both the Front Range and the skyline of downtown Denver, and through urban areas where the canal is paved and used mostly by joggers and bikers. For its length, you will be seeing the lush vegetation typical of a prairie pond: cottonwoods, Queen Anne's lace, and wild asparagus. You will also see geese and a variety of species of ducks, as well as magpies, meadowlarks, prairie dogs, and even foxes and pheasants in open areas.

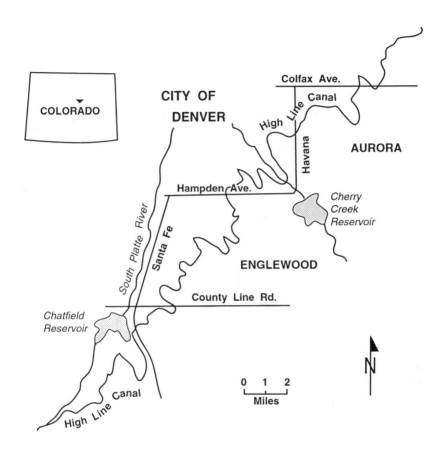

You will also hike through or around several parks, residential areas, and golf courses, and the flowers that some residents grow in their backyards during the summer months will highlight your walk.

The wonderful gift of an ambitious man who thought he was providing just an irrigation ditch, the High Line Canal is a narrow strip of country Denverites can enjoy year round without having to leave town: a place to see the changing leaves in autumn, walk in the snow in wintertime, first notice the appearance of the greenery of spring, and enjoy the cool shade of the cottonwoods in summer.—*Caryn Boddie*

Hikers on the High Line Canal Trail.

HIKE 17 *MONUMENT VALLEY TRAIL*

General description: A day hike through the City of Colorado Springs along Monument Creek.

General location: Colorado Springs, north of the central business district.

Maps: Colorado Springs Parks and Recreation Department Map.

Length: Several options exist for day hikes of varying lengths. Eventually, the trail may go from Rampart Reservoir on the north to North Cheyenne Canyon on the south and connect with several side trails.

Elevations: Little elevation gain.

Special attractions: An exceptional finger of open space extending into the City of Colorado Springs; excellent view.

Best season: Year round.

For more information: Colorado Springs Parks and Recreation Department, 1401 Recreation Way, Colorado Springs, CO 80905; (719) 578-6640.

The hike: The Monument Valley Trail takes you along Monument Creek from Bijou Street at its southern end to Monroe Street at its northern end (soon to extend farther in both directions). You'll pass parks and residential areas and have scenic views in all directions on this exceptional strip of open space.

The Monument Valley Trail with downtown Colorado Springs in the background.

At this writing, you should begin your hike at Bijou Street. Take Interstate I-25 to the Bijou Street exit and head east to Cascade. Park along the street near a small park and walk down the hill to the trail following Monument Creek (it goes along both banks), the headwaters of which are in the rolling country north of Colorado Springs and which join Fountain Creek farther south—the route Zebulon Pike once followed from Pueblo.

As you start walking, look up to the west. You will have an excellent view of Pikes Peak, rising massive above the city. The peak has inspired people for centuries, including the Ute Indians who believed that the Great Spirit was restless one day so he took a large stone, gouged out a hole in the sky and

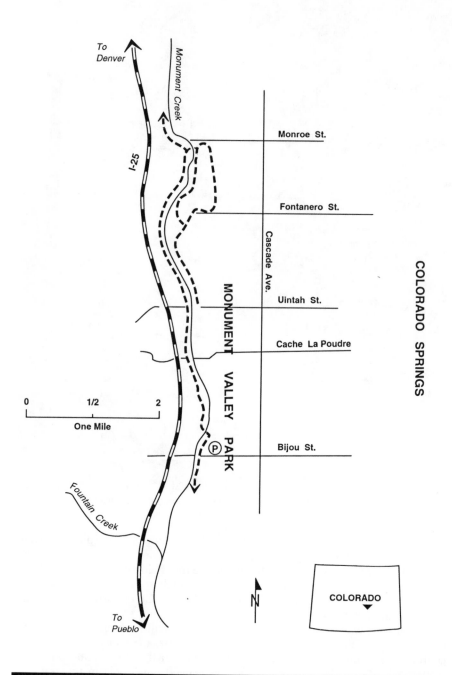

poured ice and snow into the hole until he had made a great peak.

To the northeast as you hike along, you will have views of the foothills and mesas; to the east you will be able to see Pulpit Rock, a unique geologic formation; to the south is the skyline of downtown.

Between Bijou and Cache La Poudre Streets, on the west side of the creek, you will see a softball/baseball field, volleyball courts, a large group picnic shelter and other public recreation facilities. Farther along, near Uintah Street, there is a duck lake on the west side, as well as an historical sundial and a pinetum (an arboretum of pine trees) and some tennis courts on the east side of the creek. The Colorado College campus is nearby to the east, as well.

Continue north of Uintah Street into North Monument Valley Park. Beyond the baseball field is the Monument Valley Fitness Trail, which circles around the north end of the park and past a scenic overlook and a geologic column. This was a gift from William Jackson Palmer, founder of Colorado Springs and a wise man who banned horses and vehicles from this park in its early days, sensing that people needed open space and parks to walk in.

The Colorado Springs Parks and Recreation Department has great plans for this trail and others in this city. For an up-to-date description of future revisions and additions to the trail system, contact their office as listed above.
—*Caryn Boddie*

HIKE 18 *ARKANSAS RIVER TRAIL*

General description: A wide, paved trail along the Arkansas River.
General location: The City of Pueblo.
Maps: City of Pueblo Trail System Map.
Degree of difficulty: Easy.
Length: Will be approximately twenty miles long when completed; offers opportunities for several shorter day hikes.
Elevations: Little elevation gain from the confluence of the Arkansas River and Fountain Creek at 4,650 feet.
Special attractions: A scenic and easily accessible trail along the river bottom of the Arkansas River; many species of birds and waterfowl; accessible to the wheelchair-bound.
Best season: Year round. For more information: The City of Pueblo, Parks Department, 860 Goodnight Ave., Pueblo, CO 81005; (719) 566-1745.

The hike: This river trail system through the southern Front Range city of Pueblo will be an extensive system when completed taking you from the El Paso County Line and Colorado Springs on the northeast to Pueblo Reservoir at the trail's southwest end.

A good starting point is on the Arkansas River Trail at the Audubon Nature Center west of Pueblo Boulevard on West 11th Street. To reach it, take State Highway 50 (Canon City Highway) west to Pueblo Boulevard. Go south on the boulevard for about three miles to the Arkansas River Valley. Pass over a railroad on a high bridge and turn right (west) at the foot of the grade on 11th Street. Follow 11th Street west for one mile and park at the Nature Center at the foot of the hill beside the river. You can hike either way on the trail, but we recommend going west toward Pueblo Reservoir, a hike of about 3.5 miles one way.

As you hike west from the Nature Center, you will be hiking along the cottonwood-lined river bottom of the Arkansas River. There you may see birds and wildlife, including beavers, whose mud paths cross the trail as they fell trees and build their dams. Deer and an occasional bear may be seen on the western end of the trail.

The Pueblo Reservoir at the end of your 3.5-mile hike is a typical reservoir, but with limestone cliffs and flat-top buttes rimming its irregular seventeen-mile shoreline and the Greenhorn and Sangre de Cristo mountains forming an alpine backdrop to the west. Prickly pear cactus are found there, along with cottonwoods and willows. There are red-tailed hawks in the area, too, as well as the occasional rattlesnake.

From the Reservoir, return to your starting point and, if you like, head the other direction to Pueblo's City Park, and on to Runyan Lake and Fountain Creek. There is a crossing at Fountain Creek. A proposed trail will someday connect the Arkansas River Trail with the Fountain Creek Trail, which follows Fountain Creek north from Plaza Verde Park to University Boulevard.
—*Frances C. Carter*

HIKE 18 *ARKANSAS RIVER TRAIL*

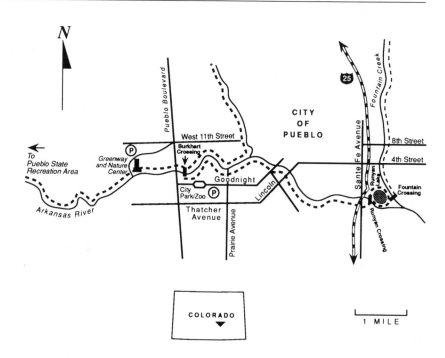

HIKE 19 *NORTH CANYON*

General description: A day hike in a prairie canyon in the Commanche National Grassland.

General location: Thirty miles southwest of Springfield.

Maps: Tubs Springs and Campo SW USGS quads; Comanche National Grassland Map.

Degree of difficulty: Easy.

Length: Four miles one way.

Elevations: 4,200 to 4,450 feet.

Special attractions: Short-grass prairie; many species of birds and wildlife; wildflowers in spring; many small canyons to explore; Indian pictographs.

Best season: Spring.

For more information: Comanche National Grassland, 27162 Highway 287, P.O. Box 127, Springfield, CO 81073; (719) 523-6591.

The hike: Perhaps writer Willa Cather said it best when she compared the plains to a wild horse that couldn't be tamed; that ran wild and kicked things to pieces. The country that makes up the Comanche National Grassland is like that. Though there are many successful farms in the area, there is also evidence of the many other people who tried to tame this land and failed. Old equipment and battered structures that used to be homesteads dot the land.

The beauty of the Comanche National Grassland is subtle and you must get out on the land to appreciate it. North Canyon is located in the southern-most portion of the area where the rolling short-grass prairie has been dissected by erosion to form a series of small canyons. There is a variety of wildlife and vegetation to be discovered here, as well as evidence of the Indian peoples who left their history in the form of pictographs.

To reach North Canyon, take U.S. Highway 287 south from Springfield about seventeen miles. At the point where the highway bends to the east, turn right on County Road M. You will also see a sign for the Carrizo Picnic Area. Follow this gravel road west for about eight miles and turn left on County Road 18. Follow Road 18 south for about seven miles to where it mends to the left, and you come to a ranch house. Take the small dirt road that is across from the ranch house south into Picture Canyon for .5 mile. Park just inside the fence and cattle guard, which marks the national grassland boundary.

Begin hiking on the jeep road and bear right at the fork. (The left fork takes you about 2.5 miles into Picture Canyon—a once interesting canyon where the original Indian pictograhs have been carved and painted over with graffiti. A real disappointment.)

As you hike away from Picture Canyon and towards North Canyon, think of all the people who have come before you to this wild land. In fact, recorded history of the inhabitants of this area begins about 1535 A.D. At that time the Mescalero Apache were known to live herre. However, recent investigations in the canyons of southern Baca County indicate that this area was inhabited as early as 385 A.D. from 1540 to 1727 the Spanish explored and occupied the area. Around 1700 the Ute Indians came from west of the Rockies and were followed by the Comanches. It was not until the 1800s that white man came into the area to trade with the Indians. They were followed by

Rock window in North Canyon.

the cattlemen in the late 1800s and the farmers in the early 1900s.

Follow the jeep road up and over a small saddle to the west. Go straight at another fork in the road and drop down into a small canyon, which will connect you with North Canyon (Holt Canyon on the USGS map). From here you can explore in anyh direction you like, but a good destination would be Cave Spring. From the intersection with North Canyon, hike south about 1.5 miles until you come to an old homestead. The fenceline, a few hundred feet to the south marks the Oklahoma border, while the side canyon to the west contains Cave Spring. Drink at your own risk.

Prairie flora on the grasslands consists mainly of short-grass on the hard land (buffalo grass and blue grama are the primary species) and mid-grass, occurring mostly in sandy areas (sand drop seed, side oats grama, little blue stem, western wheat grass, sand sage, and yucca are common). Wildlife on the grasslands includes 275 different species of birds including quail, pheasant, dove, bald eagle, golden eagle, ducks, geese, hawks, and road runners. Mountain lion, bear, deer, antelope, fox, coyote, and bobcat are among the mammals found in the area.

Be sure to take plenty of water with you and wear good stout boots. Keep an eye out for rattlesnakes as you're hiking. You can return the way you came or explore some of the other canyons before heading back to your car.—*Caryn, Peter and Crystal Boddie*

HIKE 19 *NORTH CANYON*

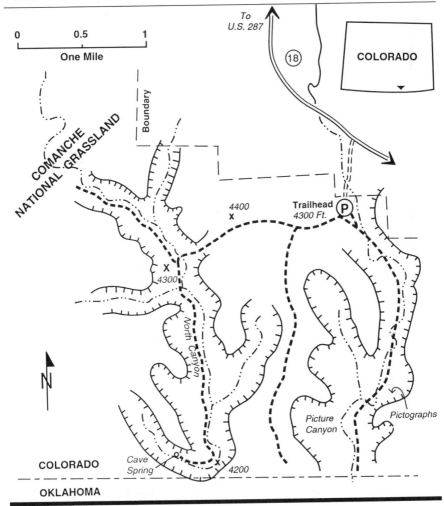

Old homesteader's cabin in North Canyon.

HIKE 20 *APISHAPA CANYON*

General description: A variety of day hikes in the spectacular prairie and canyons of the Apishapa State Wildlife Area. Requires some rock scrambling and off-trail hiking to descend into the canyons.
General location: Twenty-five miles east of Walsenburg.
Maps: Jones Lake Spring and Sun Valley Ranch quads.
Degree of difficulty: Easy to difficult.
Length: Varies from two to seven miles depending on route.
Elevations: 5,100 to 5,600 feet.
Special attractions: Spectacular prairie canyons and wildlife including: pronghorn antelope, mule deer, bighorn sheep, wild turkeys, prairie falcons, and other raptors.
Best season: Spring and fall.
For more information: Colorado Division of Wildlife, Area 11, 200 Reservoir Rd., Pueblo, CO 80105; (719) 561-4909.

The hike: The Apishapa Canyon is one of several small but spectacular canyons which break the otherwise featureless expanse of prairie in southeastern Colorado. The Huerfano, Apishapa, Purgatoire and Cucharas rivers all drain the eastern side of the Spanish Peaks and the Culebra Range and head northeast to join the Arkansas River. As each river crosses the prairie it cuts a deep canyon (relative to the plains topography) through the resistant Dakota sandstone formation. Of these canyons, only the Apishapa is presently open to public access within the Apishapa State Wildlife Area, one of the oldest wildlife areas in Colorado.

To reach the Apishapa State Wildlife Area, take State Highway 10 northeast from Walsenburg approximately 8.5 miles. Between mileposts 16 and 17, look for the State Wildlife Area sign and turn south onto a county road. Follow this road and the wildlife area signs (you want the north property area) for approximately 16.5 miles to the Apishapa State Wildlife Area boundary. Turn right into the wildlife area and follow the main road another 1.7 miles to a gravel parking area. The county roads to this point are passable to passenger cars in any season when dry. Under wet conditions, the Division of Wildlife prohibits vehicle travel anywhere beyond the parking area, and a four-wheel drive vehicle may be necessary even to reach that point.

From the parking area a number of hiking options are available; but some require careful route selection and some rock-scrambling to enter and exit the canyons. For the closest point to view or descend into the canyons, follow the jeep road uphill and to the south approximately 0.7 mile to the high point of the mesa. From here you can see that the gently sloping topography, controlled by the resistant Dakota sandstone, has been cut by the Apishapa River and several tributary streams.

This area is a true transition zone with species representative of prairie, desert, and foothills. The surrounding short-grass prairie is interspersed with pinon, juniper, and the misshapen and menacing cholla cactus. The rare shelter and greenery of cottonwoods can be found in the riparian habitat of the canyon bottoms, and the occasional ponderosa pine is reminiscent of past climatic conditions.

From the high point, follow the jeep road to the southeast and east .5 mile to the edge of Jones Lake Canyon. From this vantage point you can see the junction with Apishapa Canyon about .5 mile to the east and 350 feet below. You have the choice of following along the canyon rim or finding a safe route to descend to the canyon bottom—note that you can descend, but it is not particularly easy and requires some rock-scrambling.

While exploring the canyon walls look for prairie falcons and other raptors, but please do not disturb any nests you may find. Big horn sheep, which once roamed these canyons as evidenced by Indian pictographs, have been reintroduced by the Division of Wildlife. Note that these animals are particularly sensitive to the presence of humans, so please keep your distance. Roadrunners, scaled quail, rattlesnakes, wild turkey, mule deer, pronghorn antelope, and soft-shelled turtles in the canyon bottom are also denizens you may encounter in this wild area. Mountain lion and bobcats are present but rarely seen. And, the area supports a large population of bluebirds in the winter.

Two options for longer hikes: descend into the Apishapa Canyon near the east boundary of the wildlife area by way of Buckletton Canyon; or make a loop along the canyon bottoms between this entry point and the previously described route to Jones Lake Canyon.

To hike into the canyon at the eastern end, hike or drive (requires a high-clearance vehicle and dry road conditions) along the jeep road east from the parking area approximately 3.2 miles to an old homestead cabin near the east boundary. From this cabin it is an easy rock scramble down into Buckletton Canyon and the junction with the Apishapa River. Depending upon river state, the river bed and canhon can be easily followed from this point upstream. In about one mile you'll come to a rock pinnacle in a large side alcove of the canyon, both carved by a now-abandoned meander of the Apishapa River.

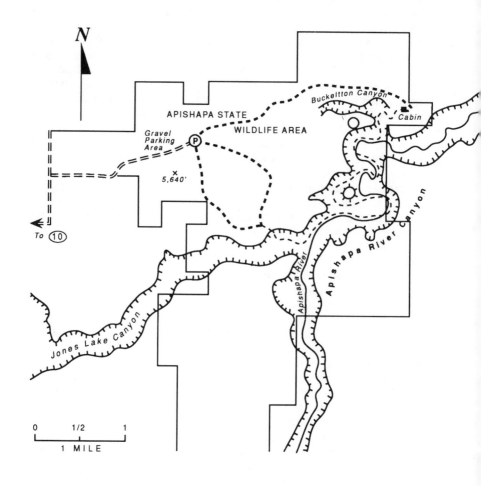

You are free to explore the canyons upstream of this point, but please remain within the wildlife area boundary. Use your best judgment in ascending and descending the canyon walls and in following the stream in the canyon bottom. Primitive camping is permitted in the wildlife area, but use care if you camp, and please respect the wildlife. Also, you may want to contact the Division of Wildlife before your hike for road condition and hunting season information.—*Peter Boddie*

The Mountains

"With all their infinite variations, the mountains comprise not only heaving waves of forest, but jutting cliffs, abysmal gorges, and deep sunless canyons, vast open parks and tiny arctic meadows, small blue lakes, gushing warm geysers, mineral springs, cold trout pools, lacy falls, heavy cataracts and great soggy marshes, cones and craters of extinct volcanoes, bristling hogbacks, rolling hills of sage and cedar, high groves of aspen, immense flat-topped mesas, solitary bluffs and weirdly eroded buttes."

This passage by writer Frank Waters really says it all. The following hikes, grouped not by range but by region, are meant to show you Colorado's mountains "with all their infinite variations."

HIKE 21 *WAHATOYA TRAIL*

General description: A day hike or overnighter to a saddle separating the Spanish Peaks and an additional longer route around the West Peak.
General location: Approximately twenty miles southwest of Walsenburg.
Maps: Spanish Peaks, Cuchara, Cucharas Pass, and Herlick Canyon USGS quads; San Isabel National Forest Map.
Degree of difficulty: Moderate to difficult.
Length: From five to fifteen miles one way.
Elevations: 8,500 to 11,500 feet.
Special attractions: The Spanish Peaks; unique geologic features.
Best season: Summer and fall.
For more information: San Isabel National Forest, San Carlos Ranger District, 326 Dozier St., Canon City, CO 81212; (719) 275-4119.

The hike: This hike takes you to the saddle between two important landmarks of south-central Colorado: the Spanish Peaks. You also have the option of circling the peaks to the south and west.

Located east of the Sangre de Cristo Range, the Spanish Peaks have been of importance to Indians, Spanish explorers and settlers at various times in history, and are also known worldwide for their unique volcanic geology. The Indian tribes of southern Colorado believe that all life gets its nourishment from the "Huatollas," these mountains they call the "Breasts of the World." They say that all clouds are born here and hence the life-giving moisture that feeds us all. Indeed, these two peaks rise spectacularly above the plains like some gigantic cleavage. The East Spanish Peak is 12,683 feet high. The West Spanish Peak, more famous, is 13,626 feet.

To reach the trailhead for the Wahatoya Trail, drive into the quaint town of La Veta. Stay on State Highway 12 and take the dirt road to the left (east) just south of town, before you cross the Cucharas River. This is Wahatoya Road, but isn't marked as such. (Anyone in town can direct you if you get lost.) The road winds through the countryside for about two miles, past Town Lakes on the right and around a sharp turn to the left. Turn right after approx-

HIKE 21 *WAHATOYA TRAIL*

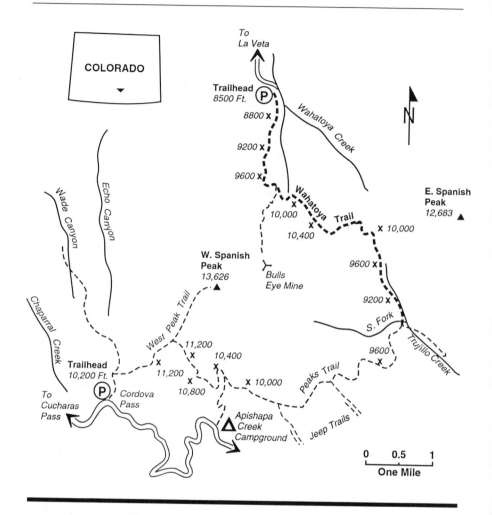

imately .5 mile. From here to the trailhead it is about ten miles. Park your car near the San Isabel Forest sign at the top of the long hill before you go down into the canyon. Be sure and walk over to the edge of Lover's Leap and look down into Wahatoya Canyon before you start out.

From the Forest Service sign you climb to the saddle between East and West Spanish Peaks. The sign at the beginning of your hike indicates that Trujillo Creek, located on the other side of the saddle, is a three-mile-hike. This is wrong. It is about five miles to the saddle and 1.5 miles to Trujillo Creek.

As you begin your hike, you will follow a four-wheel-drive road which ends at the Bulls Eye Mine. About 1.5 miles up the road, turn to your left. There is a Forest Service sign marking the trail turnoff.

If you go straight ahead you will come to the mine, once a thriving, active, working mine, containing no small amount of gold and silver. As you ascend this old jeep trail you will appreciate the tenacity of those old miners who hauled equipment, food, and the various necessities of life up this grade on a regular basis. The mine is privately owned. It is never a good idea to explore old mines.

From here to the saddle, the trail climbs much more gradually and crosses several small tributaries to Wahatoya Creek. If you are making a short over-night trip, there are some good camping spots along this stretch of the trail, but you should select one a good distance from both the streams and the trail.

As you wind your way up and over the saddle, you will come across an avalanche chute and a large rock slide. You should have good views of the peaks from here.

Soon you will head down to the South Fork of Trujillo Creek and a small meadow where there is a cabin. This is a good place to turn around if you are making a day hike. If you plan to continue on, around the south and west sides of West Spanish Peak, follow the trail to the left past the cabin. This is the Peaks Trail, which will take you west towards Apishapa Pass (Cordova Pass) and a side trail to Apishapa Campground. You could car shuttle to either of these points for a long one-way hike of between eleven and thirteen miles from the Wahatoya trailhead.

At Apishapa (Cordova) Pass you will intersect the West Peak Trail taking you to the summit of West Spanish Peak (see the West Spanish Peak hike description).

If you are ambitious, you can hike down along the west slope of the peak into Echo, Wade, and Chapparal Canyons where there are many interesting rock formations and Chapparal Falls. This is a beautiful and little-used area. However, you cannot get out of the bottom of these canyons which end in private land. You will have to retrace your steps to Apishapa Pass and/or all the way back to the Wayatoya trailhead. Be sure to have a topo map if you continue on into this area.

The Spanish Peaks and surrounding area have been proposed as a wilder-ness area. After visiting the area, you may want to encourage your congresspersons to support it as such.—*Leslie Hicks*

HIKE 22 *WEST SPANISH PEAK*

General description: A day hike taking you to the summit of West Spanish Peak and/or the circuitous Apishapa Trail at the base of the mountain.
General location: Twenty miles southwest of Walsenburg.
Maps: Cuchara, Cucharas Pass, Herlick Canyon and Spanish Peaks USGS quads; San Isabel National Forest Map.
Degree of difficulty: Moderate.
Length: Five miles round trip to West Spanish Peak summit; 8.5 miles on Apishapa Trail.
Elevations: 9,700 to 13,626 feet.
Special attractions: Solitude; beautiful views; interesting geology.
Best season: Spring, summer or fall.
For more information: San Isabel National Forest, San Carlos Ranger District, 326 Dozier St., Canon City, CO 81212; (719) 275-4119.

The Devils Stairway, one of the volcanic dikes radiating from West Spanish Peak.
U.S. Forest Service photo.

The hike: A hike up the western of the two Spanish Peaks or "Breasts of the World," as they were called by the Indians who so revered them, is a hike up a very distinctive landmark, culminating with beautiful views of surrounding country and the unique volcanic geology of the area.

To reach the trailhead, drive west on State Highway 160 from Walsenburg and turn south on State Highway 12 through La Veta and Cuchara. The highway continues over 9,941 foot Cucharas Pass.

At the summit of the pass, turn left on the good gravel road. Follow it through the beautiful forest of spruce and fir for six miles to Cordova Pass at 11,248 feet (formerly called Apishapa Pass and still noted that way on the USGS quad). Park beneath the trees in the large parking area provided and look for the gate and sign on the north side of the road. The sign reads, "West Peak Trail" and the gate is there to keep motorbikes out.

You begin your hike as the trail winds along an almost-level ridge offering good views for 1.5 miles until you come to a sign pointing to the right (east) and downhill and labeled "Apishapa Trail." (The Apishapa trail marked on the Cucharas Pass quad is wrong. The trail really begins 1.5 miles from Cordova Pass, at elevation 11,600 feet.) At this point, you can either continue on to climb the West Spanish Peak by continuing on the West Peak Trail, or you can follow the Apishapa Trail in a circle of 8.5 miles, which will lead you back to your parking spot.

The latter is an excellent trail and well-marked. It takes you down four miles, almost 2,000 feet, through forest cut by some streams, where wildflowers grow. It takes you past several volcanic dikes and ends at the gravel road which you followed over Cordova Pass. From there you will need to hike about 4.5 miles back up the road to your car. On your way up, you will pass Apishapa

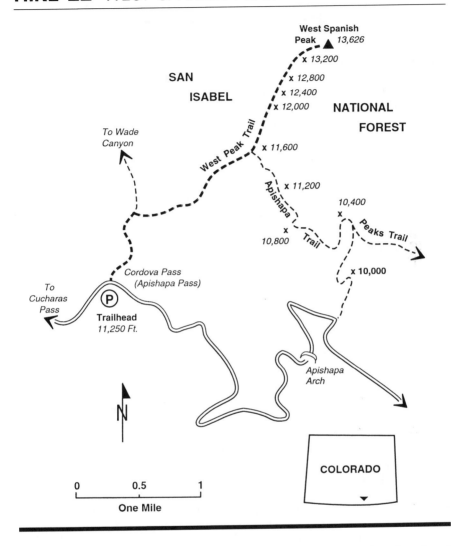

Arch, a hole in a dike through which a road passes. The road is closed and blocked to motorized vehicles.

The West Peak Trail takes you to the edge of timberline where you will see West Spanish Peak to the east. The trail becomes indistinct as it enters the boulder field on the west side of the peak, but any route you choose from here to the summit is safe. You will probably tend to follow the distinct east-west ridge to the top. The rock is safe and stable, but stout hiking boots are advisable. Once atop West Spanish Peak, be sure to sign the register and mark the date you arrived at the summit of this amazing 13,626 foot peak, rising so sharply from the flatlands below. Spend some time taking in the views.

East Spanish Peak is only 3.5 miles away and beyond it are the Great Plains. To the west is the Sangre de Cristo Range and to the north are the Wet Mountains and the Wet Mountain Valley.

At the base of the mountain you will see volcanic dikes (vertical rock walls) radiating out like spokes from the hub of a wheel. These walls, formed by extrusions of molten lava forced through crevices beneath the earth's surface and left standing when the surrounding rock eroded away, are hundreds of feet high and many miles long. They are very uncommon and known to geologists the world over. The Spanish Peaks, themselves, are intrusives, having been forced up from beneath the earth. Enjoy these fantastic views and then return as you came.—*Janina and Don Janes*

HIKE 23 *WEST CHAMA TRAIL*

General description: A day hike or overnighter along the Chama River into the upper Chama Basin.

General location: Approximately seven miles north of Chama, New Mexico; about thirty-five miles southwest of Antonito, Colorado.

Maps: Chama Peak 15 minute USGS quad, Rio Grande National Forest Map.

Degree of difficulty: Moderate.

Length: Eight miles one way.

Elevations: 8,800 to 10,800 feet.

Special attractions: Access to the upper Chama Basin with its steep and colorful volcanic cliffs; waterfalls; beautiful colors in fall.

For more information: Rio Grande National Forest, Conejos Peak Ranger District, 21461 State Highway 285, La Jara, CO 81140, (719) 274-5194.

The hike: The West Chama Trail leads you along the Chama River up into the beautiful Chama Basin, one of the most scenic areas in the Rio Grande National Forest and in the San Juan Mountain Range.

To reach the trailhead, take State Highway 17 southwest from Antonito into New Mexico or drive seven miles north from Chama, New Mexico, on 17 to the Chama River Road (Forest Route 121). The Lobo Ranch is a good landmark at the intersection. Take this road north through private property for six miles to the Rio Grande National Forest boundary. At the forest boundary, take the left fork of the road to the campground beside the river. The road is closed on the east bank of the river. It may reopen eventually. Ford on foot and go about two miles to West Chama Trail, which begins at the road closure.

The trail climbs steeply away from the Chama River along a small tributary stream bordered by stands of aspen that are spectacular in the fall. As the trail leaves this tributary and follows the Chama River to the confluence of the East and West forks, it stays high above the river and passes through dry subalpine meadows and more stands of aspen and then through virgin spruce-fir forests. A spectacular view of the entire valley is afforded from the trail above the confluence.

While the glacial valleys of the Conejos Plateau Area are steep and narrow, the Chama River Valley is wide and spacious. Steep cliffs of colorful volcanic

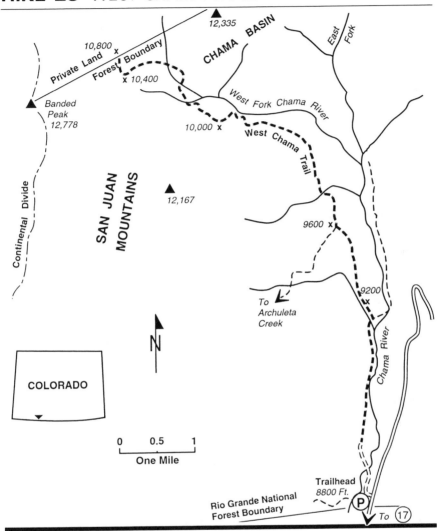

and sedimentary rock intricately eroded, surround the valley. Waterfalls cascade over the cliffs from the plateau above.

The gentle slopes which descend from the foot of the cliffs to the river below are covered by forests of aspen, interspersed with spruce and fir. Fingers of forest creep up the ravines dissecting the cliffs. Willows and cottonwoods follow the river as it meanders through the grasslands of the lower valley. At the trailhead of the West Chama Trail, the valley narrows and narrowleaf alder and willow dominate the streamside vegetation.

Massive Banded Peak, a local landmark, rises to your left as you continue the strenuous climb up the trail to the Forest Boundary and the Continental

Divide. Here, at the trail's end, you have superb views of the Chama Basin and south into New Mexico.

This is not only a very scenic area, but a historic one as well. To the west is the Tierra Amarilla Land Grant and to the south is the route of the Cumbres and Toltec Railroad, a narrow gauge steam route which runs from Antonito, Colorado, to Chama, New Mexico.

Water and camping sites are abundant along the entire length of the trail, but drinking water should be treated before consumption. Fishing is good for rainbow and cutthroat trout in the Chama River. Be extremely careful in fording the river during spring runoff.

After enjoying the view from this, the headwaters of the West Fork, return as you came.—*U.S. Forest Service*

HIKE 24 *RUYBALID LAKE*

General description: A good overnight backpack or strenuous day hike to a high lake overlooking the Conejos River Canyon.
General location: Thirty-five miles southwest of Alamosa.
Maps: Spectacle Lake USGS quad; Rio Grande National Forest Map.
Degree of difficulty: Moderate.
Length: Seven miles roundtrip.
Elevations: 8,800 to 11,200 feet.
Special attractions: Beautiful lake and excellent views of the Conejos River Canyon, the San Luis Valley, and the Sangre de Cristo Mountains.
Best season: Early summer through late fall.
For more information: Rio Grande National Forest, Conejos Ranger District, 21461 State Highway 285, La Jara, CO 81140; (719) 274-5193 or 5194.

The hike: This hike takes you into the beautiful South San Juan Wilderness in an area of high, forested plateaus, lakes and deep canyons on the southeastern edge of the San Juan Mountains. Ruybalid Lake is perched on the edge of one of these plateaus overlooking the deep glaciated Conejos River Canyon.

To reach the trailhead, take U.S. Highway 285 south from Alamosa for about twenty-five miles. At Antonito, go west on State Highway 17 along the Conejos River. After approximately fifteen miles, turn right onto the gravel road which follows the Conejos River to its headwaters near Platoro reservoir (the turn is well marked). After eight miles, you will pass through a small settlement and see a sign reading, "Ruybalid Lake and No Name Lake." Turn left at this sign, cross the Conejos River and park in the area provided. The trail leaves from the south end of the parking area, goes downstream for a hundred yards or so, then leaves the river bottom area and climbs the steep canyon wall.

The Conejos River Canyon is a deep, U-shaped, glacial valley incised about 2,000 feet into the relatively flat-topped basalt plateau which extends eastward from the Continental Divide. You will have some nice views of the Conejos River, winding its way through the lush meadows in the canyon bottom as you climb the switchbacks to the top of the plateau. The climb up this slope looks short on the maps, but is actually about two miles. There are twelve long switchbacks, a short break, then eighteen more short, steep switchbacks to the top. There isn't much water along the way, and if it weren't

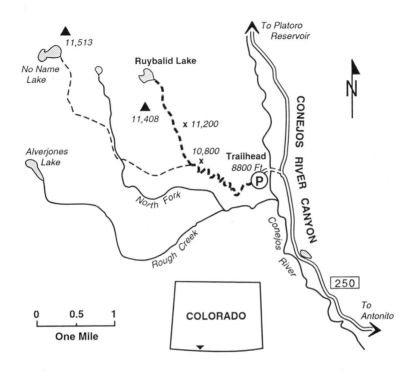

for the occasional views, this portion of the hike would have to be considered just a necessary evil on the road to your destination.

Once you reach the top, the trail breaks into some openings and levels off. Several hundred yards along, there is a sign where the trails to No Name Lake and Ruybalid Lake diverge. (The sign looks as though it may not be there for long, however.) The trail to the left goes to No Name Lake, while the Ruybalid Lake trail goes straight across the meadow. The Forest Service and USGS maps both show this intersection rather far up the North Fork of Rough Creek, with the trail to Ruybalid Lake traversing a saddle in a low divide. This is incorrect. Actually, the trails diverge shortly after you reach the top of the plateau and the Ruybalid Lake trail travels along the east side of the low divide. Once you take the fork to Ruybalid Lake, it's easy to lose the trail as it crosses the meadow, but you should be able to pick it up again on the opposite side. Ruybalid Lake is reached about 1.5 miles after the trails diverge. The lake is deep and rimmed on three sides by rocky cliffs. A rise in the ground surface of only ten feet or so separates the lake from the Conejos River Canyon, so you are able to look out to the east toward the historic San Luis Valley, through which Ute Indians, Spaniards, trappers, explorers, miners, and settlers have all passed at one time or another. This is a good campsite, away from the lake edge and with this beautiful view. There are few other sites between the lake and the canyon. Fishing is fair at the lake for brook trout.

The cliff area behind the lake makes for some good exploring. A good "cross country" route to No Name Lake leads up a small valley north of the lake onto the cliffs and then west-northwest through the woods. The woods are relatively thin here and it's difficult to get lost because you will intercept either the trail to No Name Lake or the edge of the canyon. There are several small, but scenic, ponds along the way.

Extended hikes may be taken west along the top of the plateau from the No Name Lake trail. The plateau rises in elevation to the west to 12,000 feet where the Continental Divide crosses it. There are many other fine lakes in this backcountry and hiking is easy between them, but the trails are unreliable because they are so infrequently used by hikers that they are difficult to discern from cattle and game trails. For this reason, a topo map is a must if you plan any extensive trips into the South San Juan Wilderness.—*Bill Bath*

HIKE 25 *WOLF CREEK PASS DIVIDE TRAIL*

General description: An easy day hike or the starting point for an extended backpack along the Continental Divide in the San Juan Mountains.
General location: About fifty miles west of Alamosa and 60 miles east of Durango.
Maps: Wolf Creek Pass and Spar City 15 minute USGS quads, Trails Illustrated Weminuche Wilderness map.
Degree of difficulty: Easy.
Length: As long as you want.
Elevations: Follows the Continental Divide at between 11,000 and 12,000 feet.
Special attractions: Easy access to the Continental Divide; spectacular views; beautiful wildflowers; good opportunities to see wildlife.
Best season: Summer.
For more information: Rio Grande National Forest, Del Norte Ranger District, 13308 W. Highway 160, P.O. Box 40, Del Norte, CO 81132; (719) 657-3321.

The hike: This hike takes you west and northwest along a portion of the Continental Divide Trail from the top of Wolf Creek Pass. The trail is easily accessible and takes you immediately into the beautiful timberline country along the Continental Divide. You will have spectacular views of the surrounding mountain ranges as you hike into the Weminuche Wilderness Area.

To reach the trail, take U.S. Highway 160 southwest from Del Norte or northeast from Pagosa Springs to the summit of Wolf Creek Pass. Just on the east side of the pass, look for a gravel road, which climbs the north mountain to the Lobo Overlook at an elevation of about 11,700 feet and overlooks Wolf Creek Pass. The road is steep but accessible to passenger cars once the snow has been cleared in late spring or early summer.

Park in the area provided at the end of the road. Begin your hike by walking

The San Juan Mountains.

down past and to the west of the microwave tower, staying on the ridgetop through timber until you encounter the trail where it leads out across an alpine meadow. From here the trail is easy to follow, except where it may disappear into snow drifts if you are hiking early in the summer season.

Within the first .5 mile, you may come across side trails which descend both north and south from the divide. These side trails are indicated differently on both the USGS and Forest Service Maps and are difficult to follow.

About .75 mile along, the trail drops down on the south side of the divide to avoid the steep ridgetop. The trail then traverses a beautiful bowl above Wolf Creek. At this point you may notice some timber cuts across the valley on the slopes of Treasure Mountain. They are clearcuts, but have been made in irregular shapes to approximate natural openings in the forest. These are a far cry from the square blocks so commonly associated with clearcutting in the past.

As you climb back toward the ridgetop and pass several outcroppings of rock, look for indications of the volcanic geology of this area. Extensive deposits of volcanic breccia and lava cover most of the San Juan Mountains.

After you reach the ridgetop, you will descend by way of a long meadow to a saddle along the divide. This would make a good destination for a short day hike or provide a good camping spot if you plan on going farther.

The possibilities for longer hikes are unlimited along this trail, which takes you through meadows of unsurpassed beauty, full of wildflowers, and provides you with spectacular views through its length. The trail will eventually extend all the way from the New Mexico border to the Wyoming border, following both existing trails and trail sections yet to be built as it traces the Continental Divide through the state. You may continue as far as Silverton, some sixty miles away, or just to Archuleta Lake, eight miles farther. There are side trails to be explored, too. Or you can always simply return as you came.—*Peter, Caryn and Crystal Boddie.*

HIKE 25 *WOLF CREEK PASS DIVIDE TRAIL*

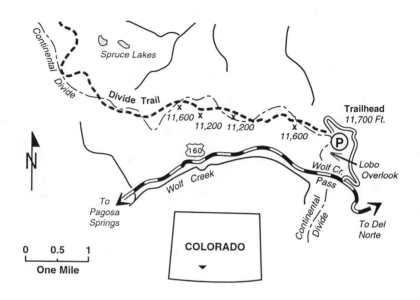

HIKE 26 *PIEDRA RIVER TRAIL*

General description: A day hike or overnighter into the forested canyon of the Piedra River on the southern edge of the San Juan Mountains.
General location: About eighteen miles northwest of Pagosa Springs.
Maps: USGS Devil Mountain, Bear Mountain, and Oakbrush Ridge quads.; San Juan National Forest map.
Degree of difficulty: Easy.
Length: About 9.5 miles one way.
Elevations: 7,100 to 7,600 feet.
Special attractions: Beautiful tall ponderosa pine and blue spruce, wildflowers, butterflies, interesting geology, good fishing along the Piedra River, and the rare possibility of seeing river otters.
Best season: Spring or early summer.
For more information: San Juan National Forest, Pagosa Ranger District, P.O. Box 310, Pagosa Springs, CO 81147, (719) 264-2268.

The Hike: This gentle hike along the Piedra River at the southern edge of the San Juan Mountains provides an opportunity to explore a large mountain river and canyon ecosystem, which provides habitat for the endangered river otter. You can make a short day hike or a longer trek between upper and lower trailheads with the shuttle of a car. You can also make a loop trip of about twelve miles. This trail also provides access to a number of

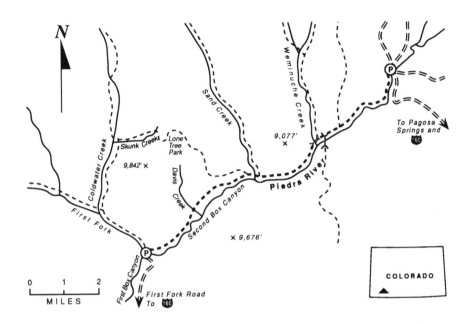

trails into various tributary canyons and valleys of the Piedra.

To reach the upper trailhead drive west from Pagosa Springs about two miles on US Highway 160. Turn right on Piedra Road (Forest Route 631). Follow it northwest, keeping on the main road at all forks, for about 14.5 miles to the Piedra Picnic Ground and the trailhead. Park just across the bridge. The trail is above the parking lot and goes south on the west side of the river. At this end of the trail you have the option of an easy 2.5-mile hike to the footbridge across the Piedra.

To reach the lower Piedra River trailhead, take US Highway 160 about twenty-two miles west from Pagosa Springs or about twenty-one miles east from Bayfield to the First Fork Rd. where the highway crosses the Piedra River. Take the First Fork Rd. north along the east side of the Piedra River for approximately twelve miles to the point where it ends at the bridge across the Piedra River. Ample parking is available.

After you walk across the bridge over the Piedra River, turn right on the trail and hike upstream. You will hike along a very hot, dry, south-facing slope where short grass, oakbrush, and very tall ponderosa pine grow. The trail, which has been packed down by horses and riders, becomes a bit steeper. Soon you have a view of the Piedra River below.

Considered for wild and scenic designation, the river traverses lower and middle elevation ponderosa pine forest still in primitive condition. Alternately included and excluded in various wilderness proposals, this type of area is not well-represented in the wilderness system in Colorado and would be an important addition. Of particular threat are timber sales proposed for the upper benches northwest of the Piedra Canyon which presently provide roadless area contiguous with the Weminuche Wilderness.

In this area the Piedra River and its tributaries, First Fork, Sand Creek, and Weminuche Creek, have cut canyons into nearly flat-lying sedimentary rocks mostly of Jurassic and Cretaceous ages. Above, the forested benches between the canyons are capped by the resistant Dakota sandstone while the lower canyon and valley sides include the red sandstones, mudstones, shales, and conglomerates of Permian Age. However, because of gentle folding, the Piedra River has in places exposed the underlying hard Precambrian rocks, which you will glimpse along your hike. These more resistant rocks have formed steep inner canyons locally termed box canyons.

The first box canyon is located just downstream of the trailhead and is visible on the drive in. Second Box Canyon is located approximately three miles upstream along the trail and additional Precambrian rocks are exposed along the canyon where Weminuche Creek joins the Piedra.

The trail ascends away from and descends to the Piedra River a couple of times. Watch for river otter along the banks. They were transplanted here in 1978 by the Colorado Division of Wildlife and the San Juan National Forest. You will cross a small creek, hike up away from the river in a steep pitch, still surrounded by lots of oakbrush and starting to get into Douglas fir.

As you hike, notice the sweet-smelling yellow clover, wild roses, geraniums, and iris, butterflies, and purple mountain asters. Watch for poison ivy in some places. Look for lupine and blue spruce along the riverbanks.

You'll hike through a parklike area, and then climb up, up and away from the river. You will soon cross Davis Creek, which is signed. Then you will come to a fork in the trail, a good spot to turn around.

For a loop hike you could go left at this junction onto the trail to Lone Tree Park, then descends along Skunk Creek to Coldwater Creek, down to First Fork, and to your starting point. This would be a twelve-mile hike and you might want to make it an overnighter, finding a good camping spot somewhere about half way.—*Caryn Boddie*

HIKE 27 *HERMOSA TRAIL*

General description: A day hike or backpack taking you along the canyon of Hermosa Creek in the San Juan Mountains.
General location: Fourteen miles north of Durango.
Maps: Hermosa, Monument Hill, Elk Creek, Electra Lake, and Hermosa Peak USGS quads; San Juan National Forest Map.
Length: Up to twenty miles one way.
Degree of difficulty: Easy.
Elevations: 7,600 to 8,800 feet.
Special attractions: A completely roadless area; the trail follows a long canyon

from which you will have ever-varying vistas; provides access to many side trails in the area.

Best season: Spring, fall, and early winter (when not snow covered).

For more information: San Juan National Forest, Animas Ranger District, 110 W. 11th Street, Durango, CO 81301; (303) 247-4874.

The hike: Hermosa Trail is at once one of the best and one of the most heavily used trails in southwestern Colorado. However, since it is twenty miles long, it has room to absorb many people.

You'll find the hiking good on the Hermosa Trail any time of the year when the snow is off, but hunting season is the poorest time to hike it. (This is great elk and deer country and during October and the first half of November the area is taken over by the hunters. Hikers should wear blaze orange during these months.)

Day hikes can be done from either end of the trail with the hiker returning the way he came. Backpackers should count on being out at least one night; two or more are necessary to traverse the entire canyon. There are also many side trails out of the canyon which can be explored, making a whole week in the area worthwhile for those who want a longer stay. The south end of the trail is most-used and easiest to get to. To find it, go ten miles north of Durango (or forty miles south of Silverton) on US Highway 550 to the unincorporated settlement of Hermosa. At the north end of the town the narrow gauge railroad crosses the highway. Just south of the crossing several yards, a road turns west off the highway. Take this road for about thirty yards until it dead-ends into a road paralleling the highway. Turn right (north) on this road and follow it to its end in four miles. The first half of the road is paved, the last half gravel. At the end of the road, park off to the side and begin your hike.

The trail starts directly at the end of the road and dips steeply for about twenty yards, then meets the main trail, which you take to the right. This point should be carefully noted for the sake of return, because you can easily miss this exit and find yourself not only bypassing your car, but entering private property.

Once on the main trail, you will find hiking quite easy for the first five miles, with only small ups and downs. It takes you through heavy stands of timber and along the side of the mountain, giving you a view far down below into the Hermosa Creek Canyon and up on both sides to the high mountains. You can see the La Plata Mountains to the west and south with several summits above 13,000 feet.

After five miles, the Dutch Creek Trail takes off to the right, joining Dutch Creek a mile up and eventually winding its way in a northerly direction to the top of the ridge at an altitude above 10,000 feet. One can hike the ridge trail several miles in either direction.

When the Dutch Creek Trail turns north, the Hermosa Trail swings left and down a long hill, some of it steep. After a mile, there is a fine Forest Service bridge across Dutch Creek. There is good camping nearby. Also at this point, you are back down to the level of Hermosa Creek where fishing is fair, mainly for rainbow trout. The Clear Creek Trail leads to it and up the other side into the La Platas. The main trail continues on without crossing Hermosa Creek and climbs high above the creek again. Several miles farther along it returns to stream level.

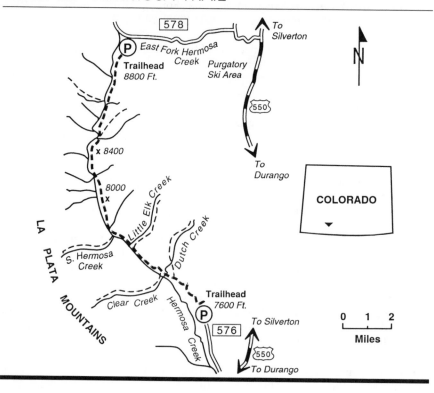

The canyon changes as you continue. At times, it is narrow with low cliffs on each side. At other times, there are grassy spots near the creek. Near the north end, it widens out into a large, open park. Most of the way, the trail is quite clear, but a few miles from the north end, it is sometimes grassy enough to be lost temporarily.

At one point, near an old cabin, there is a grassy spot obscuring the trail for a short distance. At this same point there is a side trail crossing the creek west over a dilapidated log bridge and going up a side canyon. If you find this spot, resist the temptation to cross the bridge and continue south on the east side of the canyon. You should pick up the trail again.

The north end of the trail can also be taken in and out a suitable distance for day hikes. Actually, if you want to hike the full length of the Hermosa Trail, the north to south route is easier since there is a net loss of 1,000 feet in elevation in that direction. For easy day hikes, however, the south end is slightly better since the north end drops steadily for several miles, making the return uphill. In spite of the favorable drop for a southbound full-length trip, it is not all downhill. The long Dutch Creek hill mentioned above will have to be climbed. Also, there are a couple of other long climbs before that.

To find the north entrance, take U.S. Highway 550 twenty-eight miles north of Durango and twenty-two miles south of Silverton to the Purgatory Ski Area Road. It goes steeply west up to the ski headquarters in .5 mile. At the east end of the ski parking area, a small road turns right (north) uphill. Follow it as it winds 2.5 miles to the top of a ridge in a mostly westerly direction. At the top, a left turn will take you to the Purgatory Powder House. Follow the main road to the right. Half a mile later, a road runs downhill. Follow it down into Hermosa Park for five miles where a little road turns left (south) off the main road and crosses the East Fork of Hermosa Creek. In .25 mile, the road ends. Park here out of the way and begin hiking on the trail through a small gate.

Late September or early October, just before the main hunting season starts, is an especially nice time for this end of the route since there are many aspen on the north side of Hermosa Park and at various points along the trail. The aspens are a brilliant gold at this time, set against a dark green background of conifers. There are many side trails off the main trail, some of which may not be well maintained, but are worth the exploring time; each of them with their own fascinations.—*Paul Pixler* (Paul Pixler is the author of *Hiking Trails of Southwestern Colorado*, published by Pruett Publishing.)

HIKE 28 *CHICAGO BASIN*

General description: An overnight hike into the Chicago Basin and Needle Mountains with the added excitement of a ride on the Durango and Silverton Narrow Gauge Railway to reach the trailhead.

General location: About thirty miles north of Durango, twenty miles south of Silverton.

Maps: Columbine Pass and Mountain View Crest USGS quads; San Juan National Forest map, Trails Illustrated Weminuche Wilderness map.

Degree of difficulty: Moderate to more difficult.

Length: Eight miles one way, not including access by rail.

Elevations: 8,100 to 11,000 feet.

Special attractions: Spectacular views of the rugged Needle Mountains and three fourteen-thousand-foot peaks: Eolus, Windom and Sunlight; and a fun train ride.

Best season: Summer.

For more information: San Juan National Forest, Animas Ranger District, Federal Building, 110 W. 11th Street, Durango, CO 81301; (303) 247-4874.

The hike: This hike into the spectacular Needles Mountains and Chicago Basin in the San Juan Range north of Durango, combines the unique opportunity to ride one of the West's classic railways and to climb on an improved trail into some pretty rugged country.

The Needle Creek trail may be reached by the Rockwood Railroad shuttle or via the Durango and Silverton Narrow Gauge Railway. The train departs from Durango. After a ride of about an hour it makes a stop at Needleton Bridge. This is one of two points at which the train stops for hikers, and Chicago Basin hikers should disembark here. Be sure the conductor knows you are hiking from Needleton when you board the train. Also, ask him what flagging motion to use to stop the train when you want to reboard after your hike. The Rockwood Railroad shuttle goes from Rockwood to Elk Creek and back twice each day, passing Needleton en route. Call the D&SNGR at

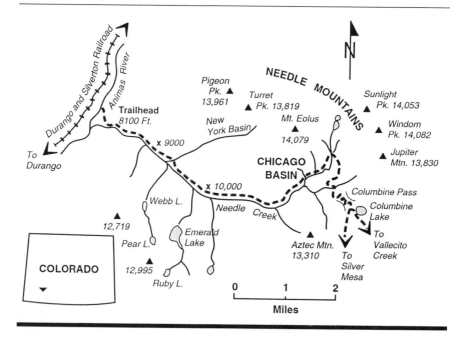

(303) 247-2733 for specific information on times and fares.

After watching the old coalfire steam engine head on its way to Silverton, proceed across the Needleton Bridge which crosses the Animas River here, and find a trail that passes to the right of the remains of an old log cabin and heads to the south. Within about one-half mile, the trail comes to a junction. The right fork continues along the Animas River to the south, after crossing Needle Creek. The fork to the left is the trail to Chicago Basin, and follows the north bank of Needle Creek all the way to timberline. Within two miles the trail crosses a major drainage from New York Basin which descends from the north. Though there are side trails which cross Needle Creek at several points along the seven-mile route to Chicago Basin, the easiest and most direct route is the trail along the creek's northern (lefthand) bank.

As the trail climbs the narrow valley of Needle Creek through thick stands of pine, spruce and fir, the sharp, knife-edge ridges of the Needle Mountains begin to reveal themselves. The vista becomes superb as the trail approaches the upper basin near timberline. From any of the numerous campsites in the grassy, sparsely wooded meadows in the basin, three of Colorado's fourteen-thousand-foot peaks dominate the skyline. To the northwest is Mount Eolus at 14,083, beyond and to the north lies Sunlight, 14,059, and Windom, at 14,087.

Because Chicago Basin gets heavy use, campers should be particularly careful to use low impact camping methods. And you should purify the water you find, which is plentiful. No open fires are permitted.

Return as you came. Give yourself plenty of time to reach the rail stop at Needleton. Find out what time the train will be returning when you buy your tickets. Also be prepared to flag the train as it approaches.—*Chris Frye*

HIKE 29   ICE LAKE BASIN

General description: A day hike or overnighter into the spectacular Ice Lake Basin above timberline.

General location: Eight miles west of Silverton.

Maps: Ophir USGS quad; San Juan National Forest map.

Degree of difficulty: Moderate.

Length: 3.5 miles one way.

Elevations: 9,900 to 12,250 feet.

Special attractions: Spectacular alpine basin with lakes, waterfalls, high peaks and interesting volcanic and glacial geology.

Best season: Summer and early fall.

For more information: San Juan National Forest, Animas Ranger District, 110 W. 11th St., Durango, CO 81301; (303) 247-4874.

The Hike: The Ice Lake Basin hike in the San Juan Mountains west of Silverton provides easy access to high lakes in a broad basin above timberline. Surrounded by 13,000-foot peaks, the Ice Lake Basin is aptly named, often holding snow well into summer. Spectacular waterfalls highlight this hike.

To reach the trailhead, take U.S. Highway 550 northwest from Silverton about two miles to the South Fork Mineral Creek road. Follow this road approximately six miles and look for the trailhead sign on the right just past South Mineral Campground. There are several parking spots along the road between the campground and the point where the road crosses Clear Creek.

From the road the trail climbs steeply with numerous switchbacks for about 0.4 mile through timber to the base of Clear Creek Falls. After crossing the creek another set of switchbacks brings you to a point about midway up the falls and a spectacular view down the valley. It is possible to cross the falls at this point on the remnants of an old jeep road and connect with the jeep road to Clear Lake.

From the falls the trail climbs through open meadow with many wildflowers and passes remnants of old mining operations. The red rocks visible below and on the adjacent lower valley slopes include red shales, mudstones, sandstones, and conglomerates of the Permian Age Cutler Formation. All of the cliffs above you are formed of volcanic tuffs, ash flows, mudflows, conglomerates and sandstones of Tertiary age.

Near the upper end of the meadow, the trail reenters timber and passes a spectacular waterfall—a good spot to stop for a snack. After another steep climb and more switchbacks, the trail breaks into the open again just below the cliff above which lies Lower Ice Lake Basin. Here is a good opportunity to examine the volcanic rocks close up. You can see that these rocks were deposited as violent ash flows and mud flows similar to those that occurred during and after the eruption of Mount St. Helens in Washington. The thousands of feet of surrounding cliffs in this part of the San Juan Mountains were built up over millions of years of this volcanic activity.

Once you top this first cliff, the trail levels out and crosses Lower Ice Lake Basin, a good destination for a shorter trip. With alternating forest and meadow, Lower Ice Lake Basin offers numerous secluded camping spots; one advantage it has over the windy and exposed Upper Ice Lake Basin. (To avoid

HIKE 29 *ICE LAKE BASIN*

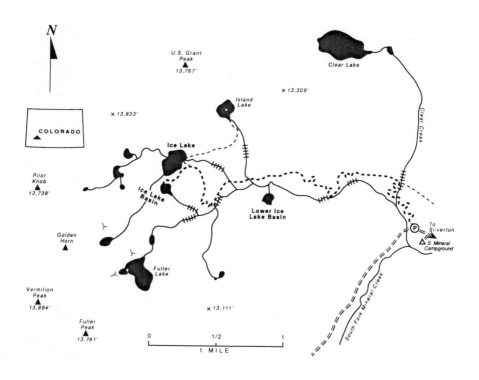

Ice Lake below Fuller and Vermilion peaks.

environmental damage and find seclusion, it is best to camp away from the lakes here and in the upper basin. Camping stoves are also recommended in this fragile area.)

As you reach the upper end of Lower Ice Lake Basin, the roar of waterfalls from the cliffs above increases. In succession the trail passes waterfalls that drain from upper basins containing Island Lake, Ice Lake, and Fuller Lake. Located anywhere in the vicinity of a city, each of these waterfalls would be a major tourist attraction. Here in the backcountry of the San Juans they haven't even been named.

As the trail climbs up the cliff at the end of Lower Ice Lake Basin, it passes right by the last of the three waterfalls, which has cut a deep cleft along a fracture in the cliff. Above this falls, the trail makes a final, strenuous 0.5 mile climb to Ice Lake. Surrounded by "thirteeners" including from south to west Fuller Peak (13,761 feet), Vermilion Peak (13,894 feet), Golden Horn (13,760 feet), and Pilot Knob (13,373 feet), the basin presents you with many opportunities for hiking, climbing, and camping.

To the north and across the outlet stream from Ice Lake, a faint trail to Island Lake can be seen traversing the base of a cliff. Located in a separate alpine basin, Island Lake offers a good alternative destination. Also, from Ice Lake to the south and southwest are several smaller lakes and the larger Fuller Lake; all easily visited by cross-country hikes across the open tundra of the basin. Elevation gains on these routes are moderate.

Climbs of the surrounding peaks range in difficulty from moderate (Fuller Peak) to difficult (Pilot Knob, a technical climb). Depending on snow conditions, any of the climbs could require an ice axe and may best be climbed in late summer.—*Peter Boddie*

Hiking in the San Juans.

HIKE 30 *LIZARD HEAD TRAIL*

General description: A steep day hike or backpack into the heart of the San Miguel Mountains.

General location: Approximately sixty miles north of Cortez; fourteen miles south of Telluride.

Maps: Mount Wilson USGS quad; Uncompahgre and San Juan National Forest maps.

Degree of difficulty: Moderate.

Length: Approximately 3.5 miles one way, but offering the possibility for a longer backpack.

Elevations: 10,280 to 12,080 feet.

Special attractions: Spectacular view of the San Miguels with their intriguing geology; interesting and beautiful hiking through conifer forest and aspen groves, beautiful wildflowers and many species of mushrooms.

Best season: Summer through early fall.

For more information: Uncompahgre National Forest, Norwood Ranger District, 1760 East Grande Ave., P.O. Box 388, Norwood, CO 81423; (303) 327-4261.

HIKE 30 *LIZARD HEAD TRAIL*

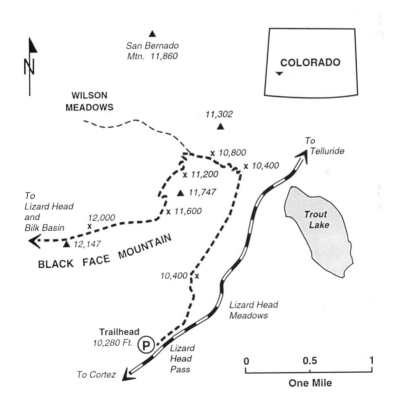

The hike: A hike along the Lizard Head Trail in the heart of the San Miguels is a hike into some of Colorado's most rugged and beautiful country. You will travel through meadows alive with wildflowers, through thick conifer forests where mushrooms, moss and lichens grow profusely, and through beautiful aspen groves. When you reach the ridgetop that is your destination, you will be more than glad you made the trip. The scenery is fantastic; the famed Lizard Head juts into the sky to the west.

To reach the trailhead, drive south on State Highway 789 from Montrose to Ridgeway. Turn west at Ridgeway on Highway 62 and follow it until you reach the junction with State Highway 145. Turn south on 145 and follow it to the summit of Lizard Head Pass. You can also drive north from Cortez on 145 to the summit of the pass. Park in the area provided at the Lizard Head Pass sign on the west side of the highway. Begin your hike by following the dirt road to the northeast about .10 mile. Look for the trail marker and the trail itself taking off to the left.

The first mile of the trail is fairly level (you even lose some elevation) as you contour the east side of Black Face Mountain. You will be hiking through beautiful aspen groves and open parks where you can look down into the valley eastward.

Soon you will enter the Lizard Head Wilderness Area, where you will begin to ascend steeply through heavy stands of spruce and fir, and then intercept the old trail coming up from the highway below. It is still indicated this way on the topo map. You will cross the old trail several times on your climb. Please do not use it, as the Forest Service is trying to revegetate it.

Try to pick out the different species of wildflowers as you make your way along the switchbacks that take you steeply up the mountainside: there are mountain asters, Indian paintbrush, larkspur, chiming bells, as well as a variety of mushrooms, lichens and moss.

The spectacular Lizard Head in the San Miguel Mountains.

Once up this steep pitch, you will reach a small clearing and a fork in the trail. A sign directs you straight ahead to Wilson Meadows or left to the Lizard Head Trail. Go left and you will again begin to climb, switching back many times until you reach the ridgetop. Watch for glimpses of the Lizard Head to your right as you climb through the trees. Once on the ridgetop, the trail becomes indistinct. Look to your right and you'll see it emerge on the far side of a small meadow. Watch for the posts ahead of you as you continue on to your destination, as the trail disappears and reappears several times as you walk across the tundra. The views you'll have as you climb this ridge leading to the summit of Black Face Mountain (12,147 feet) will have been well worth your effort. To the west is the unmistakeable Lizard Head, volcanic rock rising some 500 feet from the mountaintop as a lone pinnacle; beyond it are rugged Gladstone Peak and Mount Wilson; to the northwest is Wilson Peak and to the northeast is Sunshine Mountain. Below you to the north is Wilson Meadows, an area inviting to elk and backpackers alike.

Should you want to continue on backpacking, you can follow the Lizard Head Trail along the ridge south of the Lizard Head and then northward down Bilk Basin along Bilk Creek to State Highway 145, where you will have had to shuttle a car before you started out. Otherwise, return as you came.
—*Caryn, Peter and Crystal Boddie*

HIKE 31 *BEAR CREEK NATIONAL RECREATION TRAIL*

General description: A full day hike or backpack through a wonderland of varied geological formations and diverse vegetation.
General location: Two miles south of Ouray.
Maps: Ouray, Ironton, Handies Peak, and Wetterhorn Peak USGS quads; Uncompahgre National Forest map.
Degree of difficulty: Moderate.
Length: 4.2 miles one way with the possibility of a longer backpack.
Elevations: 8,440 to 11,200 feet.
Special attractions: Interesting geology; beautiful wildflowers.
Best season: Late spring, summer and fall.
For more information: Uncompahgre National Forest, Ouray Ranger District, 2505 S. Townsend, Montrose, CO 81401; (303) 249-3711.

The hike: The Bear Creek National Recreation Trail takes you through country that has been referred to as "the little Switzerland of America," leading you over a variety of geologic formations to the Yellow Jacket Mine near timberline and on to Engineer Mountain Pass. It is only one in a system of trails in this part of the Uncompahgre National Forest. You can extend your hike by taking other, connecting trails to expand your experience of these verdant mountains.

You begin your hike near the nestled town of Ouray, once a mining town with a population of several thousands. Drive south from the town on US Highway 550 for two miles until you come to a tunnel. Trail parking for the Bear Creek National Recreation Trail is on the south end of the tunnel and east side of the highway. The trail itself begins on the west side of the highway and leads you over the tunnel and then, after a short walk, starts to switchback

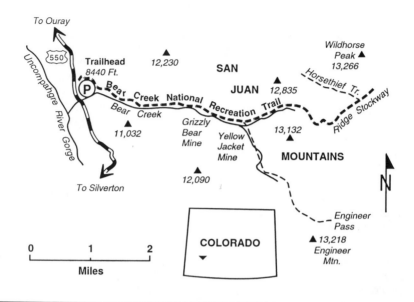

through a forest of white fir and Douglas fir, interspersed with stands of aspen that are glorious in the fall. It was once the site of intensive mining activity. There are many abandoned mines throughout the area, including the Grizzly Bear and Yellow Jacket mines.

There are a total of thirteen switchbacks over loose talus in the first mile, a real chore, but well worth the effort. The talus slope is composed of quartzite and slate. This is the Precambrian Uncompahgre Formation, which is only exposed in this area south of Ouray. Climbing away from the Uncompahgre Formation, you come upon the San Juan Formation, composed of volcanic tuff cut by veins of pyrite and containing rich deposits of silver, lead, and zinc sulfide.

At the top of the switchbacks, you will see a sign for those descending, which reads, "Do not cut the switchbacks or throw rocks." Approximately 300 feet from the sign there is a small boulder slide to cross. The trail then levels and takes you under an overhang that runs with water at times and is lush with wildflowers such as mountain aster, yarrow, and wild geranium. Then it winds along a ledge high above Bear Creek.

When the Bear Creek Trail was built in the late 1800s by miners as access to claims along Bear Creek and an alternate route over Engineer Mountain, it was a substantial, well-built route hewn into the rock ledges and supported by log and rock cribbing. It is not unsafe today, either, though deterioration has occurred in some of the original cribbing and pinning. New supports have been added, replacing portions that were hazardous.

Soon the trail crosses two stream beds that may be flowing in spring and early summer and you can cross small patches of snow, depending on the

Bear Creek Trail in 1916. U.S. Forest Service photo.

previous winter's snowfall. After the trail levels out and takes you through open green meadows and cool green stands of aspen, you will come to a small steel shack on the left side of the trail and discarded mining equipment on the right. After another minute on the trail, you will see the Grizzly Bear Mine on the right, along Bear Creek. Please do not go near the mines. It is private property and can be dangerous. Continue through more woods to the first major stream crossing. The trail is marked on both sides of the stream by wooden posts topped with orange metallic diamonds. After you carefully cross the stream, hike up through more lush green meadows and over a portion of the trail that is narrow (watch your step), then cross another stream and continue to an avalanche area with a lot of deadfall. Do not head up to your left along the bank where a worn area on the hill appears as a trail. Cross the avalanche area and continue on the trail through intermittent forest and meadow until you arrive at the Yellow Jacket Mine where you will find evidence of mining history in the form of buildings, equipment, shafts, and adits still remaining. Again, do not take chances by going to close to the mine or equipment, and be sure to keep children close at hand.

At the mine, the trail forks. A turn to the left will take you along the Ridge Stock Driveway to a fork on the Continental Divide. A left turn there will take you onto the Horsethief Trail, which winds northeast to Dexter Creek, an overnight hike. This makes a good backpack loop provided you shuttled vehicles to Dexter Creek before you left. (To do so, drive north from Ouray on US Highway 550 to Forest Route 871, taking you to Lenore Lake. Drive past the lake to the trailhead.)

A turn to the right at the Yellow Jacket Mine will take you southeast to the Continental Divide and Engineer Mountain Pass. The trail becomes vague above timberline, but you will not become lost. Follow the switchbacks above the mining debris. A double-track jeep trail becomes evident above timberline; follow that to the divide. As you go ever higher, look for the large rock glacier on the north-facing slope, and notice the grasses, sedges and forbs typical of this alpine tundra. Also keep an eye open for marmots, the ever-elusive pika, grouse, and ptarmigan at this high altitude. Once at the summit of Engineer Mountain Pass, take time to look around. You have a spectacular 360-degree view of the mountain summits and lakes of the San Juans. And there is time to rest, as time stands still.—*Jeanne Vallez*

HIKE 32 *CIMARRON RIVER LOOP*

General description: A two to three day backpack on an extended loop route through the Big Blue Wilderness.
General location: Approximately twenty-five miles southeast of Montrose.
Maps: Courthouse Mountain, Wetterhorn Peak, Uncompahgre Peak and Sheep Mountain USGS quads; Uncompahgre National Forest Map.
Degree of difficulty: Moderate.
Length: About a twenty-two mile loop.
Elevations: 9,275 to 12,400 feet.
Special attractions: Long, scenic backpack through the Big Blue Wilderness; interesting geology; old mine; opportunities to see elk and deer; great views of fourteeners, Uncompahgre and Wetterhorn Peaks.
For more information: Uncompahgre National Forest, Ouray Ranger District, 2505 S. Townsend, Montrose, CO 81401; (303) 249-3711.

The hike: The Middle Fork Trail along the Middle Fork of the Cimarron River, combined with the East Fork Trail along the river's East Fork, forms an excellent two to three day backpack loop in the Big Blue Wilderness in the San Juan Mountains.

To reach the trailhead, drive east from Montrose on US Highway 50 for about twenty miles to the Owl Creek Cimarron Road going south (Forest Route 861). Follow this road south past Silver Jack Reservoir until the road makes a big turn west. About .25 mile past the junction with the West Fork Road (Forest Route 860), turn left on Middle Fork Road (still Forest Route 861) and follow it 6.4 miles to the parking area at the end of the road. Since you will be doing a loop trip, you will need to shuttle cars to the trailhead of the East Fork Trail or plan on hiking an extra eight miles or so to your car. To shuttle, follow 861 back to the East Fork Road and follow it for two miles to the

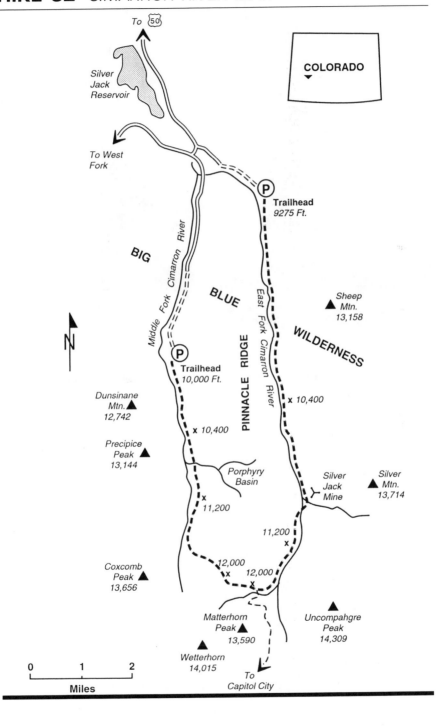

Wetterhorn, Matterhorn and Coxcomb peaks. U.S. Forest Service photo.

trailhead in the open meadows—the last .5 mile is pretty rough and narrow.

The Middle Fork Trail begins on the right side of the parking area near the river. For the first six miles it parallels the Middle Fork of the Cimarron River and walking is easy. In early summer, a few bogs must be crossed within the first .5 mile of the trail, but they are usually dried up by mid-July. Two miles from the trailhead, you'll cross a stream where water from the Porphyry Basin to the east joins the Middle Fork. The old foot bridge is no longer useable and the trail is routed to an easy crossing. An old trail to the Porphyry Mine in Porphyry Basin takes off near the crossing and might make a nice day trip. But stay away from the mine.

You are hiking into the Big Blue Wilderness, beautiful and wild, and surrounded by mines. It includes two fourteeners—Wetterhorn and Uncompahgre Peaks—the latter being the highest mountain in the San Juan Range. Throughout this area, you will find examples of the complex volcanic geology typical of the San Juans. Pinnacle Ridge, which separates the Middle and East Forks of the Cimarron River, is an especially interesting and spectacularly eroded ridge formed of volcanic breccia.

About two miles past the Porphyry Basin you will begin the steep climb to the pass below Wetterhorn and Uncompahgre Peaks, from which you will descend into the valley of the East Fork of the Cimarron River. As you make the top of the pass, stop and take in the panorama. To the west you will see Redcliff, Coxcomb, and Precipice peaks. To the south is Matterhorn Peak;

to the southwest, Wetterhorn Peak; and to the southeast, Uncompahgre Peak.

At the top of the pass the trail is indistinct and marked only by rock cairns. Follow the drainage downhill towards the basin below Uncompahgre Peak and you will easily locate the East Fork Trail.

The East Fork Trails follows an old mining road for much of its length and is one route for domestic sheep grazing the alpine country. Bands of sheep are driven by herders along the trail beginning in July. Water, though plentiful, must be considered unsafe to drink unless treated. As you make your way from the tundra down into the spruce and fir forests beginning at 11,600 feet elevation, watch for elk and deer.

At the base of Silver Mountain you will come upon the remains of the Silver Jack Mine, along with other evidence of past mining activity. The mining of metallic ores such as gold, silver, copper, lead and zinc has been an important industry in and around this area since 1875. The mining camps of Lake City, Telluride and Ouray once had populations of several thousand people.

The last portion of the East Fork Trail is easy walking along the river to your destination and, if you shuttled cars, to your vehicle. Otherwise, you'll have to walk the two miles down to Forest Route 861 and then hike up to the Middle Creek trailhead.

Please be careful to camp below timberline and use your backpacking stove instead of building fires. Also remember to camp at least 200 feet away from trails and water and enjoy this beautiful backpack through high mountain country.—*U.S. Forest Service*

HIKE 33 *STEWART CREEK*

General description: Day hike or overnighter in the La Garita Wilderness.
General location: Forty miles south of Gunnison.
Maps: USGS Elk Park, Stewart Peak, San Luis Peak, and Half Moon Pass; Saguache County map.
Degree of difficulty: Easy to moderate.
Length: Six miles one way to the saddle below San Luis Peak.
Elevations: 10,400 to 13,200.
Special attractions: Lesser-used trail in the La Garita Wilderness; provides access to a climb of 14,014 ft. San Luis Peak and other high peaks; can be made into a loop trip along a portion of the Colorado Trail.
Best season: Summer.
For more information: Gunnison National Forest, Cebolla Ranger District, 216 N. Colorado, Gunnison, CO 81230; (303) 641-0471.

The hike: The Stewart Creek Trail leads you into the La Garita Wilderness and gives you access to San Luis Peak, one of the more easily climbed fourteeners. On this hike you will feel that you are in a wilderness even though it is not one of the most difficult trails you'll tackle. This is a good trail to take for an introduction to backpacking and mountain climbing. You can also extend the hike to a longer loop by crossing the saddle between Organ Mountain and San Luis Peak and connecting with the Colorado Trail along Cochetopa Creek and back to the Eddiesville trailhead.

To reach the trailhead from Gunnison take US Highway 50 east to Colorado

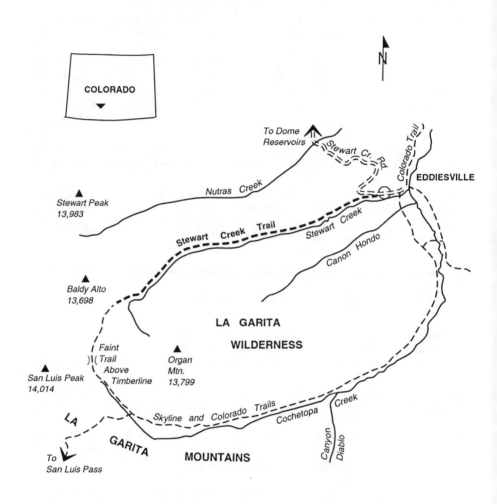

COLORADO

N

To Dome
Reservoirs

Stewart Cr. Rd.

Colorado Trail

EDDIESVILLE

Nutras Creek

▲
Stewart Peak
13,983

Stewart Creek Trail

Stewart Creek

Canon Hondo

▲
Baldy Alto
13,698

LA GARITA

WILDERNESS

Faint
Trail
Above
Timberline

▲
Organ
Mtn.
13,799

▲
San Luis Peak
14,014

Skyline and Colorado Trails

Cochetopa Creek

LA

GARITA

MOUNTAINS

Canyon Diablo

To
San Luis Pass

0   0.5   1

One Mile

Highway 114. Go through Cochetopa Canyon, turn right at the road to Dome Reservoirs and the Old Agency Work Center. Continue on just past Upper Dome Reservoir and turn right onto Forest Route 794. Follow this to the Stewart Creek Route Take the Stewart Creek Route about 5 miles until you see the sign for the Stewart Creek trailhead. The road deadends in only about .25 mile beyond the Stewart Creek trailhead at the Eddiesville trailhead, where you should park if you want to do a loop hike via the Colorado Trail.

As you start out on the Stewart Creek Trail you pass an extensive area of willows and beaver ponds. Look for signs of beaver activity old and new.

In the first two miles the trail is well maintained and fairly easy, passing through forest. Look for unusually tall bristlecone pines on the south-facing slope. After two miles the valley begins to open up with some small meadows and glimpses of Organ Mountain, San Luis Peak, Baldy Alto, and the large above-timberline bowl at the head of the valley.

The trail gradually steepens and disappears when you reach timberline after about four miles. If you're backpacking you may want to camp in this area.

For a climb of San Luis Peak or Organ Mountain, aim for the saddle between these two peaks to the southwest. From the top of the saddle it is a fairly easy climb to the top of San Luis Peak.

Or, you can descend via a faint trail into the Cochetopa Creek drainage. About one mile down from the top of the saddle you will intersect the Skyline Trail, which provides the combined route for the Colorado and Continental Divide trails. From this point it is about seven miles back to the Eddiesville trailhead.—*Peter Boddie*

Stewart Creek from the trailhead.

HIKE 34 *EAST BELLOWS TRAIL*

General description: A long day hike or overnighter taking you to Wheeler Geologic Area, Halfmoon Pass and the La Garita Wilderness.

General location: Approximately ten miles southeast of Creede.

Maps: Pool Table Mountain, Halfmoon Pass, and Wagon Wheel Gap USGS quads; Rio Grande National Forest Map.

Degree of difficulty: Moderate.

Length: About 8.5 miles one way.

Elevations: 10,400 to 12,500 feet.

Special attractions: Beautiful, high-plateau meadows of the La Garita Mountains; unique geologic features; good fishing for small brook trout.

Visitors to Wheeler National Monument in the 1930s. U.S. Forest Service photo.

Best season: Summer and fall.
For more information: Rio Grande National Forest, Creede Ranger District, 3rd and Creede Ave., P.O. Box 270, Creede, CO 81130; (719) 658-2556.

The hike: The East Bellows Trail takes you up the East Fork of Bellows Creek to spectacular Wheeler Geologic Area and on up to Halfmoon Pass with its beautiful views and beyond to the La Garita Wilderness. To reach the trailhead, drive southeast from Creede for 7.3 miles or 14.4 miles northwest of South Fork on State Highway 149 to Forest Route 600 (Pool Table Road), located on the north side of the highway, then approximately 9.5 miles northwest on Pool Table Road to the Hanson's Mill camping area.

Begin your hike by following the old jeep road in a northeasterly direction. After about .25 mile, the road will fork. Follow the left (west) fork of the road for about one mile down into the East Bellows Creek drainage. The foot trail will begin just before this road crosses the creek. After crossing the creek (you'll have to wade it as the bridge is gone, so be very careful, particularly in early summer), the trail heads up the west fork of East Bellows Creek (Canon Nieve). In about .5 mile, there is a fork in the trail which is signed. Take the fork heading west, which will make a gradual climb of about four miles through open parks and scattered timber before joining the four-wheel drive access road to Wheeler Geologic Area. Follow the road west for about one mile to its end at a pole fence in a small meadow below the area.

The unique, picturesque features of the geologic area are about .25 to .5 miles north from the end of the road. The foot trail to Wheeler will quickly meet the West Bellows Creek Trail. Follow the sign directions and continue up West Bellows Creek Trail. Just before reaching the lower base of the geologic formations, you will come to the junction of this trail with the Wheeler-Wason Trail. Take the fork heading north and in 150 yards you will arrive at the base of the beautiful Wheeler Geologic Area formations.

Named for Captain George M. Wheeler, who in 1874, was in charge of the surveying and exploration work being done in this part of Colorado by the War Department, the Wheeler Geologic Area was proclaimed a National Monument by President Theodore Roosevelt in 1908. The scenic geologic area occupies 640 acres, about sixty acres of which consist of formations of volcanic tuff, crumbled and eroded by wind and water into fantastic shapes.

The Ute Indians called the area "The Sand Stones," and tribal renegades are said to have used the strange place as a hideout. Others have called it, "The City of Gnomes," "The White Shrouded Ghosts," "Dante's Lost Souls," "Beehives," "Temples," and "Phantom Ships." Whatever you choose to call them, you'll be amazed at this conglomeration of pinnacles, domes, and spires of rock surrounded and hidden by mountains.

The rock itself is a moderately coarse volcanic tuff (debris blown into the air from volcanic vents), which settled here. Individual particles of this debris may range in size from dust flakes to blocks two or three feet across. They have not been cemented together or firmly compacted.

As the rains and snows have fallen upon the easily eroded material, the water has carried away much of the finer debris. Larger blocks have remained as capstones for sharp spires or pinnacles, which stand alone when the surrounding unprotected material has been washed away. Slight differences in texture or in the amount of compaction results in the development of the different shapes and forms. Also, vertical joint cracks weaken the beds at

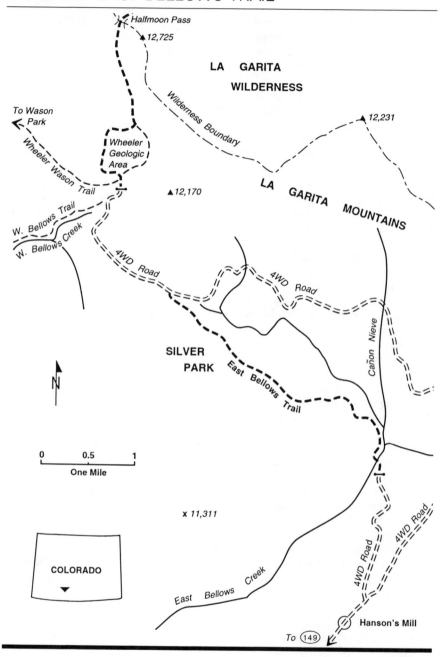

intervals and these can form what appear to be hooded ghosts.

After enjoying the formations, follow the trail past a shelter house (be sure to stop and sign your name to the guest register), through a stand of timber, and climb above the formations. Some magnificent views are available before you conquer the crest of the La Garita Mountains at Halfmoon Pass, about one mile way, and arrive finally at the La Garita Wilderness Area, beautiful and rugged, beckoning you to spend some time. Then return as you came. —*Peter, Caryn, Crystal, and Robin Boddie.*

HIKE 35 *FREMONT'S CAMPS*

General description: A day hike or short overnighter in the La Garita mountains.
General location: About twenty miles northwest of Del Norte.
Maps: From Cathedral Campground: USGS Pine Cone Knob and Pool Table Mountain quads. From Groundhog Park: Pine Cone Knob, Pool Table Mountain, Bowers Peak, and Mesa Mountain USGS quads; Rio Grande National Forest Map.
Degree of difficulty: Moderate.
Length: From Cathedral Campground, 3.5 miles; from Groundhog Park, eight miles one way.
Elevations: 9,400 to 12,400 feet.
Special attractions: Historic site of John C. Fremont's winter camps.
Best season: Summer.
For more information: Rio Grande National Forest, Del Norte Ranger District, 13308 W. Highway 160, P.O. Box 40, Del Norte, CO 81132; (719) 657-3321.

Earlier visitors to Fremont's Camps. U.S. Forest Service photo.

HIKE 35 *FREMONT'S CAMPS*

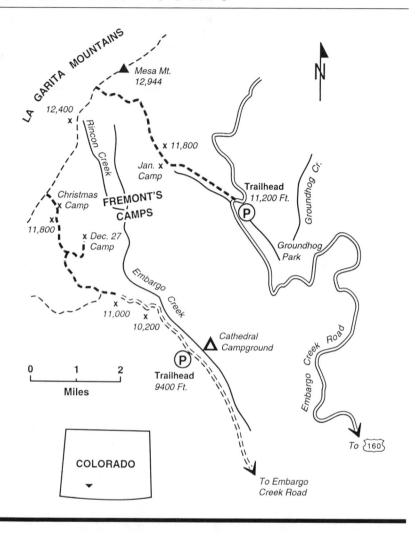

The hike: In the winter of 1848, General John Charles Fremont made a disastrous attempt to cross the mountains of southern Colorado in the dead of winter. These two trails—one long and one short—lead to the historic site of his Christmas camp and to the December 27 camp nearby. The first trail is 3.5 miles and the second is eight miles one way. The trails were scheduled for reconstruction in 1990.

From Cathedral Campground: To reach this trailhead, drive west of Del Norte on State Highway 160 to Embargo Creek Road (Forest Route 650). Go right (north) and cross the Embargo (Granger) bridge, then continue north on the Embargo Road, following the signs to Cathedral Campground.

Beginning at the campground, you will hike on jeep road #640 for about

The La Garita Mountains around Mesa Mountain. U.S. Forest Service photo.

2.5 miles. Approximately .5 mile of the road is on private land; please respect it. Approximately .5 mile after the end of the jeep road is the junction of the Big City Trail and the Fremont Trail. The sign directs you to the right and to Fremont's camp.

The trail passes through aspen stands, offering a view of the cliffs and rocks for which Cathedral Campground is named. It then climbs fairly steeply through stands of Douglas fir, then up into spruce and fir stands, and finally, into alpine meadows. During July, many wildflowers appear in the meadows. About 1.5 miles after the trail junction is another sign giving directions to the Fremont camps. The December 27 camp is to the right .5 mile and the Christmas camp is .5 mile past the sign on the same drainage, in the last string of trees.

From Groundhog Park: To reach this trailhead, follow the same directions as to Cathedral Campground, except once on the Embargo Creek Road, you should follow the signs to Groundhog Park. The hike begins where the road crosses Groundhog Creek. Follow the trail up the creek to Mesa Mountain. In one of the fingers of timber on the left side of the draw, below timberline, lies another of Fremont's camps, where his party apparently stayed on its way out of the area in January. From the ridge of Mesa Mountain, the view is extensive in all directions. Travel southwest along the ridge, until you reach the sign to Fremont's Christmas camp. The camp is about .25 mile off the ridge towards the creek.

When the "Pathfinder," as Fremont was called, left St. Louis to find a railroad route through the Central Rockies, to California, he was certain that he could make it through the mountains during the height of winter and that this accomplishment would prove that a railroad could make it through in winter, as well. He headed west from Pueblo in November 1848 with thirty-six men and 120 mules into particularly harsh weather that made the La Garita

Mountains even more impassable than they would have been during a normal winter. There was even heavy snow cover on the floor of the usually dry San Luis Valley.

Although the exact route Fremont took into the mountains isn't clear, several camps around Mesa Mountain are known. There you'll see stumps of trees cut by the expedition at the snow level—at a depth of four to six feet—and the remains of one of the party's sleds. Diaries from several expedition members described the camps, including the Christmas camp where, after managing to cross the summit of the La Garitas, Fremont decided to turn back, recross the mountains, and head down to the Rio Grande River.The diaries tell a sad but fascinating tale. The party became stranded in the high country. For several weeks the only food was mule, while Fremont, with ponies secured from the Indians, was able to reach Taos and the famous Kit Carson, who went back with a rescue party to find a few men making their way across the San Luis Valley. Eleven of them had died of hunger and exposure. The rest made it to Taos and safety and, although Fremont continued on to California in 1849, he never found the hoped-for route across the southern Colorado Rockies.

The diaries can be read at the Del Norte Ranger District office or the museum in Del Norte where relics of the equipment used by the expedition are housed.
—*Curtis Bates*

HIKE 36 *RINCON LA VACA & RIO GRANDE PYRAMID*

General description: Moderate day hike with the option of a long day hike or overnight trip. Could include a climb of Rio Grande Pyramid.

General location: About thirty miles southwest of Creede in the Weminuche Wilderness.

Maps: Rio Grande National Forest Map; Weminuche Pass USGS quad.; Trails Illustrated Weminuche Wilderness map.

Degree of difficulty: Moderate to more difficult.

Length: 5.5 miles one way to Rincon La Vaca (eleven miles roundtrip); ten miles one-way to Rio Grande Pyramid (twenty miles roundtrip).

Elevations: 9,300 to 10,800 feet to Rincon La Vaca; 9,300 to 13,821 feet to climb Rio Grande Pyramid.

Special attractions: Excellent entry point for the vast Weminuche Wilderness; access to the Continental Divide Trail; wildflowers in spring; aspen in fall; chances to see elk, deer, black bear; relatively easy access to spectacular alpine terrain.

Best season: May and June for wildflowers, late June through August to hike up Rio Grande Pyramid, September for colorful aspens.

For more information: Rio Grande National Forest, Creede Range District, 3rd and Creede Ave., Box 270, Creede, CO 81130, (719) 658-2556.

The hike: Drive twenty-four miles south from Lake City on Colorado Highway 149 or twenty miles west from Creede. Turn west on Forest Service Route 520 and proceed eleven miles to Thirty Mile Campground where there is a trailhead.

A short distance from the signed trailhead, Squaw Creek Trail forks off. Stay on the Weminuche Creek Trail. Pass Rio Grande Reservoir dam, follow

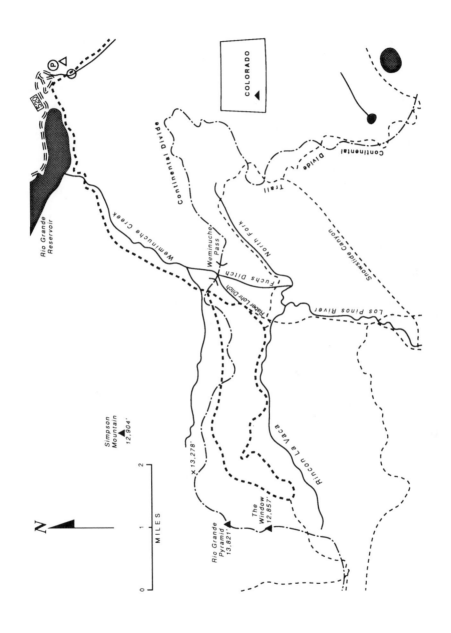

the contour of the land up above the reservoir through the aspen. Sometimes there is quite a bit of horse traffic from commercial stables on this part of the trail (mostly day trips), so you may have to step off the trail for horses. Columbines are abundant here in spring.

The trail bends left abruptly up Weminuche Creek Canyon and is moderately steep for a while. The trail is built through a rockslide, then crosses a small stream, just before crossing Weminuche Creek on a bridge at about mile two. The creek here is an impressive torrent in the peak run-off season, increased further by the diversion into Weminuche Creek from Los Pinos River via the Raber Lohr Ditch. The trail continues up quite steeply for a bit, then the valley opens up into the broad meadows of Weminuche Pass. From this point up to Rincon La Vaca the trail is much more gentle.

The trail stays well above Weminuche Creek for about two miles, crossing two streams (the second is the larger) coming off Simpson Mountain. Weminuche Creek is encountered at about mile 4.5 and must be forded. There can be a lot of water in the spring, but the wading isn't difficult.

Weminuche Pass is crossed a short distance beyond the creek (a very gentle Continental Divide crossing). Pack horses are often seen grazing in the grassy meadows near the Pass.

The trail parallels the Raber Lohr Ditch for about .5 mile, bends right, joins with the Continental Divide Trail, then heads up Rincon La Vaca. Rincon La Vaca is a good place to stop if you are day hiking. It's a good camping spot if you are continuing.

This is good elk and deer country, but they are usually higher up after early June. Weather permitting, a good view of Rio Grande Pyramid will be visible where the forest opens up. Proceed across the bottom of an avalanche chute, then climb up the moderately steep incline to continue on toward the peak.

To climb Rio Grande Pyramid, leave the trail at a broad switchback at timberline, skirt the willows on the left and hike up to the ridge where a large, square-cut window becomes visible. The trail coming directly up the ridge from Weminuche Pass is joined at about 12,300 feet and continues to the summit of the pyramid (about four miles from lower Rincon La Vaca). The climb is rocky and steep in places, but not difficult for experienced hikers. Red Cloud, Sunshine, Uncompahgre, Wetterhorn, Mt. Sneffels, Mt. Wilson, Wilson Peak, the Grenadiers and the Needles can all be seen from the summit in good weather.—*Mountain Miser, Ltd.*

HIKE 37 *EAST SIDE DUNE TRAIL*

General description: A pleasant day hike along the eastern edge of the Great Sand Dunes or a longer hike into the Sangre de Cristo Mountains.

General location: Approximately thirty miles northeast of Alamosa.

Maps: Medano Pass and Mosca Pass USGS quads; Great Sand Dunes National Monument; Rio Grande National Forest Map.

Degree of difficulty: Moderate to difficult.

Length: From three to ten miles one way.

Elevations: 8,300 to 13,297 feet.

Special attractions: Great Sand Dunes; good views of surrounding mountain ranges; disappearing creeks.

Best season: Spring and fall.

For more information: Great Sand Dunes National Monument, Mosca, CO 81146; Rio Grande National Forest, Conejos Peak Ranger District, 21461 State Highway 285, La Jara, CO 81140; (719) 274-5193.

The hike: This hike takes you into an intriguing and unique area in southern Colorado, long the focus of many legends and superstitions: the Great Sand Dunes. The trail follows a jeep road but offers you a good chance to disappear for awhile like the creek that runs through the shifting sands.

To reach the trailhead, drive east from Alamosa about fourteen miles on US Highway 160. Then go north on State Highway 150 about twenty miles to the Great Sand Dunes National Monument Visitors Center. From the parking lot area proceed northwest on the Medano Pass Road on foot. It is easy hiking along this four-wheel drive road, which follows Medano Creek at the eastern edge of the sand dunes. You can also follow the creekbed.

Legend, mystery, and superstition have long surrounded these shifting hills of sand. Some say there are huge, web-footed horses that race over the dunes at night. On a moonlit night, they say, you can see them. Bands of wild horses may actually roam the edges of the dunes, but web-footed they're not, just broad-hooved. They were probably brought here by the Spaniards in the 1500s.

When the wind blows over the dunes, it is said you can hear voices. The Indians who came often to the dunes called them the "singing sands" for this reason.

Medano Creek follows the eastern edge of the dunes for many miles. Then it disappears. Like the creek, many humans are rumored to have disappeared into the sands, as well as whole flocks of sheep and whole wagon trains, mules and all.Whatever you think of the legends surrounding the dunes, you will, no doubt, be very impressed by the mountain ranges that surround them. To the north and east is the Sangre de Cristo Range. To the west across the San Luis Valley are the San Juans. It was once believed that the sand dunes were formed from deposits from Medano Creek and other creeks flowing out of the Sangre de Cristos. Now it is believed that the sand came originally from the rocks that make up the San Juans. Streams brought them down to the San Luis Valley, the only true desert in the Southern Rockies. The winds— prevailing westerlies—picked up the sands and carried them eastward and when the winds rose to funnel through Medano and Mosca passes in the Sangre de Cristos, the sand was dropped in the dune area. Sometimes violent

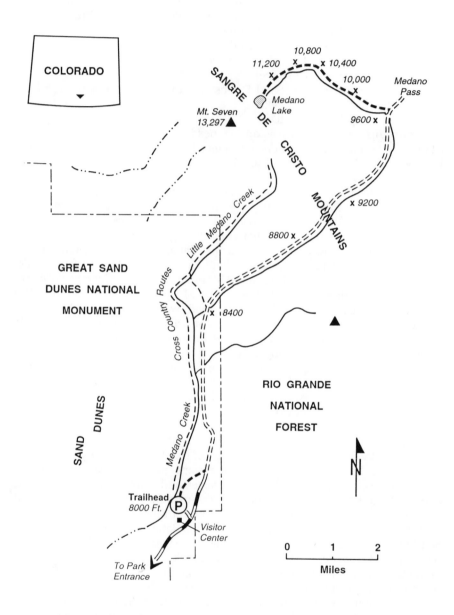

COLORADO

SANGRE DE CRISTO MOUNTAINS

10,800
x
11,200 x x 10,400
x
10,000
x
Medano
Pass

Medano
Lake

Mt. Seven
13,297 ▲

9600 x

x 9200

Little Medano Creek

8800 x

GREAT SAND
DUNES NATIONAL
MONUMENT

Cross Country Routes

x 8400

▲

RIO GRANDE
NATIONAL
FOREST

SAND DUNES

Medano Creek

N

Trailhead
8000 Ft. P

Visitor
Center

To Park
Entrance

0   1   2

Miles

winds rage out of the mountain canyons to the east, too, creating strange shapes out of the sand.

Following the jeep trail (or creekbed) along the edge of the dunes, you will observe the constant battle between the shifting sands, the flowing water and the forest vegetation for control of this area. The sand is dropped here by the wind and in the spring Medano Creek carries it away. But late in the year, the creek becomes lost in the sand. In places, new trees take root, stabilizing the dunes and in other places are covered and die, leaving only their eerie skeletons behind, half covered with sand.

Near the junction of Medano and Little Medano Creeks (about four miles along), the jeep road turns eastward and climbs to Medano Pass. At this point, you can continue on the road to Medano Pass and eventually intercept a trail to Medano Lake, located on the northeast side of Mt. Seven. This hike would necessitate a backpack.

Or you can follow the Little Medano Creek Trail through varied terrain. It begins by heading north from the campground near site #62. It continues to the Dunes Overlook and through Escape Dunes until it crosses Medano Creek and ends at an overlook just beyond Little Medano Creek. This trail would make a nice loop hike with a return to the campground by way of the jeep road or Medano Creek.

Camping is good in the trees, but not allowed in the dunes. A campground is provided at the dune headquarters. Be sure to take water with you.

Enjoy your exploration of the dunes (you can climb atop them more easily when it has rained a bit) and then return as you came.—*Brian Dempsey*

HIKE 38 *HORN LAKES*

General description: An overnighter to alpine lakes in the heart of the rugged Sangre de Cristo Range.
General location: About forty-five miles southeast of Salida.
Maps: Horn Peak USGS quad; San Isabel National Forest Map.
Degree of difficulty: Moderate.
Length: Five miles one way.
Elevations: 9,000 to 11,800 feet.
Special attractions: Deep glacial valley and cirque lakes; thick forests and abundant wildflowers at lower elevations.
Best season: Summer.
For more information: San Isabel National Forest, San Carlos Ranger District, 326 Dozier Ave., Canon City, CO 81212; (719) 275-4119.

The hike: The Sangre de Cristo Range, which extends some 150 miles from Salida southeast into New Mexico, is visible from much of southeastern Colorado as a jagged, unbroken ridge. This hike takes you into the heart of this range and into the San Isabel National Forest.

To reach the trailhead, drive east on State Highway from Salida or west from Canon City. Turn south on State Highway 69 to the town of Westcliffe. From Westcliffe, go south approximately three miles on Highway 69, turning right onto Schoolfield Road, a paved road with signs to Alpine Lodge and Alvarado Campground. Follow this road for .9 mile and turn left onto Colony

HIKE 38 HORN LAKES

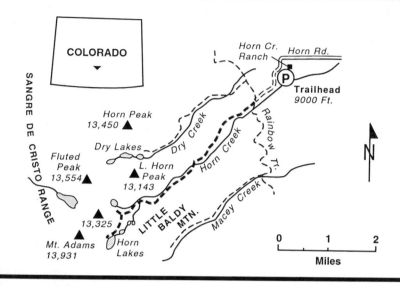

Lane, another paved road. After two miles, turn right onto Horn Road for about 4.5 miles to its end near the Horn Creek Ranch. Bear right at the entrance to the ranch and continue about a hundred yards to the trailhead and a parking area.

There is a four-wheel drive road leaving the parking area to the left and a footpath going off to the right. The easiest route is along the closed four-wheel drive road, which is windy and stony, but not steep. The road terminates after about .75 mile at the Rainbow Trail, which parallels the eastern side of the mountain range at lower elevations for much of its length and offers access to the Dry Lakes Valley to the north and the Macey Lakes Valley to the south.

From the Rainbow Trail, the Horn Lakes Trail continues straight uphill on the old four-wheel-drive road. It climbs at a moderate rate for the first 1.75 miles up the right (north) side of the Horn Creek Valley. The trail is generally within a few hundred yards of Horn Creek as it passes through dense forests of aspen, ponderosa pine and Douglas fir. The forest is interrupted occasionally by open, grassy meadows which offer some superb views back towards the Wet Mountains to the east. During mid-July, these meadows are brimming with many kinds of wildflowers, including several varieties of penstemon, wall flower, yellow pea, wild rose, and columbine. All in all, this lower stretch of the trail is quite enjoyable as you gain about a thousand vertical feet.

After the trail crosses to the left (south) side of Horn Creek (no bridge), it climbs steeply for about 1.25 miles. The forest is rather dense here and you can't see far up or down the valley. The trail is rough and several muddy areas may be encountered along this section.

This steep stretch ends rather abruptly when you cross Horn Creek. (Again, there is no bridge, but the creek is much smaller here than downstream.) From here, you leave the dense forest and pass through gently rolling, high alpine meadows and two valleys become visible. The main Horn Lake is at the end of the valley straight ahead. The trail becomes rather rugged, but not too steep, and in places, passes through thick willows. In short, your progress along this stretch may be slower than you'd expect. As you go this slower pace, watch for occasional bristlecone pines and take in the views: they're awe-inspiring.

There are numerous small lakes and ponds below the main Horn Lake and some good camping spots. The lake itself is very scenic, edged by cliffs and with a small island in the middle. We do not recommend camping near the lake. Like many other high alpine lakes in Colorado, this lake could be easily scarred by careless campers.

For those who like "top of the world" mountain views, a short day trip may be made by climbing the ridge to the north of Horn Lakes. The best route begins about .5 mile below the main lake. The climb is steep, but not dangerous. From the top of the ridge you get a good view of four "four-teeners:" Crestone Needle, Crestone Peak, Humboldt, and Kit Carson Peak. This southern view is particularly impressive, but the views to the north along the backbone of the Sangre de Cristo Range and the views into the San Luis Valley to the west and the Wet Mountains to the east are equally impressive. This ridge also provides access to 13,931 foot Mt. Adams, which is about .5 mile to the southwest. This climb can be made without a rope, but it is not recommended.—*Bill Bath*

HIKE 39 *ST. CHARLES PEAK*

General description: A day hike up the second highest peak in the Wet Mountains.

General location: Approximately forty miles southwest of Pueblo.

Maps: St. Charles Peak USGS quad; San Isabel National Forest Map.

Degree of difficulty: Easy.

Length: Ten miles round trip.

Elevations: 9,050 to 11,784 feet.

Special attractions: Pine, spruce and fir trees; small stream; excellent views from the summit.

Best season: Summer and fall.

For more information: San Carlos Ranger District, 326 Dozier Ave., Canon City, CO 81212; (719) 275-4119.

The hike: This hike takes you to the summit of St. Charles Peak, the second highest peak in the Wet Mountains, a southern continuation of the Front Range west of Pueblo. To reach the trailhead, take State Highway 78 southwest to Beulah (twenty-six miles). Instead of driving into Beulah, take the highway (now Pine Drive) southwest for twelve miles to its junction with State Highway 165. Turn north on 165 and in less than one mile park in the area provided on the right side of the road. The trailhead is directly across the road.

The trail leads you west and up onto a ridge, then drops a few feet and crosses a small stream. A series of switchbacks leads you to another stream crossing and through evergreen forests up to a pass at 10,050 feet. The trail then descends a bit, crosses a boggy place, then climbs again westward with more switchbacks to another pass at 10,800 feet.

HIKE 39 ST. CHARLES PEAK

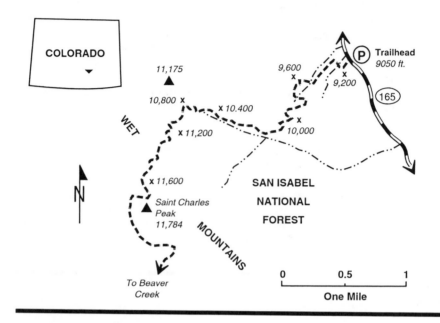

Turning south-southwest (left), the trail now switchbacks to a small, rocky point with a good view of the summit. Beyond, at 11,480 feet, one climbs out of the thick woods to open tundra with timberline trees, wildflowers, rocks, and a good view.

Follow the ridge, go through more forest and then begin to follow the trail around the western side of the summit dome. At this point, leave the trail and hike carefully across the tundra to the obvious top of St. Charles Peak.

From here you could follow the trail generally southward down Beaver Creek to Lake Isabel Campground and a waiting vehicle, which you would have had to shuttle before your start.

You can also descend the western side of the mountain to a logging road leading to the Ophir Creek Road. A shuttle would be needed in that case as well.

The view from the summit is excellent. To the west is the Wet Mountain Valley—a structural valley—separating the Wet Mountain Range from the Sangre de Cristo Range that you can see in the distance. To the east are the Great Plains. Enjoy the view and then return as you came.—*Frances C. Carter*

HIKE 40 *TANNER TRAIL*

General description: A solitary day hike into the Wet Mountains, culminating in an alpine meadow with views of both the eastern plains and western Sangre de Cristo Mountains.

General location: Twelve miles south of Canon City.

Maps: Curley Peak USGS quad; San Isabel National Forest Map.

Degree of difficulty: Moderate.

Length: Four miles one way.

Elevations: 7,362 to 9,600 feet.

Special attractions: Terrific views both east and west; lush vegetation; little-used although open to motor bikes.

Best season: Summer and fall.

For more information: San Isabel National Forest, San Carlos Ranger District, 326 Dozier Ave., Canon City, CO 81212; (719) 275-4119.

The hike: The Tanner Trail to Curley Peak in the San Isabel National Forest is a trail well worth hiking if you are seeking a short day hike featuring an abundance of mountain wildflowers, varied mountain terrain, and an escape from the heavily traveled trails in the northern mountain ranges.

To reach the trailhead, drive to Canon City and turn south from the city's main street onto 9th Street (Colorado 115). Turn right (west) at the Lakeside Cemetery and then left (south) onto Fremont County Road 143. Follow this road about twelve miles past a golf course and a large mill and continue going toward the Oak Creek Campground. The trailhead is reached about one mile

The Sangre de Cristo Mountains from the Tanner Trail. Chuck Kall photo.

HIKE 40 *TANNER TRAIL*

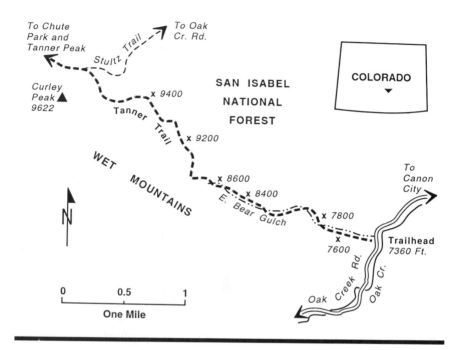

To Chute
Park and
Tanner Peak

To Oak
Cr. Rd.

Stultz *Trail*

Curley
Peak ▲
9622

Tanner *Trail*

x 9400

SAN ISABEL
NATIONAL
FOREST

COLORADO
▼

x 9200

WET
MOUNTAINS

x 8600
x 8400
E. Bear Gulch
x 7800

To
Canon
City

x
7600

x
7600

Trailhead
7360 Ft.

Oak Creek Rd.

Oak Cr.

N

0   0.5   1
One Mile

before the campground. It is on your right and marked by a poorly placed sign, which is somewhat overgrown by brush so look closely for it. There is no parking area, but it is not difficult to pull safely off the road.

The trail begins at 7,362 feet and climbs to 9,600 feet, mostly within the first 2.5 miles. It is sometimes covered with loose rock which makes for difficult walking. As you begin your hike make a mental note to watch for rattlesnakes.

The early part of the trail winds up East Bear Gulch through shady mountain forest. Scrub oak, aspen, blue spruce, Douglas fir, juniper, and pinon pine are all along the route, as are a surprising variety of wildflowers and butterflies. Tall tansy asters, Indian paintbrush, wallflower, harebell, pinedrops, scarlet gilia, and an intriguing variety of mushrooms are easily identified.

After an ascent of about two miles, you will begin to have a view of the eastern plains. Continuing upward, this view will be complimented by a western view of the Sangre de Cristo Mountains and the intervening Wet Mountain Valley. At about three miles, the trail stretches out into a lovely mountain meadow providing an easy walk of another one mile or so to the high point of the trail. Curley Peak is a stony nob that is seen a few hundred feet from the Tanner Trail. The trail does not actually lead to its summit, but it is an easy side trip. The view here southwest to the Sangre de Cristos is nothing short of spectacular.

If you wish to continue on for a longer hike from here, you can follow the

Tanner Trail to its intersection with the Tanner Peak Trail in 3.5 miles and in 4.5 miles, the Stultz Trail which returns some eight miles to the Oak Creek Grade Road about four miles north of the Tanner Trail trailhead.

Be sure to carry a supply of drinking water with you; little is available along the way. And enjoy this opportunity to spend an entire day on a little-used mountain trail.—*Chuck and Babs Kall*

HIKE 41 *GARNER CREEK*

General description: A day hike or overnighter to the crest of the Sangre de Cristo Range.
General location: About thirty-five miles southeast of Poncha Springs.
Maps: Valley View Hot Springs USGS quad; Rio Grande National Forest Map.
Degree of difficulty: Difficult.
Length: About 4.5 miles one way with opportunities for peak ascents and an extended backpack.
Elevations: 8,700 to 13,588 feet.
Special attractions: Great views; access to high peaks.
Best season: Summer.
For more information: Contact Rio Grande National Forest, Saguache Ranger District, 444 Christy Ave., P.O. Box 67, Saguache, CO 81149; (719) 655-2553.

The hike: This hike takes you up the western flank of the Sangre de Cristo Range and provides you with many great views, as well as access to several high peaks. A topographic map, a good sense of direction, and some sturdy hiking boots will be invaluable to you on this hike.

To reach the trailhead, take US Highway 285 south past Poncha Springs, over Poncha Pass and into the San Luis Valley to the town of Villa Grove. Go four miles south of the town to the junction of 285 and State Highway 17. At the junction there is a dirt road running east (Forest Route 964). Follow it for 6.9 miles to the "Y," then go south and right about one mile. You will first pass a jeep road with a sign marked "Hot Springs Creek" on your left. Continue to the second jeep road on your left with a sign for the Garner Creek trailhead. (A turn north at the "Y" will take you to Valley View Hot Springs.) The first .2 mile of this road (up to the first gate) is private land, and it is .5 mile to the trailhead. Park somewhere along the short jeep road up the draw and begin your hike.

The San Luis Valley, which you will be hiking away from, is a flat-floored desert park created as a giant rift valley. Near the point at which you left the county road is the surface expression of an extensive fault, which marks the distinction between the mountains and the valleys. On the east of the fault, the Sangre de Cristos have been uplifted and on the west the valley floor has dropped. Over millions of years the valley has been filled with thousands of feet of sediments. Today, badger, pronghorn antelope, deer and rattlesnakes make it their home.

As you hike up Garner Creek Draw, keep to the south on all tributaries. You will ascend from your parking spot at 8,700 feet to the crest at 12,650 in 4.5 miles. Keep an eye out for deer, elk and possibly bobcat as you climb.

You may want to try your luck fishing Garner Creek. However, it is rated only fair for small brook trout.

At the pass where small mammals like the marmot and pika make their homes, you can proceed northwest to the summit of Cottonwood Peak (13,588 feet) about one mile away via an old mining road going nearly all the way to the summit, or turn southeast to Thirsty Peak (13,217 feet). Then you can continue south over Lakes Peak (13,382 feet) to Electric Peak (13,621 feet), which is directly above Banjo Lake to the east.

From the summits of these peaks your views will be of the Wet Mountains to the east, and the intervening Wet Mountain Valley; the San Juan Mountains to the west and the intervening San Luis Valley. Along the Sangre de Cristo Range (the name means "Blood of Christ" and refers to the red glow the mountains take on at sunrise and sunset) as you look to the southeast, you will see many fourteeners, including Kit Carson Peak (14,165 feet), Crestone Peak (14,295 feet) and Humboldt Peak (14,064 feet). Beyond them is the Crestone Needle (14,191 feet) and, at the western base of the range, the Great Sand Dunes. Far to the southeast are Little Bear and Blanca peaks and Mt. Lindsey. Beyond that lies New Mexico.

Returning along the ridge to Garner Pass you could conceivably follow the Garner Trail east past Silver Lake (fair fishing for small natives) and Rainbow

HIKE 41 *GARNER CREEK*

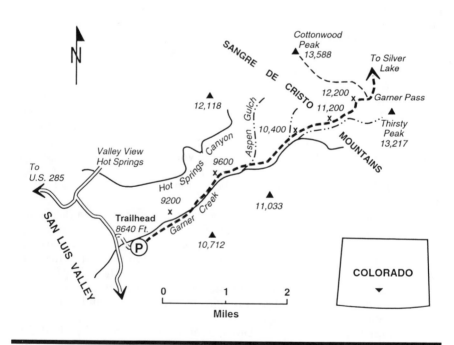

Lake (fair fishing for ten to fourteen-inch rainbow trout) to Lake Creek Campground on San Isabel Forest Route 300, making a long backpack out of your trip. To do so, however, you would have to shuttle vehicles before you leave by driving southeast from Salida, taking US Highway 50 east to State Highway 69 and then going south past the town of Hillside and bearing right when State Highway 69 turns southeast, to take Forest Route 300 to Lake Creek Campground.

Otherwise, return as you came, hiking down the Garner Creek Trail to your vehicle.—*Brian Dempsey*

HIKE 42 *MT. OURAY*

General description: A short, but steep, day hike to the summit of Mt. Ouray in the Sawatch Range.

General location: About fifteen miles southwest of Poncha Springs.

Maps: Pahlone Peak and fifteen minute Bonanza USGS quads; San Isabel National Forest Map.

Length: About 3.5 miles one way.

Degree of difficulty: Moderate.

Elevations: 10,800 to 13,971 feet.

Special attractions: A short climb to a peak with a summit just short of 14,000 feet; beautiful views; many wildflowers.

Best season: Summer.

For more information: San Isabel National Forest, Salida Ranger District, 230 W. 16th St., Salida, CO 81201; (719) 539-3591.

The hike: This hike takes you to the summit of a "near fourteener" in the Sawatch Range. Named after the great Ute Indian chief, Mt. Ouray stands at 13,971 feet and is reached by a short but steep climb, beginning near Marshall Pass. This could also be the starting point for a long hike along the Continental Divide to Monarch Pass, which would require a car shuttle.

To reach the trail to the peak, drive south from Poncha Springs on US 285 for five miles and turn right (west) on Chaffee County Road 200 (Forest Route 243) at Mears Junction (Marshall Pass Road). After about .25 mile turn right towards O'Haver Lake on Forest Route 243, then turn right at the Marshall Pass sign. From there it is about ten miles to the top of the pass as you follow the scenic route of the old Denver & Rio Grande Railroad. About .25 mile before the summit of the pass is the sign for the Crest Trail at an old jeep road to the right. Park across the road from the trailhead.

Begin your hike by following the upper of the two jeep trails at the trailhead, away from the meadows and marshy area on the south side of the road where Poncha Creek has its headwaters and where wild iris grow. The trail switches back two times and heads into a forest of spruce-fir, then climbs at a moderate grade until it reaches a ridgetop. From this point the summit of Mt. Ouray looms above you to the northeast. To the west are the tributaries to the Gunnison River. You are straddling the Continental Divide. After you cross the cattle guard, continue along the road for about .25 mile paralleling the ridge.

The easiest route to the peak summit is to leave the road where it makes a sharp bend to the right, cross the fence and climb through intermittent meadow and forest up the broad ridge to the northeast. After a good steady climb, you will reach timberline and shortly after that, the terrain flattens out to a broad saddle, which connects to Mt. Ouray. This saddle with its many wildflowers would make a good destination in itself.

Once across the saddle, you will reach the summit after a steep, rocky climb of .75 mile, which may necessitate some scrambling, but is not dangerous.

From the summit you can see the peaks of the Sawatch Range to the north, the Elk and the West Elk Mountains to the northwest, the Gunnison Valley to the west, the Cochetopa Hills to the southwest and the San Juan Mountains beyond, the San Luis Valley to the south, the Sangre de Cristo Range to the southeast and the Arkansas Valley to the east with the summit of Pikes Peak in the distance. It is truly a spectacular view. Directly below you on the east side of the peak is the fantastic Devil's Armchair. Legend has it that Chief Ouray's spirit sits in the chair to watch over the country below. Notice Chipeta Mountain to the northwest, named for the chief's wife.

HIKE 42 *MT. OURAY*

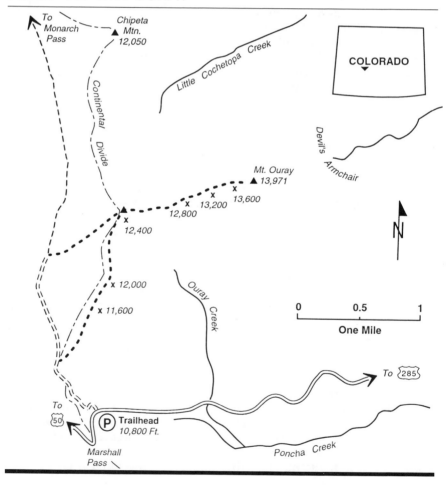

After enjoying the view, return as you came. Should you decide to make the long ten-mile hike to Monarch Pass (US Highway 50), continue north along the jeep road which you left to climb Mt. Ouray. The road ends about one mile farther along and becomes the Monarch Trail. This portion is included as part of both the Continental Divide National Scenic Trail and the Colorado Trail.—*Peter, Caryn and Crystal Boddie*

HIKE 43 *HENRY LAKE*

General description: A backpack to Henry Lake, an alpine lake in the proposed Fossil Ridge Wilderness Area.
General location: Approximately twenty miles northeast of Gunnison.
Maps: Matchless Mountain, Taylor Park Reservoir and Fairview Peak USGS quads; Gunnison National Forest Map, Trails Illustrated Pearl Pass and Gunnison NE.
Degree of difficulty: Moderate.
Length: Twelve miles round trip.
Elevations: 9,140 to 11,704 feet.
Special attractions: A beautiful alpine lake nestled right at the base of Henry Mountain and offering good fishing; numerous private campsites and spectacular views; good opportunities to see deer and elk.
Best season: Summer and fall.
For more information: Contact Gunnison National Forest, Taylor Ranger District, 216 N. Colorado, Gunnison, CO 81230; (303) 641-0471.

The hike: This hike beginning at Lottis Creek Campground, a Gunnison National Forest recreation site, and ending at Henry Lake at the base of 13,254-foot Mt. Henry, offers scenic campsites, fair fishing for eight- to twelve-inch cutthroat and some large rainbow trout, and access to the summits of mountain peaks.To reach the trailhead, drive north from Gunnison on State Highway 135. At the town of Almont, turn right onto the Taylor Canyon Road and follow it fifteen miles up the canyon to Lottis Creek Campground. (Watch for bighorn sheep on your drive up. They can sometimes be seen across the river to your left.) Once at the campground, take the second right entrance and follow the road through the overflow camping area for .25 mile to the signed trailhead. Lottis Creek Campground may also be reached by driving over Cottonwood Pass, through Taylor Park, and four miles down Taylor Canyon from the dam.

Once at the trailhead, be sure to sign the register before starting out. Then, rather than hiking up Lottis Creek into Union Canyon (a very nice day trip), cross over the creek on the log bridge and begin following the trail up South Lottis Creek.

The trail climbs south through the timber, along the east side of South Lottis Creek. It remains fairly level, with only an occasional steep section. A small, rocky clearing at 9,950 feet and about 2.5 miles up the trail makes for a nice resting or lunch spot. A bit over a mile above the clearing, the trail crosses a small creek coming from the left, down off the west side of 12,459 foot

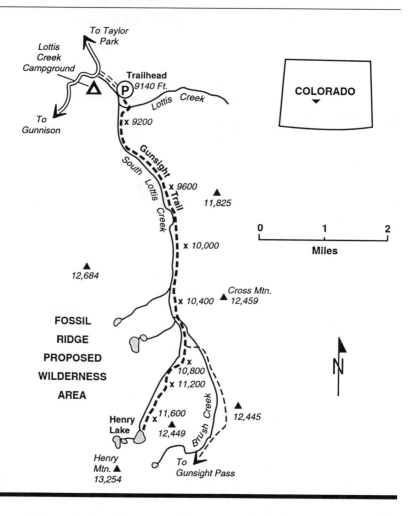

foot Cross Mountain. For those in no hurry to reach Henry Lake, camp may be set up here. From the creek crossing, it is another .5 mile to the junction with the trail to Gunsight Pass. The pass is three miles up Brush Creek and makes for a nice day hike. It is little used, however, and may require a bit of route-finding ability.

Taking the right fork, continue steeply up the last 1.5 miles to Henry Lake. The trail continues to climb along the east side of South Lottis Creek, directly below the northeast ridge of Henry Mountain. The final half-mile is the steepest, as is often the case when reaching an alpine lake in Colorado. But, as soon as you crest the top and view the lake, there is no doubt the pull was worth it.

Level campsites are abundant, both in clearings and in the timber. Please camp at least 200 feet away from the lake, as this is a very fragile environment and easily impacted. Areas near the small lakes directly west of Henry Lake also make for nice campsites.

Once settled, it is time to try the fishing, gaze at the views, or for the more energetic, climb to the broad summit of Henry Mountain. Whatever you choose to do once at the lake, you will certainly enjoy the scenic alpine setting and likely leave vowing to return for a more lengthy visit next time. —*Chris Gore*

HIKE 44 *MILL-CASTLE TRAIL*

General description: A backpack into the West Elk Wilderness, culminating in a panoramic view from the top of Storm Pass. General location: Approximately fifteen miles northwest of Gunnison.
Maps: Squirrel Creek and West Elk Peak quads; Gunnison National Forest Map, Trails Illustrated Black Mesa.
Degree of difficulty: Moderate.
Length: Nine miles one way.
Elevations: 9,000 to 12,450 feet.
Special attractions: Good views of The Castles and other rock formations, of the Baldys and of the Elk Range fourteeners; opportunities to see elk and deer.
Best season: Summer and fall (be especially careful during hunting season).
For more information: Gunnison National Forest, Taylor River District, 216 N. Colorado, Gunnison, CO 81230; (303) 641-0471.

The hike: The Mill-Castle Trail takes you into the heart of the West Elk Wilderness to Storm Pass where there is a spectacular view of the unique rock formations of the Castles. The trail also provides access to further backpacking opportunities.

To reach the trailhead, drive three miles north of Gunnison on State Highway 135. Turn left onto the Ohio Creek Road and drive nine miles to the Mill Creek Road, which turns off to the left just before the paved section of the Ohio Creek Road ends. Turn onto the Mill Creek Road and go four miles to its end where the Forest Service maintains a locked gate just before the wilderness boundary. With careful driving and dry conditions, passenger cars can make it this far. But, if you find the going too rough, park your car lower and begin your trip at that point.

As you start out, continue to follow the old road, now closed to motor vehicles. Be sure to have a member of your party sign the Forest Service register before you begin your hike.

You will pass the West Elk Wilderness boundary sign and the trail sign and soon the old road becomes a trail. Shortly above this point, you make the one and only crossing of Mill Creek. The trail then climbs a steep bank, continues above the creek, and then enters a stand of aspen. Keep alert for deer and elk. Immediately, you will begin to see beautiful, serene campsites off towards Mill Creek to your left, but keep on going. It is still about six miles to Storm Pass.

Concern about *Giardia* makes drinking untreated, unboiled water from Mill Creek a poor idea. Drinking water should be filterd, treated, or boiled.

The Castles. U.S. Forest Service photo.

Once in the trees, it becomes obvious that the trail is gaining elevation. As it does, you will gain exciting glimpses of the rock formations to the north. The West Elk Mountains, like the San Juans to the south, are primarily of volcanic origin and the extensive deposits of ash and lava in them have been eroded into a spectacular array of cliffs and pinnacles. Before you know it, the trail has brought you up far enough to be at eye level with these interesting rock walls. Be sure to locate the rock figure there resembling an upright creature. It can be seen watching hikers near the western end of the formations.

By now, you have left enough miles behind you to make for a short, enjoy-

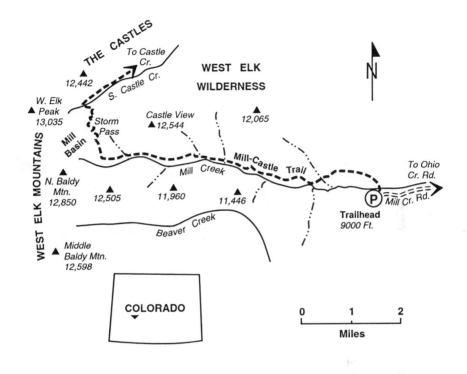

able trek up to Storm Pass tomorrow. You can begin searching for campsites or wait until you have reached the end of the trees and entered Mill Basin. When selecting a site, look away from the trail, water, and over-used areas. And when you move on, leave your site as litter-free and undisturbed as when you found it.

As you leave the trees and begin climbing into Mill Basin, you will notice the trail becoming less distinct. At this point, you will find yourself relying on rock cairns to point out the route. Consulting the West Elk Peak quad map as you move upwards will help assure you of following the proper route. Keep looking for deer and elk in Mill Basin. Soon the trail, marked by a large rock, heads to the north, and reaches the foot of Storm Pass. At this point, the trail again becomes distinct, as it switchbacks up the final steep pitch to the pass.

Even before reaching the top, as you travel the switchbacks and gain elevation, you will begin anticipating the view ahead. At the top, looking to the north, The Castles appear close enough to touch. Nowhere else are you able to view The Castles from such a vantage point. Further north, the Elk Mountain fourteeners are clearly visible (most noticeably the Maroon Bells). For

The Castles from Mill-Castle Trail. Chris Gore photo.

those wishing to continue, the trail drops steeply from the pass to join South Castle Creek, eventually reaching Castle Creek. From here, the Lowline Trail will take you north over Beckwith Pass to the Kebler Pass Road or south back to Mill Creek Road, where you can connect with your vehicle. The Lowline Trail also provides access east to the Ohio Pass Road, via the Swampy Pass Trail. Vehicle shuttles would be necessary for those hiking out to either Kebler Pass or Ohio Pass Roads.

Whether you choose to adventure further, visit only as far as Storm Pass, or simply day hike Mill Creek, the wildlife, rock formations, and scenic beauty and solitude of the West Elk Wilderness are sure to please in many ways. —*Chris Gore*

HIKE 45 *COPPER CREEK*

General description: A day hike or overnighter in the Maroon Bells Snowmass Wilderness near Crested Butte.
General location: About eight miles north of Crested Butte.
Maps: USGS Gothic and Maroon Bells quads; USFS/BLM Gunnison Basin map; Trails Illustrated Pearl Pass and Maroon Bells maps.
Degree of difficulty: Moderate.
Length: Five miles.
Elevations: 9,800 to 11,800 feet.

Special attractions: Beautiful Judd Falls near the beginning of the hike, wildflowers, high alpine glaciated Copper Basin and Copper Lake, access for longer hikes to Conundrum Hot Springs and the Aspen side of the Wilderness Area.

Best Season: Summer and fall.

For more information: Gunnison National Forest, Taylor River Ranger District, 216 N. Colorado, Gunnison, CO 81230. (303) 641-0471.

The hike: The Copper Creek trail north of Crested Butte makes for an easy stroll into the Maroon Bells Snowmass Wilderness with a beautiful waterfall within the first half mile, or a start of a more challenging backpacking trip over the crest of the Elk Mountains into the East Maroon or Conundrum Creek valleys on the Aspen side. Spectacular glaciated mountain topography, wildflowers, waterfalls, and wilderness are your rewards in either case.

To reach the Copper Creek trail, take the Gothic Road from Crested Butte past the Crested Butte Ski Area to the town of Gothic. Continue on past Gothic approximately .3 mile, turn right onto the National Forest access road and follow it to the trailhead. Both the Gunnison National Forest and USGS topographic maps show the access to the trail by way of a jeep road from Gothic. However, because this road has been closed where it crosses private land, the new trailhead was built to the north. Please respect this route closure.

From the trailhead, the trail takes a circuitous route first uphill and then back down to avoid private land and rejoins the Copper Creek jeep road at Judd Falls in about .5 mile. Judd Falls makes an easy destination for children or an easy evening walk for a moment of contemplation (there is even a rustic bench to sit on) and marks the edge of the Maroon Bells Snowmass Wilderness.

From Judd Falls, the trail follows a primitive jeep road approximately 4.5 miles to Copper Lake, where the Forest Service used to have a campground. Although located within the wilderness area, the first four miles of this road are still maintained and occasionally used to provide vehicle access to the Sylvenite Mine, an active claim that predated wilderness designation. The presence of the road only detracts slightly from the wilderness character of the valley and has the benefit of providing for easy hiking.

After a short climb from Judd Falls, the trail follows an easy grade through open forest and meadow along the north side of the Copper Creek Valley with spectacular views of the surrounding mountains. At about 1.8 miles the trail fords Copper Creek and begins to steepen. During the spring snowmelt, this crossing and two others between three and four miles along may be difficult. At four miles, the main jeep road turns off to the Sylvenite Mine and the Copper Creek trail continues on towards Copper Lake following the old campground road. The last one mile to the lake is a fairly steep climb, but well worth the effort.

Copper Lake is located above timberline at the base of the Copper Basin, a high alpine bowl ringed by 12,000 and 13,000 foot peaks. To the north of the lake is the saddle of East Maroon Pass where the Copper Creek Trail leads over to the East Maroon Creek Valley. The short but steep one-mile climb to the pass provides spectacular views of the Copper Basin and over into the East Maroon Creek Valley towards Aspen.

To the southeast of the lake the Conundrum Trail leads up a tributary valley towards Aspen.

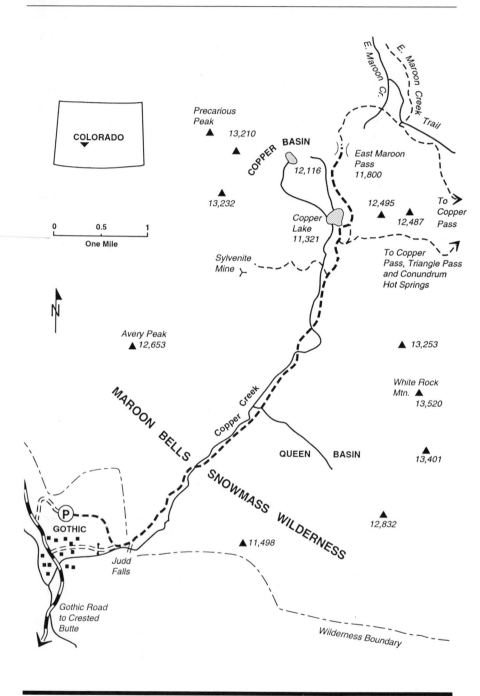

COLORADO

Precarious
Peak
▲ 13,210
▲

COPPER BASIN

12,116

13,232
▲

Copper
Lake
11,321

East Maroon
Pass
11,800

12,495
▲ 12,487
▲

To
Copper
Pass

To Copper
Pass, Triangle Pass
and Conundrum
Hot Springs

E. Maroon Cr.

E. Maroon Creek Trail

Sylvenite
Mine

0   0.5   1
One Mile

N

Avery Peak
▲ 12,653

▲ 13,253

White Rock
Mtn. ▲
13,520

Copper Creek

QUEEN   BASIN

▲
13,401

MAROON BELLS

SNOWMASS   WILDERNESS

▲
12,832

P

GOTHIC

▲ 11,498

Judd
Falls

Gothic Road
to Crested
Butte

Wilderness Boundary

To the southeast of the lake the Conundrum Trail leads up a tributary valley below White Rock Mountain and over Triangle Pass to Conundrum Creek and the Conundrum Hot Springs. Just below the summit of Triangle Pass another trail leads north over Copper Pass to the East Maroon Trail, providing a loop back to Copper Lake by way of East Maroon Pass. With a long car shuttle, it is possible to make a traverse of the Maroon Bells Snowmass Wilderness from the Crested Butte side at Copper Creek to the Aspen side by way of East Maroon or Conundrum creeks.—*Peter, Caryn, Crystal & Robin Boddie.*

HIKE 46 *DARK CANYON TRAIL*

General description: A backpack taking you through a spectacular canyon and into the high country of the Raggeds Wilderness Area.
General location: About twenty-five miles northeast of Paonia.
Maps: Paonia Reservoir and Marcellina Mountain USGS quads; Gunnison National Forest Map, Trails Illustrated Kebler Pass West.
Degree of difficulty: Moderate.
Length: Thirteen miles one way.
Elevations: 6,920 to 8,920 feet.
Special attractions: Takes you into the beautiful Ruby Mountains and Raggeds Wilderness Area; beautiful wildflowers; ends at inviting Horse Ranch Park; provides access to Oh-be-joyful Pass and North Anthracite Trail to Marble.
Best season: Late spring, summer and fall. (Ticks are terrible in the canyon before July 15.)
For more information: Gunnison National Forest, Paonia Ranger District, North Rio Grande Street, Box 1030, Paonia, CO 81428; (303) 527-4131.

The hike: Although it receives heavy use during the height of the summer season, the Dark Canyon Trail is worth hiking because it takes you into the beautiful Raggeds Wilderness Area and provides access to Oh-be-joyful Pass in the Ruby Range, an area which is under consideration for wilderness designation.

The Dark Canyon Trail in itself is thirteen miles long one way, a good two to three-day backpack which requires a car shuttle. You can extend your hike by following connecting trails. To reach the trailhead, drive northeast from Paonia on State Highway 133 to the fork in the highway just south of Paonia Reservoir, some fourteen miles. Take the right fork (Kebler Pass Road; Gunnison County Road 12) to Erickson Springs Campground. Trailhead parking is located on the south side of Anthracite Creek. A trail bridge connects the parking area with the trail on the north side of the creek.

From the campground the Dark Canyon Trail follows Anthracite Creek east into the steep-walled Dark Canyon. In the early summer season, waterfalls thunder down from cliffs and canyons high above and in the first four miles there is excellent fishing along the creek. The combined attractions of fishing opportunities and beautiful scenery mean this part of the trail receives the heaviest use.

As you reach the junction of Anthracite and North Anthracite Creeks, (the first good camping spots are here), the trail crosses two bridges—one over North Anthracite Creek, the other over Middle Anthracite Creek—and forks left and right. There is also an unmaintained trail up Middle Anthracite Creek. A hike north will take you over Anthracite Pass to an end point near Marble. A turn south follows the Dark Canyon Trail and will take you up the steep Devil's Stairway and on to Horse Ranch Park, a distance of about nine miles. This southern fork also provides access to Oh-be-joyful Pass to the east.

Take the right fork and you will begin your ascent of the Devil's Stairway, as you head around Prospect Point to your right. The trail climbs a series of switchbacks gaining approximately 1,200 feet in .75 mile for a very steep ascent. Once you top the Devil's Stairway, you will begin a gradual climb along the bench which lies at the base of the Ruby Range to the east and is drained by tributaries to Ruby Anthracite Creek to the west. At its southern end is Horse Ranch Park, your destination.

You will reach another fork in the trail about one mile along. If you go left, you will head southeast for another three miles or so to another fork. There a left turn will take you northeast to the top of Oh-be-joyful Pass, a spot befitting its name, where you will have beautiful views of the surrounding mountains of the Ruby Range. A right turn will take you south to another fork from which you can head east to Lake Irwin Campground or straight ahead to meet with the Dark Canyon Trail as it heads into Horse Ranch Park.

The most direct route to the park is simply to hike straight southward from the top of the Devil's Stairway. You will cross three major creeks—Silver, Sardine and Gold—where camping spots and water are plentiful. Be sure to camp at least 200 feet away from the streams and trail and treat your water; sheep are run in this area during the summer.

At Dyke Creek, the fourth creek you'll meet atop the plateau (you will also

The Ruby Range above the Dark Canyon Trail. U.S. Forest Service photo.

146

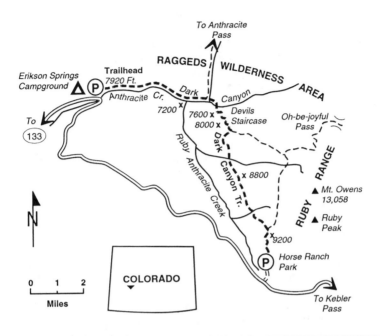

come across some small tributaries to these creeks and pass a number of ponds), you will meet a fork in the trail. A left connects you with the trail doubling back to Oh-be-joyful Pass. Straight ahead past a number of ponds is Horse Ranch Park, a beautiful, open mountain park divided by Ruby Anthracite Creek.

From here you can return as you came, or meet a vehicle that you will have had to shuttle before your start. To shuttle cars to this end point at Forest Route 826 (not posted), drive south from the Erickson Springs Campground on Kebler Pass Road (Gunnison County Road 12) past the turn off to Lost Lake Campground to Horse Ranch Park and a road going to the north. Follow this road to the trailhead.

For those who prefer a downhill hiking route you can travel the Dark Canyon Trail from Horse Ranch Park to Erickson Springs where you can meet a vehicle. However, by hiking in this direction you will miss the feeling of accomplishment and the reward of having made the ascent of the Devil's Staircase.

Whatever flight plan you set for hiking the Dark Canyon Trail, throughout your hike you will enjoy beautiful wildflowers, lush meadows of rushes, sedges, and grasses fringed by stands of aspen, forests of Douglas fir, ponderosa pine and lodgepole pine, and passes offering wide vistas of this gorgeous country. Be sure to keep your eyes peeled for deer, elk, and birds such as the brilliant mountain bluebird or gregarious gray and Steller's jays.—*Caryn Boddie*

HIKE 47 *KROENKE LAKE*

General description: A day hike along a roaring stream within a lush mountain forest, leading to a subalpine lake.
General location: Eight miles west of Buena Vista.
Maps: Mt. Harvard fifteen minute USGS quad; San Isabel National Forest Map, Trails Illustrated Collegiate Mountains.
Degree of difficulty: Moderate.
Length: Eight miles round trip.
Elevations: 9,000 to 11,600 feet.
Special attractions: Beautiful subalpine lake; fourteener, Mt. Yale.
Best season: Summer and fall.
For more information: San Isabel National Forest, Salida Ranger District, 230 W 16th, Salida, CO 81201; (719) 539-3591

The hike: This hike takes you into the beautiful Collegiate Mountain Range to Kroenke Lake in a subalpine setting surrounded by evergreens and vast mountain meadows.

To reach the trail to the lake, go west from Buena Vista on Crossman Avenue, which is Chaffee County Road 350. After approximately two miles, turn right on Chaffee County Road 361. You cannot miss this turn, since Crossman Avenue (County Road 350) deadends here. After a short while, County Road 361 will veer to the left (northwest). After 1.2 miles from your original turn onto this road, take a sharp left. You will be heading south again. Shortly afterward the road will turn west again. From this point it is approximately nine miles along an extremely bumpy road to the dead-end at the trailhead.

The trail begins by crossing North Cottonwood Creek via a wide, sturdy bridge about fifty yards from the trailhead. It then continues on the south side of the North Fork of Cottonwood Creek through a lush forest of spruce and fir with scattered small stands of aspen and stays close to the stream.

After approximately 1.5 miles, the trail will cross the stream over a second bridge. Shortly thereafter, it will cross a minor brook over some wobbly logs. As you continue on, you will occasionally have good views of the north face of Mt. Yale, which is composed of brecciated gneisses and granite. Approximately one mile after your last stream crossing via the second bridge, the trail crosses North Horn Creek.

From this point the hiker might decide to go right to Bear Lake, another four miles, or go straight ahead to Kroenke Lake. After another long mile, the trail crosses another small brook and then proceeds for less than one mile to Kroenke Lake.

All along your hike you will have seen small meadows with many wildflowers in summer. Kroenke Lake is surrounded by evergreens and is directly below the Continental Divide in a glaciated valley where there are vast alpine meadows, as well. It is a very beautiful area and the lake promises good fishing. You may want to stay awhile and just enjoy your surroundings or ascend to the summit of Mt. Yale (14,196 feet), or go to Brown's Pass on the Continental Divide, or any of the other high peaks in the area. Then you will want to return as you came.—*Pieter Dahmen*

HIKE 47 *KROENKE LAKE*

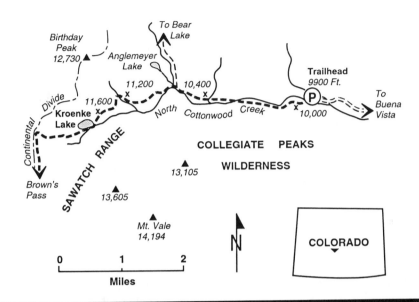

HIKE 48 *MISSOURI GULCH TRAIL*

General description: A day hike to a "hanging valley" and beyond to Elk Head Pass and the summit of Mt. Belford, a "fourteener."

General location: Approximately twenty miles northwest of Buena Vista.

Maps: Mt. Harvard fifteen minute USGS quad; San Isabel National Forest Map; Trails Illustrated Collegiate Mountains.

Degree of difficulty: Difficult.

Length: Nine miles round trip.

Elevations: 9,600 to 14,196 feet.

Special attractions: Opportunity to climb a fourteener; beautiful views of the Missouri Basin; Collegiate Peaks Wilderness.

Best season: Summer and early fall.

For more information: San Isabel National Forest, Leadville Ranger District, 2015 N. Poplar, Leadville, CO 80461; (719) 486-0752.

The hike: The Missouri Trail will truly give you a Rocky Mountain experience, taking you through stands of aspen, evergreen forest, alpine meadows and over the delicate tundra to Elk Head Pass and the 14,196 foot summit of Mt. Belford in the Collegiate Range.

To reach the trailhead, drive north from Buena Vista on US Highway 24 for seventeen miles to the Clear Creek Road just north of Clear Creek Reservoir. Turn left on this gravel road towards the ghost towns of Vicksburg and Winfield. After 7.9 miles, you should encounter the parking lot for the trailhead marked by a sign stating, "Missouri Trail Parking."

Allow at least eight hours hiking time for this nine mile round trip-you will want extra time to enjoy the views from the summit of Mt. Belford and the wildflowers you'll see as you cross the tundra.

Almost immediately after you've started your hike, you will cross Clear Creek on a sturdy bridge and head into the Collegiate Peaks Wilderness Area. After a short walk through a lush stand of aspen, you will start your ascent up a very steep slope covered with evergreens, taking on more than ten switchbacks to reach the top of the first steep portion of the Clear Creek Valley.

At the top you will enter the Missouri Gulch Valley, a hanging glacial valley. Here the trail levels off to a somewhat more gradual slope and continues thus for about .5 mile through more aspen. You will then encounter another stream as you cross Missouri Gulch on some wobbly logs and climb through a meadow where there are young aspen and evergreens growing, probably a sign that this meadow was beaten by avalanches.

At the end of this climb you will come across a miner's log cabin. A short way farther you will reach timberline and have your first view of Missouri Mountain. At this point you have hiked about two miles. Soon, the summit of Mt. Belford comes into view.

It is possible to begin the climb of Mt. Belford a mile before timberline is reached via a very steep ridge just south of a prominent gulch. This climb would save you 1.5 miles. However, if you have the time, and if you don't like steep grades, proceed to Elk Head Pass. The beautiful tundra you'll see, carpeted with wildflowers in summertime, will be worth the extra time. Please be careful in walking across the tundra, however, as it is very fragile.

From time to time you will be crossing small boulder fields. At Elk Head Pass the trail continues south into Missouri Basin.

From Elk Head Pass you have a commanding view of the Missouri Basin, which is a glacial basin with numerous cirque lakes and patches of snow surrounded by sharp mountain peaks such as Mt. Harvard, Emerald Peak, Iowa Peak and Missouri Mountain. You will also have a fantastic view of the Sawatch Range south of you with its numewrous fourteeners and the Continental Divide.

To reach the summit of Mt. Belford from Elk Head Pass, climb the ridge to your east, a gradual slope. After .3 mile on the ridge, you will have to turn north to reach the peak. From the summit of Mt. Belford, at 14,196 feet, the view is even grander than at the pass. In addition to the mountains you have already seen, you will now be able to view the Sawatch Range north of you, a group of impressive peaks including Huron Peak to the west, and the Mosquito Range and South Park to the east.

In addition to enjoyable day hikes, there are many possibilities for long backpacks in this area. It is possible to reach the Texas Creek Basin from here by crossing the Continental Divide. You can also climb the rest of the fourteeners in the immediate area: Oxford, Harvard, Columbia, Huron peak and Missouri Mountain. You will also discover many hidden basins.—*Pieter Dahmen*

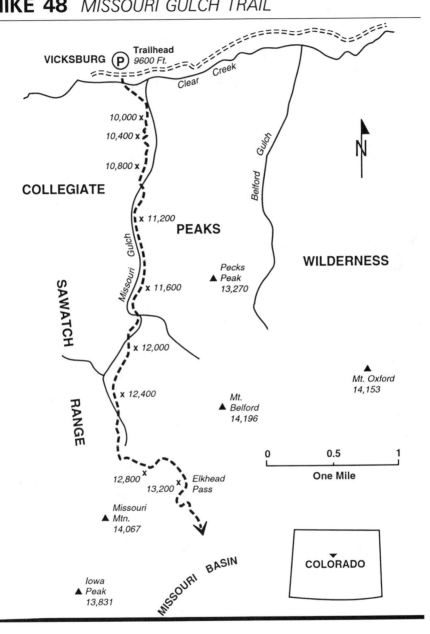

HIKE 49   *BUFFALO MEADOWS LOOP*

General description: A long day hike or overnighter to a beautiful high mountain park in the Mosquito Range.
General location: Fifteen miles southwest of Fairplay.
Maps: South Peak and Jones Hill USGS quads; Pike National Forest Map, Trails Illustrated Leadville/Fairplay South.
Degree of difficulty: Moderate.
Length: 11.5 miles round trip.
Elevations: 9,950 to 11,500 feet.
Special attractions: A beautiful loop trail in the proposed Buffalo Peaks Wilderness Area; opportunities to see elk, bear and bighorn sheep.
Best season: Summer and fall.
For more information: Pike National Forest, South Park Ranger District P.O. Box 219, Fairplay, CO 80440; (719) 836-2031.

The hike: Located at the base of Buffalo Peaks near the southern end of the Mosquito Range, Buffalo Meadows is an outstanding example of an undisturbed high mountain park, an open area of grasses and willows, surrounded by forested mountains. The open character of this area provides an unlimited supply of good camping spots, easy access to the surrounding mountains, and the opportunity to spot elk, deer and even bighorn sheep on the slopes of Buffalo Peaks.

The trail to the meadows follows a loop by way of two beautiful streams, Rich Creek and Rough and Tumbling Creek, and traverses a variety of both open and forested terrain. This wild area is part of the proposed Buffalo Peaks Wilderness and is well worth preserving for its outstanding wildlife and its uniquely gentle terrain.

To reach the trailhead to Buffalo Meadows, take US Highway 285 south of Fairplay about five miles to the Weston Pass Road (Park County Road 5). Follow this gravel road west, bearing right at a fork seven miles along and on to the Pike National Forest boundary at about ten miles. The national forest boundary is marked by a fence and cattle guard. Immediately past the cattle guard is a small parking area on the left with a sign indicating the South Fork of the South Platte River. This is the trailhead.

To begin your hike, take the footbridge across the South Fork and follow the trail upstream about 100 feet to an intersection, which marks the beginning of the loop trail to Buffalo Meadows. The entire loop is about 11.5 miles and it is an equal distance to the meadow in either direction. The trail to the left takes you up and over a ridge to Rough and Tumbling Creek, which you follow for the remainder of the way to Buffalo Meadows. Traveling the loop in this direction takes you downhill for the last portion of your hike, while a hike around the loop in the opposite direction will require a final climb of this same ridge. The trail straight ahead, as opposed to the trail to the left, follows Rich Creek to a divide overlooking Buffalo Meadows and is probably the more scenic of the two directions. If you are planning just a short day hike, this is the trail you'll probably want to take. However, for fishing, the short 1.5-mile hike over the ridge to Rough and Tumbling Creek is well worth the effort (fishing is good for small brook trout).

If you take the fork to the left, the trail climbs steeply to the top of a broad ridge with stands of aspen intermingled with spruce, limber pine, bristlecone pine and open meadows. The descent from the ridge toward Rough and Tumbling Creek offers some good views of West Buffalo Peak and the surrounding country. Continue southwesterly along the near side of the valley a little more than one mile just past the intersection with Lynch Creek where you will cross Rough and Tumbling Creek.

After crossing the creek, you enter an area where hunters have camped. The trail to Buffalo Meadows takes off to the right of this spot and goes uphill following a small tributary stream for a short distance before veering back to Rough and Tumbling Creek. If you are traveling in the opposite direction, look for the trail to the left crossing through the willows at this same well-used camping spot; if you end up crossing Lynch Creek, you've passed it.

After it enters thicker timber, the trail crosses Rough and Tumbling Creek once again. The many waterfalls visible along this section of the trail no doubt are responsible for the name of this beautiful stream. After about one mile of steeper climbing, you will reach the east end of Buffalo Meadows. It is another 1.5 miles to the junction with the trail from Rich Creek.

At Buffalo Meadows, there are many possibilities for camping and exploring. It is best to camp well away from the trail and at the edge of the forest in one of the many small side drainages, both for seclusion and for observing wildlife. Water is readily available, but should be treated, as cattle graze here.

The forest surrounding the meadows is fairly open, providing easy cross country hiking. A good destination would be the top of West Buffalo Peak, which can be climbed along a ridge from the south side of Buffalo Meadows.

The Buffalo Peaks are volcanic mountains, marking the south end of the Mosquito Range. The view from their summits includes South Park, Pikes Peak, the Sangre de Cristo Range, the Sawatch Range, and the Collegiate Peaks. If you should spot some of the small herd of bighorn sheep on your climb,

Buffalo Meadows.

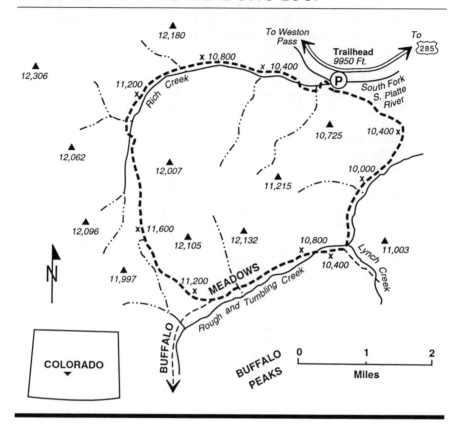

please respect the privacy of these intrusion-sensitive animals and watch them from a distance.

To return to your car by way of Rich Creek, look for the trail leaving through a saddle at the north end of the meadows. It passes through some bogs as it crosses to the east of the saddle. On the Rich Creek side of the saddle, descend one mile to a crossing of Rich Creek. After the valley bends around towards the east, the trail begins to steepen, offering a view across South Park before it drops into the forest of the lower valley. It is along this lower portion of the trail that you may notice occasional anthills that have been dug up: an indication that black bears pass this way, too.—*Peter Boddie*

West Buffalo Peak in the proposed Buffalo Peaks Wilderness.

HIKE 50 *TRAIL GULCH*

General description: A day hike or overnighter taking you into the Bureau of Land Management (BLM) Beaver Creek Wilderness Study Area.

General location: Approximately twenty miles southwest of Colorado Springs.

Maps: Phantom Canyon USGS quad.

Degree of difficulty: Moderate.

Length: Ten to eleven miles round trip.

Elevations: 6,100 to 8,700 feet.

Special attractions: A wild area with beautiful views, virtually unchanged by the influences of man; interesting geology and varied vegetation; good fishing. Best season: Late spring to early fall.

For more information: Bureau of Land Management, Royal Gorge Resource Area, 3170 E. Main Street, P.O. Box 311 Canon City, CO 81212; (719) 275-7578.

The hike: Trail Gulch takes you along Beaver Creek on the south end of the Front Range and into the BLM's Beaver Creek Wilderness Study Area.

To reach the trailhead, take Interstate 25 to State Highway 115 in Colorado Springs. Drive south on 115, 33.6 miles through Penrose to State Highway 50 and turn right (west). After 4.2 miles turn right on Fremont County Road 67 (Phantom Canyon Road). After 1.7 miles, turn right on County Road 123, then turn left on Beaver Creek Road in .3 mile. Follow this road 10.8 miles to its end and the trailhead. Park next to the fence.

Begin your hike by going through the gate and following the old road several

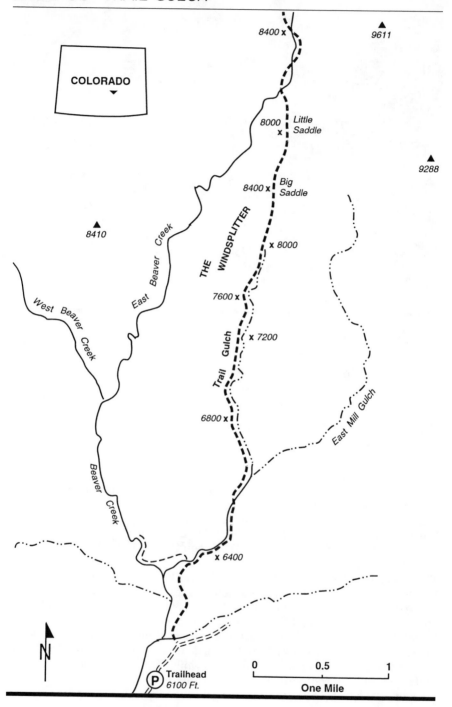

COLORADO

8400 x

▲ 9611

8000 x   Little Saddle

▲ 9288

8400 x   Big Saddle

▲ 8410

THE WINDSPLITTER

x 8000

East Beaver Creek

West Beaver Creek

7600 x

x 7200

Trail Gulch

East Mill Gulch

6800 x

Beaver Creek

x 6400

N

x 6400

Ⓟ Trailhead
6100 Ft.

0   0.5   1
One Mile

hundred yards. Then turn left near an east-west running pipeline. The trail then crosses a small, nearly dry gulch, around a steep cliff and along a fence. In another several hundred yards you will come to a fork in the trail. The left fork will lead you along the bed of Beaver Creek and eventually dead-end at a bend in the canyon. Take the right fork of the trail along a ridge paralleling Beaver Creek.

The Beaver Creek Wilderness Study Area consists of some 26,000 acres, in an area cut by very steep drainages. Beaver Creek itself is a stream of excellent water quality and sustains a good cold water fishery. Wildlife in the area includes species that thrive in this extremely rough and unroaded terrain: mule deer, bighorn sheep, mountain lion, and black bear. A pair of endangered peregrine falcons have also been sighted here, so keep your eyes peeled.

The area also contains a diversity of vegetation and interesting geology. Pinon pine, juniper, ponderosa pine, Douglas fir, white fir and spruce are some of the evergreen species present. You will also come upon stands of aspen. The major rocks in the area are granites and migmatitic gneisses and schists. The trail follows the ridge for a short way, then passes through an old ranch gate and eventually drops into Trail Gulch, where the trail again splits with the left fork heading back in the Beaver Creek Canyon while the right fork follows Trail Gulch. The valley is forested with evergreens and lush grass grows near the creek, with cactus away from the water.

About 1.5 miles along the trail you will enter a broad meadow, carpeted with clover. At its northern end, the stream surfaces from beneath an embankment offering water of good quality.

Continue the gradual ascent along the gulch for a total of 3.25 miles until the trail becomes much steeper. There are several sharp bends and then it straightens again for a very steep .5 mile to the Big Saddle. From this pretty spot you have excellent views of the cliffs of the Windsplitter to the west and of the Canon City-Florence basin to the southwest. The headwaters of Trail Gulch are near this saddle. There is no water available from this point to your destination at East Beaver Creek.

From the Big Saddle, head down the switchbacks (there is a total elevation loss of about 500 feet), through the lush vegetation at the bottom of the hill (notice the wild iris!) and begin a short ascent of 200 feet to the Little Saddle. Another short drop will take you into a small meadow bordered on the west by East Beaver Creek. This is a good place to camp. Stay at least 200 feet away from the creek and be careful in choosing your tent site. Grasses are lush and relatively undisturbed and there are several open areas of soil.

East Beaver Creek supplies water for cooking and other needs, but the water is of poor quality and tastes bad even after purification. The soils surrounding the creek are also porous and the cleaning of any dishes and dumping of liquids should be done at a considerable distance from the creek. If you want, you can follow the trail on from the meadow along East Beaver Creek and into a more developed trail designated as a seasonal use road. The road eventually follows Gould Creek and joins Gold Camp Road between Rosemont and Clyde. You would have to arrange for a car shuttle in this case. Otherwise, return as you came.—*Mary Lucas*

HIKE 51 NORTH MONUMENT CREEK LOOP

General description: A long day hike or overnighter in the foothills country of the Rampart Range.

General location: Twenty miles north of Colorado Springs.

Maps: Palmer Lake and Mount Deception USGS quads; Pike National Forest Map.

Degree of difficulty: Moderate.

Length: Fifteen miles round trip with several possibilities for short trips.

Elevations: 7,520 to 9,400 feet.

Special attractions: Easily accessible; steep canyons and interesting rock formations; good views of Pikes Peak.

Best season: Spring, summer and fall.

For more information: Pike National Forest, Pikes Peak Ranger District, 601 S. Weber Street, Colorado Springs, CO 80903; (719) 636-1602.

The hike: The North Monument Creek Trail Loop winds through the rocky and forested area of the Rampart Range. The loop trail circles the North Monument Creek Canyon, rocky and steep with numerous interesting formations that resemble shapes from eagles to Ayatollahs. In addition, the trail occasionally provides spectacular views of Pike's Peak. Portions of the trail that climb from the trailhead to above the canyon are steep, but the rest is moderate to easy hiking. It should be noted that, because of its proximity to the Front Range Metropolitan area, parts of this trail receive heavy use from four-wheelers and trailbikers.

To reach the trailhead take Interstate 25 to the Larkspur exit; the first exit south of Castle Rock. From here travel south on State Highway 18 to the town of Palmer Lake. In Palmer Lake, take the main westward road to the old waterworks. At this location there is a parking area where you can leave your vehicle and begin your hike.

A jeep road climbs westward from the trailhead into the North Monument Creek Canyon and through mountain brush and ponderosa pines for about .25 mile to the Lower Reservoir and then an additional .75 mile to the Upper Reservoir. The two reservoirs are water sources for the Town of Palmer Lake. At the Upper Reservoir the trail enters a relatively flat area, which is good spot for camping.

Several trails merge at the Upper Reservoir and care should be taken to assure proper trail selection. Travel southward along the western shore and ignore any trails leading to the north or west until you are completely south of the reservoir. Travel southward about .75 mile to another trail fork, and follow the trail to the west. You are now on Balanced Rock Trail. This trail climbs steeply to the west up a ridge above North Monument Creek Canyon for about 2.5 miles. It takes you through ponderosa pine and aspen and occasionally provides beautiful views down into the rocky canyon.

After about 2.5 miles Balanced Rock Trail reaches the ridgetop of the canyon and becomes less steep. At this point it continues westward and provides excellent views into both North Monument Creek Canyon to the north and Monument Creek Canyon to the south. Also, at strategic locations, Pike's Peak is conspicuous on the southern horizon. This portion of the trail wanders

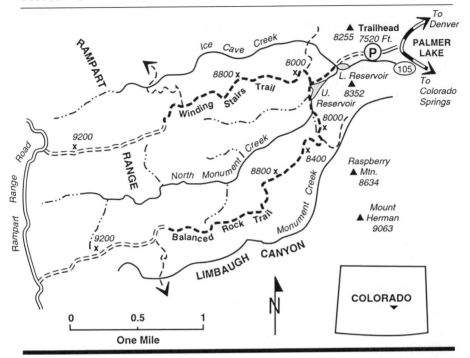

through aspen, spruce and fir. After about two miles, the trail turns into a four-wheel-drive road on which you may meet other recreational users. This road continues westward through terrain and vegetation similar to those on Rampart Range Road.

Several options are available at Rampart Range Road. The hike can be terminated at this point if arrangements have been made for transportation. As a second option, hikers can go northward along Rampart Range Road for two miles to Winding Stairs Road. This four-wheel-drive road goes eastward and narrows to a trail after about two miles. It then parallels the northern rim of North Monument Creek Canyon and goes back to the Upper Reservoir. Otherwise, hikers can return by Balanced Rock Trail to the trailhead. One note of caution: hikers should be careful in traveling the canyon bottom and should not count on camping in the bottom or hiking it for any distance. There are extensive rock formations in the canyon that make a trip down worthwhile. However, access to the bottom is limited and paths should be selected with care. The canyon bottom is filled with large boulders that make footing difficult, and there are numerous beaver ponds.—*Bill and Kay Humphries*

HIKE 52 *LOST CREEK*

General description: A day hike or overnight hike into the rugged Lost Creek Wilderness.

General location: Approximately forty miles southwest of Denver.

Maps: McCurdy Mountain USGS quad., Trails Illustrated Tarryall Mountains map, Pike National Forest map.

Degree of difficulty: Moderate.

Length: Approximately nine miles roundtrip.

Elevations: 8,000 to 9,000 feet.

Special attractions: Spectacular rock formations, extensive boulder caves, historic site.

Best season: Late spring, summer, fall.

For more information: Pike National Forest, South Platte Ranger District, 393 S. Harlan, Suite 107, Lakewood, CO 80226, (303) 234-5707.

The hike: The Lost Creek Wilderness offers some of the wildest and most rugged scenery in Colorado; it is a geologic masterpiece filled with domes, pinnacles, towers, and precariously balanced boulders. It is a very popular area and is heavily traveled during the warm months. It is also a fragile place which has suffered from overuse and abuse for a number of years. Please take special care if you visit this area for it is truly a wonderfully mysterious and beautiful place.

To reach the main trailhead take US Highway 285 southwest from Denver to Pine Junction. Turn south at Pine Junction and proceed through Pine and Buffalo Creek. Several miles past Buffalo Creek at the bottom of a long downhill stretch is the Wigwam Campground. Just past the campground turn south onto a dirt road with signs for Cheesman Reservoir, Lost Valley Ranch, Goose Creek, etc. Follow this road to and past Goose Creek Campground to the Lost Creek trailhead (all turns have been well marked by the US Forest Service). You will find a parking lot at the trailhead and, if it's not a summer weekend, you'll probably find a parking spot with no problem.

The trail takes off to the west down a short hill to a fork where you'll bear right. The trail then quickly joins Goose Creek for the next mile or so heading mostly to the west. The trail then breaks away from the creek turning to the north and quickly steepens as it heads up the valley.

Here, a short ways along the trail, you will already be in awe as giant rock formations begin to dominate much of the landscape. Mixed in with aspen groves and tall pines the rocks rise up everywhere in splendid disarray. When the trail leaves the river, you should be able to see a large pinnacle called Finger Rock, and, close by, you may spy an arch and a giant dome. The incredible scenery just gets better.

As the trail continues north it dips and darts around ridgelines slowly gaining altitude. From time to time you'll be treated to excellent views of the valley, each one better than the last.

The trail reaches a high point then drops down to a small valley where three old cabins stand vigil. These cabins date back to the turn of the century and still bear dated names from as early as 1899 on the inside walls. Actually, four cabins once stood here, then in the mid-1970's someone burned one of

Lost Creek: a geologic masterpiece. Michael Green photo.

the cabins to the ground. Later, another cabin collapsed and now two remain in decent shape with the third resembling a pile of giant toothpicks. These cabins are a fine example of what old time lumbermen could do with their broad axes—too bad people have abused them over the years. The cabins were built as part of a Denver Water Department project to build a dam in the area for Denver water supply. The crew lived in the cabins and worked at the shafthouse area, which can be found by following the trail directly behind the standing cabins.

The trail leading to the shafthouse is your first true dose of the incredibly rugged terrain of Lost Creek. Massive rocks of all shapes and sizes rise up everywhere creating images of creatures and objects for your imagination to find. Erosion has left its mark everywhere with subtle creases and folds in the rock and colorful streaks highlighting the red rock. It is a maze of narrow passageways, box canyons, and catacombs. A mysterious, secret place where trees seem to grow out of solid rock as they cling to tiny cracks, their roots straining to find soil. Here a river disappears nine different times as it snakes its way through the bizarre scenery.

You'll know you've reached the shafthouse when you come across a strange old steam engine that somehow seems to fit, the rust-colored metal almost mirroring the rock itself. It was here that a shaft was sunk to the river far below where the crew attempted to block the water's subterranean passage. This would have created a reservoir in the valley to the west appropriately called Reservoir Gulch, an especially interesting place.

Following the dam project, Lost Creek was a wildlife preserve for a number of years and poaching was quite a problem. The last wild buffalo in the west were tracked and killed by poachers in Lost Park around 1900.

Lost Creek has other interesting stories including the mysterious grave of

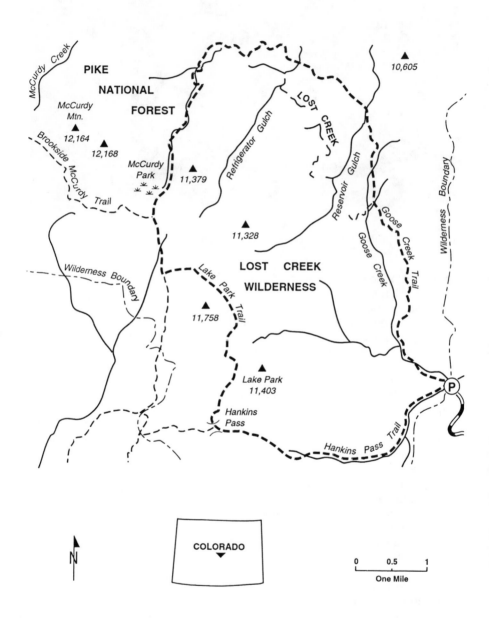

a die-hard prospector next to the old cabins. He may have been searching for the Lost Jackman Mine that, legend has it, is somewhere in the Lost Creek area and is supposed to have a load of wire gold in gleaming white quartz.

There is an old steam-powered vehicle that may have been left by the dam crew. This steamer was operational for a number of years and could be used by just about anyone to make the trip to and from the cabins. A little firewood and some water from the creek and she was ready to go. Much of the original road is now the present-day trail.

The Lost Creek Wilderness has a large population of bighorn sheep: They love the rocky terrain. It is also home to deer, elk, raccoon, owl, bobcat, and more. The most elusive is probably the bobcat, who hunts by night and has countless places to hide by day.

Lost Creek also has the most extensive boulder caves in the world with passages going everywhere. In places where the creek flows in or out of these caves, large ice formations can be seen depending on the time of year.

The Lost Creek Wilderness also has a number of other accesses which are all rich in the same kind of scenery as the Goose Creek trailhead. You'll find these accesses less crowded and quite rewarding. The Wigwam trailhead is off the same road as the Goose Creek Campground and follows Wigwam Creek. Spruce Grove Campground, Twin Eagles trailhead and Ute Creek trailhead are all on Colorado Highway 77 along Tarryall Creek and have trails leading into the wilderness area. Also, the Lost Park Campground is the start of a nice trail leading into East Lost Park. It is reached from US Highway 285 in South Park via a turnoff near Jefferson. Any of these trailheads will make for a nice outing.

Also of worth is a twenty-plus mile loop that tours a large part of the area. It is mapped out entirely on the USGS McCurdy Mountain quad.

Lost Creek is such a special place. Please enjoy it carefully so that it will remain a wilderness. See "Touching the Land Lightly" under the chapter, "Hiking Equipment and Techniques," for specific information on how to take care of this fragile place.—*Michael Green*

HIKE 53 *COLORADO TRAIL AT KENOSHA PASS*

General description: A day hike or the starting point for an extended backpack through the mountains along the north end of South Park.

General location: About sixty-five miles southwest of Denver off US Highway 285.

Maps: Jefferson and Mount Logan USGS quads; Pike National Forest Map.

Degree of difficulty: Easy.

Length: Two or more miles one way.

Elevations: 10,000 to 11,000 feet.

Special attractions: Easily accessible; offers many options for long and short hikes; beautiful aspen groves and views of South Park.

Best season: Spring, summer and early fall.

For more information: Pike National Forest, South Park Ranger District, P.O. Box 219, Fairplay, CO 80440; (719) 836-2031.

The hike: The Colorado Trail is a beautiful, long-distance route which extends

Starting down the trail.

from Denver to Durango. One particularly pretty section of the trail skirts the northern edge of South Park in the Pike National Forest.

The easiest access point is at the summit of Kenosha Pass on U.S. Highway 285 about an hour's drive southwest of Denver. From this point the trail heads southeast along the Kenosha Mountains and into the Lost Creek Wilderness Area or to the west past the Jefferson Creek campgrounds and to the summit of Georgia Pass at the Continental Divide. Many options exist for day hikes and extended backpacks in either direction.

An enjoyable day hike goes southeast from the summit of the pass. To reach the trailhead, turn onto the road across from the sign for the Kenosha Pass summit and Kenosha Campground. Follow this road across a meadow to the edge of the aspen grove where you will see the sign for the Colorado Trail. Park here.

Follow the old jeep trail south through the meadow and then east into the aspens. A short distance along, you will come to a fork where a trail marker tells you to go to the right. As you continue on through alternating clearings and aspen groves, you will have some good views of South Park. The occasional pine trees you encounter along the way are bristlecone pines, which in some areas of South Park are thought to be more than 2,000 years old.

These trees are easily identified by their dense clusters of pine needles with globules of sap or pitch, their "bristly" cones (pick one up and feel), and their often gnarled and contorted shapes.

About .5 mile along, after several small openings, you will hike a long, level stretch through an aspen grove, especially beautiful in early fall. Beyond the trunks, as you look back, there are mountains.

Again the trail enters into open areas and smaller stands of aspen. Many of the aspens grew in after ancient forest fires burned through the spruce forests

HIKE 53 *COLORADO TRAIL AT KENOSHA PASS*

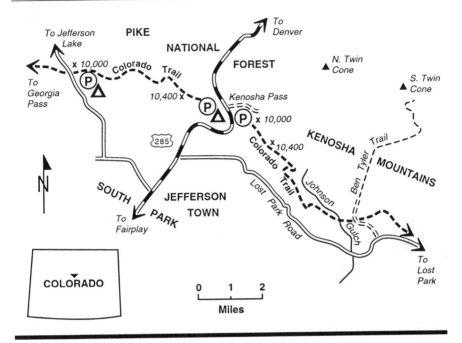

of the area. In places, the aspen stands are old and many spruce are growing in: a natural succession from aspen back to spruce once again.

The trail climbs to a saddle where you will encounter a jeep road. Follow the markers indicating the trail leading to the right and up to a ridgetop. You will hike atop this ridge for another mile and then descend to Johnson Gulch. From the ridge you have many splendid views of South Park, the Continental Divide, and the Tarryall and Kenosha mountains.

The ridgetop is a good destination for a short, easy hike of about two miles one way. Or you can continue on towards Lost Park and the Lost Creek Wilderness. In another eight miles you will reach the Lost Park Road.

An alternate route can be taken from the Kenosha Pass Campground west about seven miles to Jefferson Creek Road to which you could shuttle a car. This hike follows similar aspen, meadow and ridgetop terrain with many beautiful views.

Because the Colorado Trail is still indistinct in a few areas, you might want to check with the Forest Service for up-to-date trail routes and conditions for travel beyond the routes described here. Also, if you like this trail, you may want to get involved in supporting its maintenance.—*Peter, Caryn, Robin, and Crystal Boddie*

HIKE 54 *MOUNT SILVERHEELS*

General description: A day hike to the top of Mount Silverheels overlooking South Park.

General location: Five miles north of Fairplay.

Maps: Alma and Como USGS quads; Pike National Forest Map, Trails Illustrated Breckenridge South.

Degree of difficulty: Moderate.

Length: Five miles one way.

Elevations: 10,250 to 13,822 feet.

Special attractions: Spectacular views of South Park and many high peaks.

Best season: Summer.

For more information: Pike National Forest, South Park Ranger District, P.O. Box 219, Fairplay, CO 80440; (719) 836-2031.

The hike: A few miles northwest of Fairplay, just up Buckskin Gulch from the town of Alma, are the remains of the old mining camp called Buckskin Joe. It was here during the boom of the 1860s that Mount Silverheels, the destination of this hike, got its name.

Local legend has it that one day a beautiful dance hall girl came to town and quickly earned the nickname of "Silverheels" for the silver slippers she always wore. One winter, an epidemic of smallpox spread through the camp, killing many of the miners and leaving many others terribly scarred. Throughout the epidemic, Silverheels became nurse to the diseased miners,

Mount Silverheels.

166

traveling from cabin to cabin through the long winter. Then one day she herself contracted the disease, but after many weeks was nursed back to health and survived. When spring came, the disease had run its course and the town began to recover its once thriving nature. In appreciation of her tireless efforts, the local miners decided to take up a collection for Silverheels. They raised over five thousand dollars, but when they went to her cabin to present their gift, the dance hall girl was gone, having fled town because of her scarred face. To commemorate her beauty and her untiring charity, the miners named the beautiful peak overlooking South Park in her honor.

So, as you begin your climb of Mount Silverheels, recall the story of the beautiful dancehall girl. Picture, as well, the many mining camps which once surrounded the base of this mountain and trace the footsteps of the many miners, trappers and Indians who may have preceeded you. To reach the mountain, take US Highway 285 to the town of Como, about ten miles north of Fairplay. From the highway follow the county road northwest through town and to the turnoff to Boreas Pass Road. After about .5 mile bear left at the next fork. In about another .5 mile look for a log cabin on the left side of the road. This cabin will have the number 1187 on it. Pull off and park along the county road near the cabin. Please do not park on the private road or on private property.

Begin your hike at the small dirt road marked "Private," next to the cabin. This road leads to a house on private property across Tarryall Creek. Please respect it and don't block the road. Follow it down towards the creek and take the right fork which fords the creek. There is a small footbridge here and once you cross the creek you will be on national forest land.

Follow the jeep road across a second creek (Silverheels Creek) and up along the meadow into the trees to the right. After about .25 mile you will come to a small clearing where the jeep road forks. Take the trail down to the right into the trees and in a short distance you will again cross Silverheels Creek, then begin to climb steeply.

After the steep part of the climb, you will pass some old cabins, evidence of the mining heritage of this country. In another .25 mile the trail levels out and parallels a large opening full of willows. Follow the old road and near the upper end of this opening, look for it as it crosses through the willows. In this area the trail may become obscure. On the other side of the willows it bends to the right and climbs steeply through a thick forest of lodgepole pine and spruce. As you gain elevation, you are afforded occasional glimpses of Little Baldy Mountain and out into South Park.

When the trail bends to the west, look for limber pine along the drier south facing slopes. You will also hear the tumbling waters of South Tarryall Creek below you.

Eventually you come to a large open bowl with many wildflowers. This is an opening left by an old forest fire. Shortly after crossing South Tarryall Creek, you will reach a small saddle separating Little Baldy Mountain and Mount Silverheels. From here the trail continues on to Trout Creek, a stream which does not live up to its name. For those not wishing to make the summit climb up Silverheels, the saddle or the meadows on the banks of Trout Creek are good destinations (about 2.5 miles one way to the saddle). Keep an eye open for deer and elk in this area.

To climb Mount Silverheels follow the ridge from the saddle northwest and then west about 2.5 miles to the summit. The ridge is moderately steep and

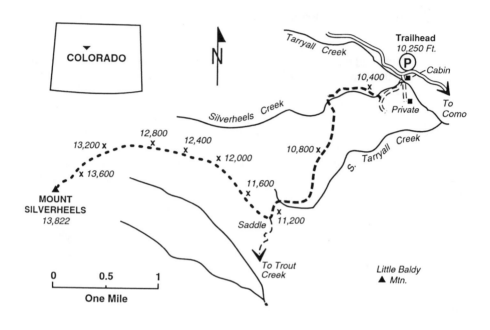

COLORADO

N

Tarryall Creek

Trailhead
10,250 Ft.

P

Cabin

10,400
x

To
Como

Private

Silverheels Creek

13,200 x

12,800
x

12,400
x

x 12,000

10,800 x

Tarryall Creek
S.

x 13,600

MOUNT
SILVERHEELS
13,822

11,600
x

11,200
x

Saddle

To Trout
Creek

Little Baldy
▲ Mtn.

0   0.5   1

One Mile

provides a good steady climbing grade. About .25 mile from the top you will encounter a false summit. Continue on southwest to the true summit. Sign the register and enjoy the view. From this vantage point you can see all of South Park, the Mosquito Range, (Mt. Bross, Mt. Lincoln, and Mt. Democrat are directly to the west), the Tenmile Range and the Continental Divide as it skirts Summit County, as well as countless other peaks and ranges. —*Peter Boddie*

HIKE 55 *HOMESTAKE MINE TRAIL*

General description: A day hike into a beautiful and historic area, ending at a high mountain lake and the Homestake Mine.
General location: Ten miles north of Leadville.
Maps: Homestake Reservoir and Leadville North USGS quads; San Isabel National Forest Map, Trails Illustrated Holy Cross and Breckenridge South.
Degree of difficulty: Moderate.
Length: Three to four miles one way.

Elevations: 10,400 to 11,700 feet.
Special attractions: Beautiful scenery; high mountain lakes; interesting history; Holy Cross Wilderness.
Best season: Summer.
For more information: San Isabel National Forest, Leadville Ranger District, 2015 N. Poplar, Leadville, CO 80461; (719) 486-0752.

The hike: Taking you up into the beautiful Holy Cross Wilderness with its gorgeous scenery and high mountain lakes, the Homestake Mine Trail also gives you a look at some of the mining works the Leadville area is famous for. To reach the trailhead, take US Highway 24 north from Leadville for about ten miles, turning left on Forest Route 100, the road to Lily Lake. Drive two miles on this road and park at the turn-about approximately .25 mile before the lake. (The road is rough for passenger cars to the turn-about and can be traveled only by four-wheel-drive vehicles beyond this point).

Be sure you're wearing good waterproof boots before you set out. There are some marshy areas at the end of the trail near the Homestake Mine that you'll have to negotiate. Begin your hike at Lily Lake by starting up the main jeep road. (There is a lesser-used one to your right.) The road will take you the entire three miles to a small, unnamed lake at the base of the Homestake Mine Area.

HIKE 55 *HOMESTAKE MINE TRAIL*

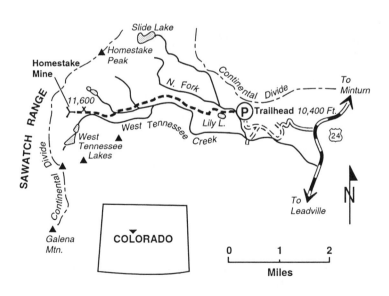

After hiking .5 to .75 mile, you will begin to skirt the edge of some high mountain meadows with streams running through them. Then, about two miles into your hike, you'll come into the Holy Cross Wilderness. Shortly beyond the wilderness sign you will see a boulder field on the right and, farther along in the trees, you will begin to see the occasional remains of the lodgings of miners who once lived here.

This area was once a thriving mining community, but it is also notorious as a slide area where loose rock from the surrounding mountain ridges buried many cabins and mines. Several people, even rescue parties, lost their lives in these rock and snow slides.

At the end of the jeep road you will come to the unnamed, high mountain lake. Above you is the Continental Divide, beautiful glacial cirques, and many snowfields.

An almost forgotten trail to the Homestake Mines (located in a large cirque) takes off to the right from here. The hiking trail to the left of the lake leads up into the cirque containing West Tennessee Lakes. Along the way, it passes many small waterfalls and affords the best view of the Homestake mining area.

Beautiful scenery, historical interest, and the fact that this trail is one of the lesser know ones combines to make this hike a truly enjoyable experience.
—*Ruth and Sandy Mooneyham*

HIKE 56 *COLORADO MIDLAND RAILROAD TRAIL*

General description: A unique day hike along the Colorado Midland Railroad Route, which passes through Hagerman Tunnel (now closed) underneath the Continental Divide.
General location: About thirteen miles west of Leadville.
Maps: Homestake Reservoir and Mt. Massive USGS quads; San Isabel National Forest Map, Trails Illustrated Holy Cross and Independence Pass.
Degree of difficulty: Easy.
Length: Five miles round trip.
Elevations: 10,950 to 11,550 feet.
Special attractions: You will be hiking along the old railroad grade of the Midland Railroad; beautiful scenery.
Best season: Summer.
For more information: San Isabel National Forest, Leadville Ranger District, 2015 N. Poplar, Leadville, CO 80461; (719) 486-0752.

The hike: The Midland Railroad Trail offers a unique hike, taking you up through the San Isabel National Forest along the old railroad bed to the Continental Divide and the old Hagerman Tunnel. To reach the trailhead, take the Turquoise Lake Road from Leadville west to Turquoise Lake. Then follow Forest Route 105 across the dam and continue on until you reach the Hagerman Pass Road turn-off four to five miles from the dam. Turn left onto this dirt road and drive another two to three miles until you come to a Forest Service sign for the old railroad route of the Midland Railroad on the left. (Watch carefully for the sign, as it is small and set back ten to twenty feet form the road.)

Park and begin your hike at the Forest Service sign, starting up the historic

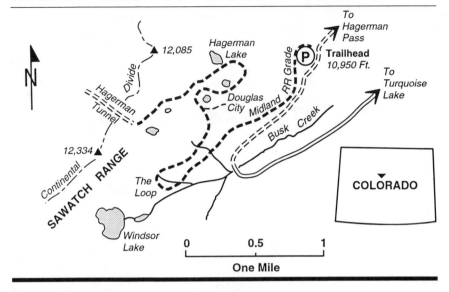

bed of the Colorado Midland Railroad, known in its day as perhaps the most scenic railroad route in America.

At the end of the first mile, you will drop into a meadow. This was the site of the famous Colorado Midland "Loop" bridge. A construction camp existed here once for the sole purpose of building a giant wooden bridge, now non-existent. Photographs of the famous bridge are abundant throughout the town of Leadville.

From the "Loop," continue on to the sign that marks a trail to Douglas City, an old railroad town now overgrown with trees. Continue on the old grade and you will come to beautiful, secluded Hagerman Lake, a great spot for camping (stay 200 feet away from the lake and off-trail) and fishing, which is fair for small cutthroat trout.

Continue on past Hagerman Lake another .75 mile and you will come to the large, cavernous opening in the rocks that is the long-abandoned Hagerman Tunnel. It once provided one of the last narrow gauge routes through the Rockies. Trains would travel through the tunnel to Lake Ivanhoe on the other side and then on to Basalt and Glenwood Springs. After having a good look, return as you came.

We're sure you'll agree this is a beautiful and interesting hike, well worth your effort.—*Ruth and Sandy Mooneyham*

Cutthroat trout. Colorado Division of Wildlife photo.

HIKE 57 *LOST MAN PASS & DEADMAN LAKE*

General description: A day hike or overnighter into the high glacial basins that feed the Roaring Fork River and one of its tributaries, Lost Man Creek, or an overnighter to Deadman Lake in the Hunter-Fryingpan Wilderness.
General location: 18.5 miles east of Aspen.
Maps: Mt. Champion, Independence Pass and New York Peak USGS quads; White River National Forest map; Trails Illustrated Independence Pass map.
Degree of difficulty: Moderate.
Length: 2.5 miles one way to Lost Man Pass; six miles one way to Deadman Lake; or 8.5 miles between trailheads.
Elevations: 10,500 to 12,800 feet, varies depending upon starting point.
Special attractions: A variety of ecotones from montane to krummholz to alpine; a number of glacial cirques and lakes; the Hunter-Fryingpan Wilderness; great scenery; two interesting and different glacially formed alpine valleys.
Best season: Summer.
For more information: White River National Forest, Aspen Ranger District, 806 W. Hallam, Aspen, CO 81611; (303) 925-3445.

The hike: The trails in the glacially formed basins that spawn the Roaring Fork River, its tributary Lost Man Creek, and the Fryingpan River make high country more than ordinarily accessible. However, because of this accessibility, the area is heavily used. Backpackers should be aware of stove-only regulations in this area and camping near the trails or any of the close-in lakes is discouraged. The trails do provide quick access to nearby country that is less heavily traveled.

The hiking alternatives in the Roaring Fork and Lost Man drainages range from the short climb of less than one mile to Linkins Lake to the full 8.5 mile traverse over Lost Man Pass between the Roaring Fork and Lost Man trailheads. You also have the option of hiking over South Fork Pass to Deadman Lake, a trip of six miles one way from the Lost Man trailhead.

To reach the Roaring Fork trailhead, take Colorado Highway 82 east from Aspen 18.5 miles to the point where it crosses the Roaring Fork River and begins the final climb to the summit of Independence Pass. From the parking lot on the north side of the highway there are trails ascending on either side of the river. The trail on the west (left) side leads to Linkins Lake, and the trail on the east (right) side leads to Independence Lake, Lost Man Pass and the Lost Man Creek drainage. Those wishing to make the full 8.5-mile horseshoe trip over the pass and down the Lost Man drainage could leave an auto at the Lost Man Trailhead, 4.5 miles west on Highway 82 (fourteen miles east of Aspen).

For a good picnic hike, or a short introduction to high country traveling, Linkins Lake is a good destination from the Roaring Fork trailhead. Follow the short trail on the west (left) side of the river, which soon leads away from the river, and climbs a short, intermediate ridge into tundra. The lake, which provides fair fishing for brook trout, is .25 mile beyond.

To reach Independence Lake or Lost Man Pass, take the trail that parallels the river on the eastern (right) bank. It follows the course of the Roaring Fork through willows and over Pre-Cambrian metamorphics and granites for 1.5 miles, then bears east and is marked by cairns up the rocky slope to the lush and marshy ground surrounding Independence Lake. Fishing in Independence Lake and in the Upper Roaring Fork is fair for brook trout.

The environs of Independence Lake demonstrate the adaptability of tundra flora to the cold, high altitude, and short growing season. The area is also an excellent study in a process of succession from alpine lakes to tundra meadows: a glacial lake slowly filled by sediment, then taken over by tundra mosses and plants to become a marsh, which may in turn be drained by the erosion of the creek to form a tundra meadow. Substantial evidence of mineralization, as well as textbook examples of glacial erosion forming cirques, moraines, and glacial lakes, is also present in the area.

The impressive walls surrounding Independence Lake to the northwest are broken by the low saddle of Lost Man Pass, another 300 vertical feet above. Hikers can minimize impact through the tundra en route to the talus-covered pass by staying on the main trail. Once you encounter the talus slopes below the pass, follow the cairns to the trail's summit at 12,800 feet.

Looking back to the south, Grizzly Peak is visible in the distance, as are several bench-like moraines containing alpine lakes, including Linkins and Independence lakes. Over the pass and to the north, the trail drops in a steep descent to Lost Man Lake. Farther north, along the jagged ridge to the right, lies South Fork Pass, and beyond it the eastern slopes of the Williams Moun-

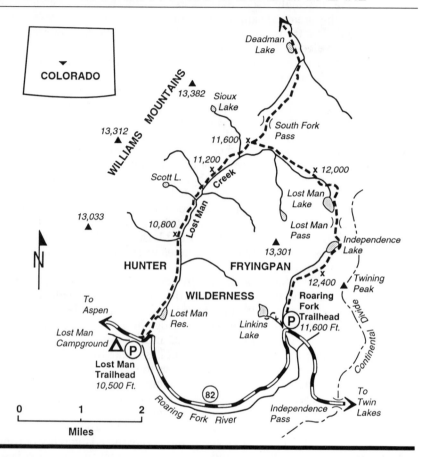

tains, which form the headwaters of the Fryingpan River.

The descent to Lost Man Lake traverses down the right hand (northerly) slope of the basin, passes the lake and becomes somewhat obscure until it reaches the meadows surrounding Lost Man Creek. The easiest traveling and the main trail lie on the west side of the creek. The trail becomes obvious once it crosses the creek at the head of the willow-covered upper valley. The remainder of the route is a leisurely grade past serpentine falls, with wide panoramas of the Continental Divide to the south, and ends just past Lost Man Reservoir at the Lost Man trailhead on Colorado Highway 82. Fishing in the reservoir is good for rainbow and brook trout. Fishing in Lost Man Creek and Lost Man Lake is fair to good for brook trout.

To make the hike to Deadman Lake, begin at the Lost Man trailhead on the north side of Highway 82. It parallels the Lost Man Reservoir outlet channel about .25 mile to the reservoir, follows the west (left hand) shore of Lost Man Reservoir through a beautiful, mature stand of spruce and fir, and then wanders through the willows and gentle meadows to the west of Lost

Man Creek, a fast, pretty stream bounding over pink and gray granites.

Within three to four miles, a comfortable walk of no more than two hours, the trail crosses one of the upper forks of Lost Man Creek. This is an ideal rest stop before the climb to the top of South Fork Pass on the switchback trail immediately to the left.

The view from the beautiful tundra of South Fork Pass is well worth the required effort. To the south lies the Continental Divide; to the north, the green slopes of the Fryingpan drainages. The trail continues northwest and descends 1.5 miles below timberline on the other side of the pass, then into a wide enchanting meadow. Across the meadow, along a faint trail marked by lonesome poles, lies Deadman Lake.

The broad expanse of the meadow and wooded hills around and below Deadman Lake are rich habitat for deer and elk, and the upper reaches of the Fryingpan offer fishing for brook trout. The area is a diverse mixture of alpine meadow, spruce-fir forest, and high country marsh. Water is readily available in the area, except on the pass, but it should be purified.

Deadman Lake itself really is dead in that it is a nonproductive fishery. This may be due to the fact that it is isolated from streams in the area, is spring fed, and is probably subject to hard freezes in winter. The lake does provide good habitat for waterfowl and a variety of mammals, and the rolling, sparsely wooded hills that surround it provide numerous attractive campsites. (Be sure to camp at least 200 feet from the lakeshore and use a backpacking stove, if possible, rather than building a fire.) What's more, the surprising mixture of meadow, woods, and steep glacially scoured ridges entices one to exploratory wandering.

One obvious topographic feature in the area below Deadman is a very large glacial moraine that forms an intricate network of ponds behind its dam of massive hardrock blocks. The river and South Fork trail continue over steep hills and through heavy timber below and beyond the moraine and upper meadows. You can return the way you came or turn east at the Lost Man Creek trail for the climb over Lost Man Pass to the Roaring Fork trailhead.
—*Chris Frye*

HIKE 58 *WEST SNOWMASS TRAIL*

General description: A day hike or backpack taking you to a saddle overlooking the Maroon Bells-Snowmass Wilderness.
General location: Approximately fifteen miles west of Aspen.
Maps: Capitol Peak and Highland Peak USGS quads; White River National Forest Map, Trails Illustrated Maroon Bells
Degree of difficulty: Difficult.
Length: About 5.5 miles one way.
Elevations: About 8,500 to 12,000 feet.
Special attractions: Magnificent views of the high peaks, including several 14,000 foot summits; dense aspen groves; pretty meadows with many wildflowers; abundant wildlife.
Best season: Summer.
For more information: White River National Forest, Aspen Ranger District, 806 W. Hallam, Aspen CO 81611; (303) 925-3445.

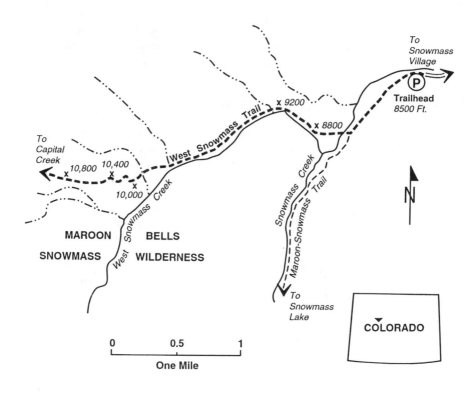

The hike: If there were a typical "Aspen-Snowmass country" trail, this would be it. It would be hard to find another one that outdoes it in sheer beauty or range of vistas and attractions, including the fact that this is a lightly-used stretch of trail in a heavily-used area. To reach the trailhead, take Colorado Highway 82 about fourteen miles northwest of Aspen. Turn south at the Forest Access sign at Old Snowmass. After about two miles, turn left at the sign for Snowmass Campground. Follow this road about ten miles to the campground. Bear right past the campground and follow the road to a parking area about .5 mile beyond. This is the trailhead for the Maroon-Snowmass Trail. From the trailhead, hike about one mile along the main trail (which leads to Snowmass Lake) until a sign directs you to the West Snowmass Trail.

The trail is as challenging as it is scenic. Almost immediately it leads across Snowmass Creek (cold and swift) and climbs sharply, switching back many times for about 1.5 miles through stands of spruce, fir and huge aspen. About halfway to the saddle, hikers will meet several non-system trails. The US Forest Service expects to improve signing in the future. For now take a topo map and follow it carefully.

Hiking the West Snowmass Trail. Elizabeth Frye photo.

Across the first ridge, the country opens into several meadows from which the higher ridges and peaks can be seen. It climbs again steeply then for another three miles to the top of the ridge between the Snowmass and Capitol Peak valleys.

As the trail climbs ever higher, it passes beneath Mt. Daly and Haystack Mountain and leads upward to timberline, eventually reaching nearly 12,000 feet in elevation at the saddle between the two mountains. From here you have clear views of such beautiful peaks as Capitol Peak (14,130 feet), the Maroon Bells (14,014 and 14,156 feet), Snowmass Mountain (14,092 feet) named for the great snowfield between its two summits, and Mt. Sopris (12,953 feet), as well as the surrounding country. This is the Elk Mountain Range with spectacular fourteeners formed of both igneous rock eroded into thin sharp ridges like those you see on Snowmass Mountain and Capitol Peak and the obvious layered, stratified rock of Castle, Pyramid and Maroon Peaks.

You can return as you came or continue on the trail as it drops abruptly for another 2.5 miles to Capitol Creek, again through stands of aspen and meadows luxuriant with wildflowers, grasses and ferns.

Especially in the upper reaches, you'll meet few, if any, hikers. It is excellent backpacking country, with numerous campsites, though steep grades and high elevations call for good conditioning, footwear and clothing. Fishing is rated fair to good in Snowmass Creek for six- to twelve-inch brook trout.

You may want to explore any of the number of trails that thread through this country, particularly the Maroon-Snowmass Trail following Snowmass Creek to Snowmass Lake where fishing is good for a few natives and rainbows usually around eleven inches. The scenery is fantastic here, too. The Capitol Creek Trail takes you through the northwest end of the Maroon Bells-Snowmass Wilderness to the Crystal River north of Redstone.—*Gib and Liz Frye*

HIKE 59 *LONESOME LAKE*

General description: A day hike or overnighter to a beautiful cirque lake in the Holy Cross Wilderness.

General location: About fifteen miles northwest of Leadville.

Maps: Homestake Reservoir USGS quad; White River National Forest Map, Trails Illustrated Holy Cross Map.

Degree of difficulty: Moderate.

Length: Nine miles round trip.

Elevations: 10,200 to 11,600 feet.

Special attractions: Beautiful high mountain lake with good fishing; roaring East Fork Homestake Creek; wildflowers; wildlife.

Best season: Summer.

For more information: White River National Forest, Holy Cross Ranger District, 401 Main, P.O. Box 190, Minturn, CO 81645; (303) 827-5715.

The hike: This hike takes you through a long, deep glacial valley and through beautiful meadows to Lonesome Lake, one of the many alpine lakes in the Sawatch Range.

To reach the trail to the lake, drive south from Minturn on US Highway 24 for about 10 miles or drive north from the summit of Tennessee Pass about 12 miles to the signed junction with Forest Route 703, leading to Homestake Reservoir. Turn southwest on this road and follow it for about 10 miles, past the Gold Park Campground and to a signed junction at the base of the Homestake Reservoir dam. Park at this junction and look for the trailhead sign next to the East Fork of Homestake Creek. From this point, the trail climbs steeply up into the hanging valley of the East Fork. As an alternative, you can follow the steep road to the crest of the dam. From here follow the aqueduct eastward into the valley of East Fork Homestake Creek. The aqueduct ends at a small diversion pond.

This diversion, a part of the Homestake Project, is one of many which capture water from tributaries to Homestake Creek and diverts it to Homestake Reservoir. From here the water flows beneath the Continental Divide through a tunnel to Turquoise Lake near Leadville. Recently, the Homestake Project has been the center of much controversy concerning a planned extension of the diversion project to Cross Creek within the Holy Cross Wilderness Area. The water ultimately is used by the cities of Colorado Springs and Aurora.

The trail continues along the west (right) side of the pond. Follow the cairns as it crosses an open area and then follows along the creek for about .5 mile through stands of evergreens. Then you will reach the first of two large meadows, this one being more than a mile in length. This beautiful spot where wildflowers bloom profusely in the summer might make a good destination if you are most interested in fishing.

Follow the trail around the west side of this mile-long meadow and then reenter the woods. You will have to climb at a little steeper grade. Soon you will pass a small stream (a good spot to rest) and then come to the second of the meadows. Follow the creek to the other end of the meadow where you will find evidence of the avalanches that may have roared down from the obvious avalanche chute during the previous winter. The trail then reenters

HIKE 59 *LONESOME LAKE*

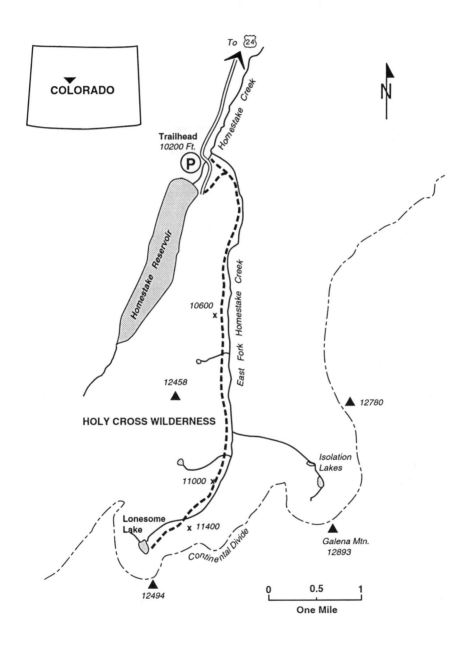

COLORADO

To 24

Homestake Creek

Trailhead
10200 Ft.

P

Homestake Reservoir

10600 x

East Fork Homestake Creek

12458
▲

HOLY CROSS WILDERNESS

12780 ▲

Isolation
Lakes

11000 x

Lonesome
Lake   x 11400

Continental Divide

Galena Mtn.
12893 ▲

12494 ▲

0   0.5   1

One Mile

the woods and begins a steady climb toward the lake. When you reach an open basin, keep to the left side for the last .5-mile climb to the grass-covered bench and Lonesome Lake. The trail is faint in several places. Watch for wildflowers and small mammals along your way, including marsh marigolds and marmots.

Lonesome Lake is one of many beautiful lakes to be found in this faulted anticline known as the Sawatch Range. Fishing is said to be good for cutthroat trout in the twelve- to fourteen-inch range. Please be sure to camp at least 200 feet away from the lake and trails to preserve the beauty of the area and be sure to watch for deer and elk on your return hike.—*Jim Haynes, Don Wagner, Tyler Garbonza*

HIKE 60 *WHEELER & GORE RANGE TRAILS*

General description: A long day hike or moderate overnighter, or a long backpack into the Gore Range.
General location: West of Dillon.
Maps: Mt. Powell, Squaw Creek, Dillon, Willow Lakes, Frisco and Vail Pass USGS quads; Arapaho National Forest Map, Trails Illustrated Vail Pass and Green Mountain Reservoir.
Degree of difficulty: Moderate to difficult.
Length: Six-mile round trip to Wheeler Lakes; 54.5 miles for the length of the Gore Range Trail.
Elevations: 8,800 to 11,600 feet.
Special attractions: Long trail with a lot of variety; beautiful views and wildflowers; big game; good fishing.
Best season: Non-peak times: midweek in early summer and fall.
For more information: Arapaho National Forest, Dillon Ranger District, P.O. Box 6207, Silverthorne, CO 80498; (303) 468-5400.

The hike: Named for Sir St. George Gore, a nobleman from Ireland who led a hunting expedition here in the 1800s with the famous Jim Bridger as his guide, this is a superb hiking and backpacking trail that runs nearly the length of the Gore Range from Mahan Lake junction in the north to Copper Mountain in the south. There are numerous possibilities for long and short backpacks and day hikes. Boulder lake and the Cataract Valley trails are the most heavily traveled, so you may want to avoid them. Be careful to practice minimum impact camping in the Eagles Nest Wilderness and on all trails. (See introductory section, "Touching the Land Lightly.")

Beginning at the southernmost end of the trail is an easily accessible portion of the trail that takes you to Wheeler Lakes (a six-mile round trip). From Wheeler Lakes you can continue on for any number of miles on the Gore Range Trail, exiting at any of the many access points.

To reach the Wheeler-Gore Range trailhead, drive to Copper Mountain at the junction of Interstate 70 and State Highway 91. Exit I-70 at exit 195. Cross over the interstate and turn east on the frontage road toward the gas station. Go past the gas station and park in the trailhead parking area on the right. Walk back over the overpass to the "No Parking" sign where the trail begins.

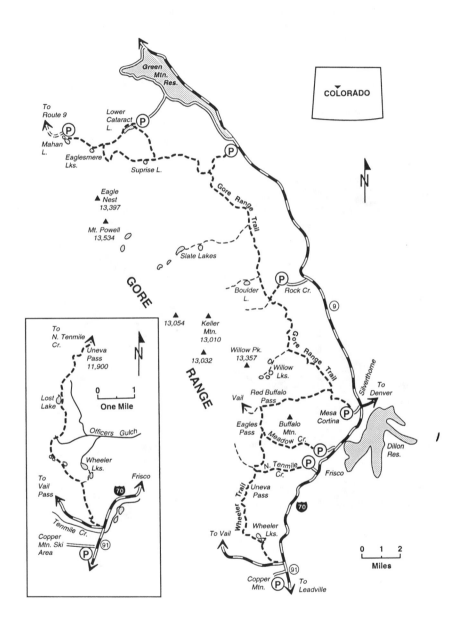

Green Mtn. Res.

COLORADO

To Route 9

Lower Cataract L.

Mahan L.

Eaglesmere Lks.

Suprise L.

Gore Range Trail

Eagle Nest 13,397

Mt. Powell 13,534

Slate Lakes

N

Boulder L.

Rock Cr.

9

13,054

Keller Mtn. 13,010

13,032

Willow Pk. 13,357

Willow Lks.

Gore Range Trail

Vail

Red Buffalo Pass

Eagles Pass

Buffalo Mtn.

Meadow Cr.

Mesa Cortina

Silverthorne

To Denver

Dillon Res.

N. Tenmile Cr.

Frisco

Wheeler Trail

Uneva Pass

70

Wheeler Lks.

To Vail

Copper Mtn.

91

To Leadville

0   1   2
Miles

GORE

RANGE

Inset map

To N. Tenmile Cr.

Uneva Pass 11,900

N

Lost Lake

0   1
One Mile

Officers Gulch

Wheeler Lks.

To Vail Pass

Frisco

70

Tenmile Cr.

Copper Mtn. Ski Area

91

At first, the trail cuts across the south-facing slope along the highway. It may seem like a strange place to begin a hike. Keep going, though, and you'll soon be climbing away from the highway and into forests of aspen, Englemann spruce and lodgepole pine. You will cross meadows where mountain asters, lupine, chiming bells, cinquefoil, and paintbrush grow abundantly.

After you've hiked a mile or so, you'll cross a small stream and, a short distance beyond, come upon the Eagles Nest Wilderness Area sign in a small stand of Englemann spruce. You are entering the wilderness at its southern edge.

The Eagles Nest Wilderness extends for over twenty miles to the north and includes some of the most rugged backcountry in Colorado. The Gore Range Trail follows the eastern edge of the Wilderness for its length. The section of the trail that will lead you to Wheeler Lakes is fairly steep.

A short way into the wilderness, you will come across a trail register. Be sure to sign it. From the register, the trail continues to gain elevation steadily. For a distance of .75 mile it leads you through spruce and pine forest and

Elk. Colorado Division of Wildlife photo.

then crosses a large meadow. At this point, the majority of the climb is behind you. Pause to look back at the Ten Mile Range and northwest across the meadow to the ridge above Shrine Pass.

The trail now continues for another .5 mile through intermittent meadow and forest and climbs steeply through a meadow to the top of a ridge. Here the view of the Ten Mile Range, including Crystal and Pacific Peaks, is even more spectacular.

At the ridgetop the trail forks. Take the right fork to Wheeler Lakes. A hike .25 mile downhill brings you to the first of the lakes. Keep going over the hill and you will come to the second and larger lake. Fishing is good here for ten- to twelve-inch cutthroat trout. However, fishermen should limit their catch, because this lake is popular and easily accessible.

There are numerous camping spots in the meadows and forest surrounding the lakes. Camp away from the water to preserve the beauty of the spot. Check with the Forest Service about campfire policies and fire danger. We recommend you use a backpack stove.

Water is available in a small stream at the northwest end of the second lake. Boil or chemically purify it before using. From the ridge at the north end of the second lake, you can look down into Officer's Gulch and Ten Mile Canyon and see Dillon Reservoir beyond. To the northwest is Uneva Pass and the Gore Range Trail winding up and over.

You may either return as you came from here or go on following the Core Range Trail for as many of its 54.5 miles as you like. Along its length, it traverses an amazing variety of terrain and provides access to numerous lakes, valleys, and trails in the rugged and spectacular Gore Range.

There are numerous access points to the trail, but you will have to arrange a car shuttle if you plan a longer hike. These access points and mileages between them as given by the US Forest Service are listed as follows (from south to north) with the appropriate USGS quads:

Copper Mountain to North Tenmile (Vail Pass quad)	10.0 miles
North Tenmile to Meadow Creek (Frisco, Vail Pass quads)	3.0 miles
Meadow Creek to Mesa Cortina (Dillon, Willow Lakes, Frisco quads)	6.25 miles
Mesa Cortina to Brush Creek (Dillon, Willow Lakes quads)	10.5 miles
Rock Creek to Brush Creek (Squaw Creek quad)	10.5 miles
Brush Creek to Surprise (Mt. Powell, Squaw Creek quads)	6.5 miles
Surprise to Eaglesmere (Mt. Powell quad)	3.0 miles
Eaglesmere to Mahan Lake Junction (Mt. Powell quad)	4.5 miles

This mileage does not include the mileages of the access trails taking you to the Gore Range Trail. One good, short hike to it in the center of the range is at Rock Creek (see description of Rock Creek).—*Peter and Caryn Boddie*

HIKE 61 *PITKIN LAKE*

General description: A day hike to Pitkin Lake in the Gore Range near Vail.
General location: Four miles east of Vail.
Maps: Vail East USGS quad; White River National Forest Map; Trails Illustrated Vail Pass.
Degree of difficulty: Moderate.
Length: About five miles one way.
Elevations: 8,400 to 11,400 feet.
Special attractions: Spectacular glacial valley with beautiful waterfalls; alpine lake; wildflowers; good fishing.
Best season: Summer.
For more information: White River National Forest, Holy Cross Ranger District, 401 Main, P.O. Box 190, Minturn, CO 81645; (303) 827-5715.

The hike: This easily accessible hike just east of Vail takes you to the beautiful setting of Pitkin Lake, a glacial bowl just below the crest of the Gore Range. Along the way the trail climbs through a steep glacial valley with stands of aspen and evergreens, alpine meadows, and picture postcard waterfalls. Because of its proximity to Vail this hike is recommended for day use, although an overnight trip would be possible.

To reach the trail to Pitkin Lake drive east on Interstate 70 from Vail Ski Area about four miles to exit 180. This exit takes you to the north side of I-70 and up a road and past several groups of condos for .3 mile to where it dead-ends. Park at the trailhead and register at the Forest Service register.

Hike along the stream for a short distance and cross the bridge at the gaging station. You will pass several condos as you begin your hike. Initially, you will climb over switchbacks that take you in a northeasterly direction. At the top of this first steep and hot pitch you head north on a good foot trail and up the Pitkin Creek Valley. (Look for a large lodgepole pine to rest under here.) As in most hanging valleys, the first part of the hike poses the more difficult pitches. After the initial exhilarating climb, the stream and trail converge to afford easier hiking and good fishing in Pitkin Creek, which has been known to yield ten- to twelve-inch brook and native trout. As the trail carves its way through the valley, aspen stands give way to evergreens and the grasses and shrubs in the meadows become shorter in resistance to the harsher conditions at higher altitudes. Please leave as little an impact on this delicate environment as you can.

About 1.5 miles up the valley the first of five small stream crossings is made. Just past the last stream crossing, some 200 feet to the east, is the first of two spectacular waterfalls on Pitkin Creek. This would make a good destination for a shorter day hike and would be beautiful in late spring or early summer. Another mile farther, just below the second falls, the trail crosses Pitkin Creek. From here it climbs steeply again up several switchbacks and then climbs less steeply for the final 1.5 miles to Pitkin Lake.—*Doug Crocker*

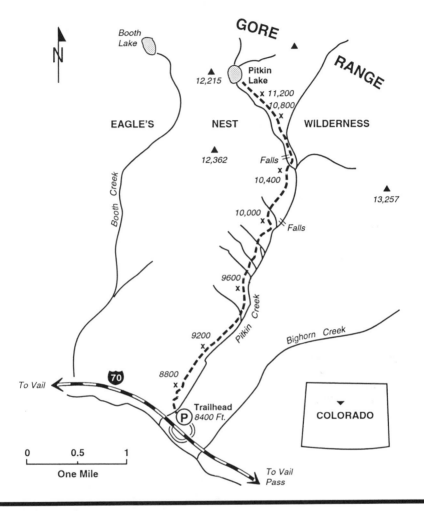

HIKE 62 ROCK CREEK

General description: A day hike to timberline in the Eagles Nest Wilderness.
General location: Eight miles northwest of Silverthorne.
Maps: Willow Lakes USGS quad; Arapaho National Forest Map; Trails Illustrated Vail Pass.
Degree of difficulty: Easy.
Length: Approximately 3.5 miles round trip.
Elevations: 9,500 to 10,200 feet.
Special attractions: Beautiful views of the Gore Range.
Best season: Summer.

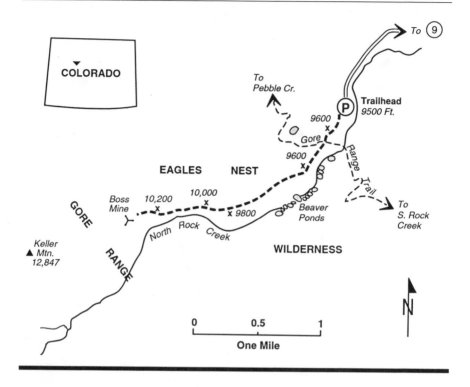

For more information: Arapaho National Forest, Dillon Ranger District, 135 Colorado Highway 9, P.O. Box 620, Silverthorne, CO 80498; (303) 468-5400.

The hike: Taking you from North Rock Creek to timberline and the old Boss Mine, the Rock Creek Trail offers an easy and enjoyable day hike into the Eagles Nest Wilderness.

To reach the trailhead, exit Interstate 70 at Silverthorne (exit 205) and drive north on Colorado Highway 9 for eight miles to Rock Creek Road just across from the Blue River Campground. Drive southwest on Rock Creek Road, turning left when you come to the fork in the road three miles along, and follow signs for Rock Creek to the trailhead parking lot at the end of the road.

Begin your hike at the Forest Service sign after taking note of the special regulations governing this wilderness area. As you follow the old jeep road away from the sign, (climbing away from North Rock Creek) you will pass a beaver pond in a small meadow. Look up to your left for a good view of one of the many unnamed peaks in the Gore Range.

Enjoy the wildflowers you see at the beginning of your hike. As you enter the forest of lodgepole pine and begin to climb toward the top of the ridge which leads eventually to the summit of Keller Mountain, you will see few of them.

The Gore Range at North Rock Creek.

Soon you will come to a crossroads. You are crossing the Gore Range Trail (see Wheeler-Gore Range Trail), which runs the length of the Gore Range. The Rock Creek Trail is often used as an access point for this trail, which, to your right, leads to Pebble Creek and to your left, continues on to South Rock Creek. (It can be followed for many miles beyond these points in either direction.) To follow the Rock Creek Trail, continue ahead up the steep old jeep road until it tapers into a trail and then past a lot of deadfall to the top of the ridge.

This is what you came for. From the edge of timberline, you have beautiful views of the North Rock Creek Valley, sculpted by glaciers. The quality of water in North Rock Creek is excellent, coming as it does from the snowfields which have remained in the cirques high atop the peaks at the head of the valley. Notice that of all the peaks you see above North Rock Creek, only one is named and that is Keller Mountain, which you can climb by continuing along this ridge.

After you spend some time taking in the rugged peaks surrounding you (and, perhaps, naming one or two just for fun) continue along the ridge to the Boss Mine, and, if you like, to the summit of Keller Mountain (13,085 feet). Then return as you came.—*Caryn Boddie*

HIKE 63 *LENAWEE TRAIL*

General description: A day hike to the ridge on Lenawee Mountain with beautiful views and historic interest.

General location: Ten miles east of Dillon.

Maps: Montezuma and Grays Peak USGS quads; Arapaho National Forest Map, Trails Illustrated Loveland Pass.

Degree of difficulty: Moderate.

Length: 3.5 miles one way.

Elevations: 10,400 to 13,204 feet.

Special attractions: Beautiful views; interesting boulder outcroppings; old mines and ruins.

Best season: Late summer.

For more information: Arapaho National Forest, Dillon Ranger District, 135 State Highway 9, P.O. Box 620, Silverthorne, CO 80498; (303) 468-5400.

The hike: The Lenawee Trail climbs from the Peru Creek Road to the summit ridge of Lenawee Mountain. This point offers a panoramic view of Summit County, including many historic mining areas and other points of interest.

To reach the trailhead, drive east on U.S. Highway 6, 6.5 miles past Dillon to the Montezuma Road. Turn right, bear left, and travel 4.6 miles to the Peru Creek Road. Turn left and look for the Lenawee Trail sign .6 mile past the creek crossing. Park along the side of the road. There is no water source along the trail, so be sure to take plenty of water with you.

From the trailhead, you climb steeply at first, then traverse westward along the north side of the Peru Creek Valley for about one mile and then the trail makes three switchbacks, heading north and taking you to the top of the ridge. As you reach timberline, take the time to look around and enjoy the alpine environment. The trail becomes less evident here and you will have to follow the rock cairns marking it.

The trail continues to the ridge near the top of Lenawee Mountain and eventually takes you to the summit at 13,204 feet. Look for evidence of the old American Eagle Mine as the trail loops to the west again and north again. (It is never a good idea to go too close to the old mines, however. **Do not let children explore alone.**) From here the views are spectacular. You can see Grays (14,270 feet) and Torreys (14,267 feet) peaks to the northeast of you, two fourteeners named for the famous botany professors from Harvard and Princeton. Below you is Chihuahua Gulch and Peru Creek. To the south is Montezuma and the headwaters of the Snake River. This entire area is dotted with hundreds of mines. Way down the valley to the west is Dillon Reservoir and beyond it, the Tenmile and Gore Ranges. To the north and directly below you is the A-Basin Ski Area and beyond it, the highway ascending Loveland Pass. To the northeast and south you can see the ridgeline of the Continental Divide extending for many miles.

After enjoying the views, return as you came.—*Caryn Boddie*

HIKE 63 *LENAWEE TRAIL*

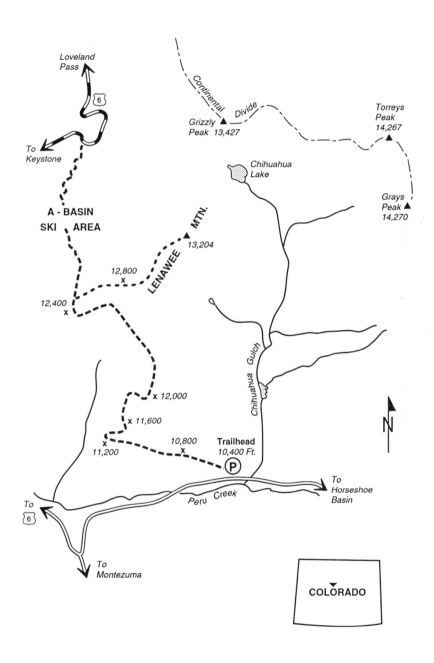

HIKE 64 *MONTE CRISTO GULCH*

General description: A short day hike from beautiful Blue Lakes above timberline into an historic mining area.

General location: About ten miles southwest of Breckenridge.

Maps: USGS Breckenridge quad.; Trails Illustrated Breckenridge South; Arapaho National Forest Map.

Length: About 1.25 miles one way.

Degree of difficulty: Moderate.

Elevations: 11,700 to 12,400 ft.

Special attractions: Beautiful lakes and scenery, good introduction to hiking above timberline, pretty alpine wildflowers, opportunity to see mining relics and imagine mining days gone by.

Best season: Summer.

For more information: Arapaho National Forest, Dillon Ranger District, P.O. Box 620, Silverthorne, CO 80498, (303) 468-5400.

The hike: This short hike above timberline in Monte Cristo Gulch in the Tenmile Range is an easily accessible introduction to the rugged glaciated terrain above timberline and the mining history of Colorado. The trail takes you from two beautiful lakes along the southern flank of fourteener Quandary Peak to a mining site in the shadow of the mountain. Along the way and at your destination you will see old mine relics and have a taste of the mining history of this area while enjoying beautiful views and wildflowers—plus, you may see snow along the trail even in midsummer.

PLEASE NOTE: It is never a good idea to get too close to old mines or to enter them. You never know how stable or unstable they are. **Never let children explore around mines.**

To reach your starting point at Blue Lakes, drive south on Colorado Highway 9 from the Bell Tower Mall in Breckenridge 7.9 miles. Turn right on Blue Lakes Road (Number 850) and look for the sign that says two miles to Blue Lakes. You'll pass a number of cabins in the beginning. Drive up to the dam where there is a big turnaround for parking. These are the Blue Lakes.

Begin your hike on the north end of the dam (right hand side as you face upvalley). While you are on the dam look to your right for a rock cairn. Then look uphill for a couple of brown rock outcroppings. Head up toward them. More cairns mark the way and the trail will become clear near the outcroppings.

Follow the trail along the southern flank of Quandary Peak, a rocky fourteener, and through willows and meadows and tundra. Some of the flowers you may see along the trail are American bistort, chiming bells, buttercups, and harebells. You will be heading toward a pass between Quandary and Fletcher Mountain to the northwest, part of the Tenmile Range. In fact, from the end of the valley it is possible to extend this hike into a climb of Fletcher Mountain (13,951). However, before climbing other of the thirteeners in the Tenmile Range or fourteener Quandary Peak, it would be a good idea to consult one of the good books on climbing the thirteeners and fourteeners (see bibliography).

In a little more than .5 mile you'll come upon two old cabins from mining

American bistort.

days gone by. Summit County, along with Park County to the south and Lake County to the west, saw extensive mining activity in the nineteenth century. In fact, gold was discovered here in Monte Cristo Gulch in 1860.

If you have a topo map with you it's fun to look to see the names of some of the mines: Monte Cristo Mine, Magnolia Mine, Russia Mine, Moose Mine, Dolly Varden Mine, Sweet Home Mine, Security Mine, Paris Mine, Buckskin Joe Mine, and so on. Some of these mines had particularly rich lodes of gold—and zinc, silver, lead, copper, and more—and had mills associated with them. Of course, there many mines on the topo without names; denoted as "Mine." But you know each one had a story in the people who came to claim and work and then leave them, whether they left with or without riches.

About .5 mile past the cabins there once was a mine. There are relics there today (otherwise known as some miner's refuse).

Enjoy imagining the mining days and taking in the view of North Star Mountain to the southeast, which is connected by a ridge (the Continental Divide) to Wheeler Mountain to the west (you probably noticed it when you started your hike at Blue Lakes). When you tire of the wind, which tends to be gusty up here, head back the way you came. As you descend, look across Upper Blue Lake at North Star Mountain. You may discern signs of mines or mining scars (whatever you prefer to call them) on that mountain's flank, too.
—*Caryn, Crystal and Robin Boddie*

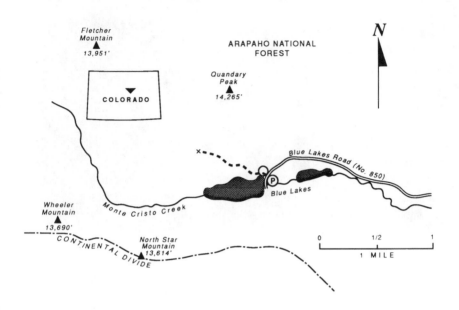

Fletcher
Mountain
▲
13,951'

ARAPAHO NATIONAL
FOREST

N

Quandary
Peak
▲
14,265'

COLORADO

▼

X ---- Blue Lakes Road (No. 850)

P

Blue Lakes

Wheeler
Mountain
▲
13,690'

Monte Cristo Creek

CONTINENTAL DIVIDE

North Star
Mountain
▲ 13,614'

0   1/2   1

1 MILE

HIKE 65 *WATROUS GULCH*

General description: An easily accessible day hike in the Front Range near the Eisenhower Tunnel.

General location: About six miles west of Silver Plume; five miles east of the Eisenhower Tunnel on Interstate 70.

Maps: Arapaho National Forest map; USGS Grays Peak quad.; Trails Illustrated Loveland Pass map.

Degree of difficulty: Easy.

Length: Day hike of 2.5 miles one way with opportunities for extended day hikes or an overnighter.

Elevations: 10,400 to 11,600 feet.

Special attractions: Easily accessible, beautiful views, many aspen promising spectacular autumn color, wildflowers. Opportunities for an extended hike on the Bard Creek Trail or for ascents of thirteeners. Nice spots for camping.

Best season: Summer and early fall.

For more information: Arapaho National Forest, Clear Creek Ranger District, P.O. Box 3307, Idaho Springs, CO 80452, (303) 567-2901.

The hike: This easily accessible and short day hike is one of the lesser used

Torreys Peak (14,267) from Watrous Gulch.

trails in this ranger district because it does not lead to a lake. Instead, it leads you to timberline for a great view and to other trails that offer opportunities for longer day hikes or overnighters and for ascents of thirteeners. It would be a good hike to take in the early fall because of the many aspen along the trail.

To reach the trailhead take Interstate 70 about six miles west of Silverplume or about five miles east of the Eisenhower Tunnel to exit 218. Follow the signs to the Herman Gulch parking area. You'll need to go under a bridge to the south side of the highway. Walk back to the north side of the highway and follow the signs to the Herman Gulch trailhead.

Start up the Herman Gulch trail. You'll see signs and a Forest Service register. You'll soon come to a fork in the trail with the Watrous Gulch trail going to your right (east). Follow it as it climbs gradually through aspen and lodgepole pine. (It should be really pretty in September.)

You'll climb about 2.5 miles with few open views until you reach timberline. You'll cross the creek in Watrous Gulch. Keep an eye open for wildflowers such as hare bells and fireweed. Stop and look back. The view is a just reward for your effort.

Baker Mountain (12,448 feet) is on your left, Mt. Sniktau (13,234 feet) is on your right in the foreground. Beyond to the southeast (far left) is Kelso Mountain (13,164 feet), which connects by a sharp ridge to pyramid-shaped Torreys Peak (14,267 feet). Continue on the trail until you come to a fork.

Notice the piles of timber that indicate there may have been a sawmill here at one time.

As you come to the fork in the trail, you have some choices to make. You can continue straight on the Watrous Gulch trail toward Woods Mountain (12,940 feet) for as long as you like. You could climb Woods Mountain and

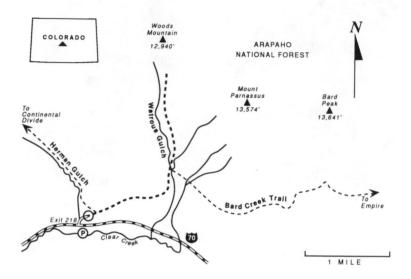

Mount Parnassus (13,574 feet) on your right by way of the saddle between them.

You might also want to go right and follow the Bard Creek Trail for a ways and then return the way you came. It follows the southern flanks of Mount Parnassus and Bard Peak (13,641 feet) and trends northeast to the town of Empire.

With some prior planning, including the shuttle of a car to the northern trailhead of the Bard Creek trail, you could do an overnighter, camping in one of the many good spots near Watrous Gulch and hiking to Empire the next day.—*Caryn Boddie*

HIKE 66 _TOO LONG TRAIL_

General description: A day hike to Bergen Peak in Elk Meadow Park.
General location: About twenty miles west of Denver.
Maps: Squaw Pass and Evergreen USGS quads; Elk Meadow Park Map.
Degree of difficulty: Moderate.
Length: 4.3 miles one way.
Elevations: 7,800 to 9,708 feet.
Special attractions: A wide diversity of ecosystems; opportunities to see wildflowers and wildlife; good views east and west.
For more information: Jefferson County Open Space Department, 18301 W. 10th Ave., Suite 100, Golden, CO 80401; (303) 278-5925.

The hike: The Too Long Trail to the summit of Bergen Peak in the Front Range near Bergen Park and Evergreen, offers a pleasant day hike through a variety of ecosystems and culminates with scenic vistas of the Front Range peaks and the eastern plains.

To reach the trailhead, drive west on Interstate 70 from Denver to Exit 252, the El Rancho exit. Turn left (south), then right to Bergen Park on State Highway 74. About .75 mile south of Bergen Park, look for a small parking area on your right. Park there and begin your hike at the trailhead.

Begin your hike through Elk Meadow on the Meadow View Trail. This .9-mile trail takes you through an environment of grasses, wildflowers and open, rolling park land. Stately, widely-spaced ponderosa pines grow in scattered stands and small mammals, such as badgers, pocket gophers, and the

Elk Meadow.

HIKE 66 *TOO LONG TRAIL*

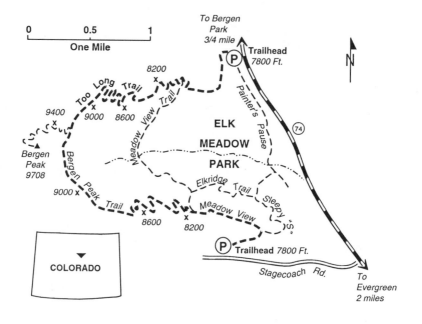

Richardson ground squirrel, make the meadow their home. Several colonies of prairie dogs are also found in the area.

As you skirt the northern edge of the meadow and begin to climb into stands of Douglas fir interspersed with aspens, you will come to a fork in the trail. A turn to the left will take you down and around the meadow. Go to the right and you will begin climbing steeply on the Too Long Trail leading to the summit of Bergen Peak. Keep an eye out for deer as you climb.

Soon you will find yourself along steep slopes forested with lodgepole pine. Keep on the lookout for blue grouse and porcupines. After 2.4 miles you will come to another fork in the trail. Take the steep right fork, which switchbacks another mile to the top of Bergen Peak.

Once at the summit of the peak you will be well rewarded for your efforts. The views are magnificent. From here you can see Mt. Evans, Mt. Bierstadt and Long's Peak in the distance and Squaw and Chief mountains before them. To the east you can see the plains and Denver.

You have a number of options for your return trip once you descend Bergen Peak to the first fork in the trail. You may return as you came along the Too Long Trail to the Meadow View Trail to the parking area. You may also follow the Bergen Peak Trail to the right (southeast) and take the Meadow View Trail north to the parking area, or south to another parking area on Stagecoach Boulevard, which will necessitate a car shuttle. Or you may take the Bergen Peak Trail to the Meadow View Trail to the Sleepy "S" Trail. This will lead you to the Painter's Pause Trail which follows the highway to the parking area.

In any case, you'll appreciate the good work of the Jefferson County Open Space people who provided all these easily accessible and enjoyable trails with the help of Denver Mountain Parks and the Colorado Division of Wildlife. Contact the department for brochures on this and other open space park and trails.—*Caryn, Peter and Crystal Boddie*

HIKE 67 *FRAZER MEADOWS*

General description: A day hike into Golden Gate Canyon State Park in the Front Range.
General location: About fifteen miles northwest of Golden.
Maps: Black Hawk USGS quad; Golden Gate Canyon State Park.
Degree of difficulty: Easy to difficult.
Length: 1.5 to 5.9 miles one way.
Elevations: 8,150 to 9,100 feet.
Special attractions: Easily accessible from Denver; beautiful foothills scenery.
Best season: Spring and fall.
For more information: Golden Gate Canyon State Park, R. Rt. #6, Box 280, Golden, CO 80403; (303) 642-3171.

The hike: This hike takes you into Golden Gate Canyon State Park on historic trails that were once traveled by gold miners, lumberjacks, and homesteaders. A visitor's center offers information on the history and natural history of the area, plus a good trail map. There is a fee to enter the park.

To reach the state park from Golden, take Colorado Highway 93 two miles north to Golden Gate Canyon Road. Turn left and continue for fourteen miles. In the park, a number of trails interconnect and offer possibilities for hikes ranging from two to about six miles one way.

One good short day hike takes you from Ralston Creek to Frazer Meadow. The trail winds through dense forests and open meadows, with beautiful views, is rated easy and offers a good getaway for those who don't have a lot of time.

To begin, park your car at the trailhead roughly .5 mile northeast of the visitor's center. From here the trail ascends an intermittent tributary of Ralston Creek. Gradually gaining elevation, it passes through thick stands of aspen and cottonwoods interspersed with blue spruce. Hiking in the fall is especially enjoyable because of the golden show these trees put on, set against the backdrop of deep green ponderosa pines.

The trail continues up the canyon, traverses the creekbed several times, then swings to the left into Greenfield Meadow. Located about .75 mile from the trailhead, the meadow is the first significant clearing you will encounter. Immediately beyond the meadow the trail forks to the right and continues uphill at a more gradual rate. The canyon becomes less steep as you proceed and the timber less dense. Outcrops formed of granitic and gneiss bedrock are interesting features along the way. At approximately 1.5 miles past Greenfield Meadow, the trail intersects Mule Deer Trail. A right turn takes you across the creek to Frazer Meadow.

Frazer Meadow, large and open, was probably once used for livestock

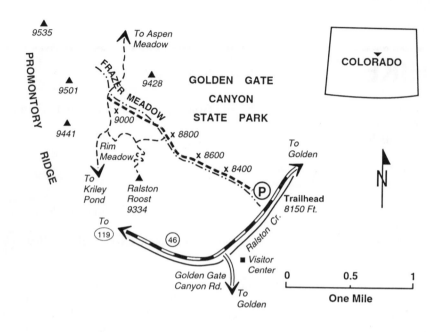

grazing and contains a partially collapsed homestead. The homestead is a large single-room house with an attached barn or storage room. Evidence of reconstruction over the years is indicated by the types of building materials used—square instead of round head nails, rough hewn instead of mill cut lumber, wooden instead of tin roofing. The homestead setting is very picturesque, with snow-capped mountains to the west, rock promontories to the north, and the serene meadow to the south.

From Frazer Meadow several other trails lead to other areas in the park. The 3.5-mile-long Mule Deer Trail will take you to Panorama Point, which offers a beautiful view of the Continental Divide. The 2.2-mile-long Coyote Trail, rated difficult, will take you back to a park road at Promontory Ridge, where you'll see interesting rock outcroppings. Several other choices are also possible (consult your maps). One strong word of caution is in order, however: In selecting alternate return routes, be careful about interpreting trail markers; they can easily be misinterpreted.

Watch for mule deer, elk, and the elusive blue grouse, as well as beaver and muskrat in stream courses. Occasionally, you will see soaring raptors and maybe coyotes, badgers, marmots, and racoons.—*Janet and Tim Shangraw*

Old homestead in Frazer Meadow. Tim Shangraw photo.

HIKE 68 *MT. NYSTROM TRAIL*

General description: An easily accessible day hike along broad ridgetops above timberline near Berthoud Pass.

General location: About forty-five miles west of Denver.

Maps: Berthoud Pass, Fraser and Byers Peak USGS quads; Arapaho National Forest Map, Trails Illustrated Rollins Pass.

Degree of difficulty: Easy to moderate.

Length: From two to eight miles one way.

Elevations: 11,300 to 12,650 feet.

Special attractions: Easy access to timberline and the Continental Divide; great views; wildflowers.

Best season: Summer and fall.

For more information: Arapaho National Forest, Sulphur Ranger District, 62429 U.S. Highway 40, P.O. Box, Granby, CO 80446-9212; (303) 887-3331.

The hike: The Mt. Nystrom Trail follows a long and broad ridge of the Continental Divide and a side ridge from Mt. Nystrom to the Mary Jane Ski Area. This route provides beautiful views of the surrounding mountains and a chance to see the spectacular wildflowers of this alpine environment. An easy access to this trail, which also provides the least elevation gain, is from Berthoud Pass. From this point you have options for short or extended day hikes and an extended backpack, as well.

To reach Berthoud Pass, take Interstate 70 west to US Highway 40 and follow it to the summit of the pass. Park at the ski lodge on the east side.

To begin your hike, cross the highway and climb the ski slopes to the top of the chairlift. For an easier start of your hike, you can take the chairlift, when it is operating most weekends and holidays during the summer.

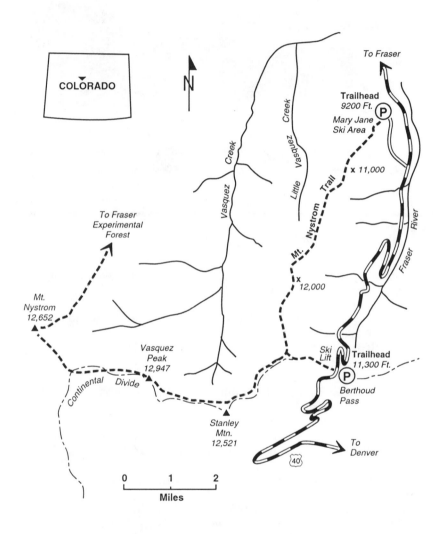

From the top of the chairlift, follow the ridge west to its intersection with another broad ridge from the north. Here you should be able to locate the Mt. Nystrom Trail, marked with rock cairns. From here out your hike will be an easy walk in either direction. To the right the trail follows the ridge for about seven miles to the Mary Jane Ski Area. You can shuttle a car to the parking lot there. To the left the trail follows the Continental Divide about two miles to Stanley Mountain and another six miles to Mt. Nystrom.

This area is part of the Vasquez Mountains and is characterized by broad, rolling ridgetops with steep-sided, glacial cirques carved into them. In general the larger cirques are found on the eastern sides of the ridges where the prevailing winds have deposited snow to form the glaciers. This pattern is repeated over and over again here.

From Berthoud Pass, Stanley Mountain is a short day hike of about 3.5 miles one way, with an elevation gain of about 1,200 feet. From the top of the mountain you can look directly south and down the path of the famous Stanley Slide, a huge avalanche chute. This is one of the most dangerous chutes in the Front Range because it crosses US Highway 40 in two separate places and can bury the highway under as much as twenty feet of snow.

From Stanley Mountain you can continue on towards Mt. Nystrom and beyond to intersect with trails to St. Louis Peak and the Fraser Experimental Forest, or you can return as you came. Whatever you choose to do, be sure to keep an eye out for signs of impending thunderstorms, as this is no place to be caught unaware.—*Brian Dempsey*

HIKE 69 *HELL CANYON*

General description: A rigorous day hike or overnighter into Hell Canyon, a steep glacial valley in the Indian Peaks Wilderness.

General location: Twelve miles east of Granby near the southern edge of Rocky Mountain National Park.

Maps: Monarch Lake and Isolation Peak USGS quads; Arapaho National Forest Map, Trails Illustrated Indian Peaks and Rocky Mountain National Park.

Degree of difficulty: Difficult.

Length: Nine miles one way.

Elevations: 8,400 to 11,400 feet.

Special attractions: Rugged backcountry with alpine lakes in a steep, glacial valley; good fishing.

Best season: Summer.

For more information: Arapaho National Forest, Sulphur District, 62429 U.S. Highway 40, P.O. Box 10, Granby, CO 80446-9212; (303) 887-3331.

The hike: Hell Canyon is very aptly named, a fact that becomes clear to anyone hiking up the unmarked trail that climbs to a saddle leading into Rocky Mountain National Park. Still, this is a hike well worth taking. Hell Canyon, as it rises above Buchanan Creek, cuts deeply into the landscape of this semi-primitive area where wildlife abounds.

To reach Hell Canyon, take US Highway 34 northeast from Granby towards Rocky Mountain National Park and Shadow Mountain National Recreation Area. About six miles north of Granby, take a right on the road which follows the southern shore of Lake Granby. Go on past Lake Granby to the road's end at Monarch Lake. Here a large parking lot serves as the trailhead for both the Arapaho Canyon and Cascade Trail systems. Follow the Northside Trail of the Cascade Trail system along the northeastern shore of Monarch Lake

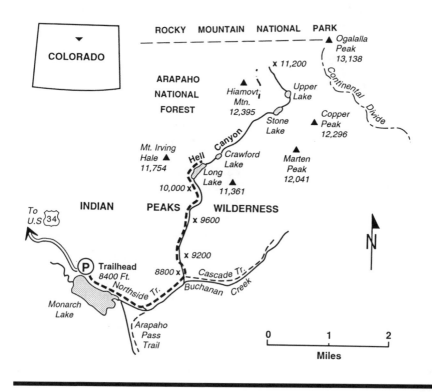

past the Forest Service cabin, then southeast to the trail register at the east end of Monarch Lake. From the register continue two miles along Buchanan Creek to the intersection with the first major drainage from the north. This is Hell Canyon. The trail begins about 100 yards before a bridge. This spot, marked by an old charred tree stump, is where you want to leave the Cascade Trail system to head up the unmarked Hell Canyon Trail.

Rumor has it that a USGS party was caught in the canyon during a mid-November snow storm while surveying. They were forced to bushwack for several days in order to make good their retreat through fresh snow and over ice that made travel precarious at best. The party demanded that the canyon be named Hell Canyon when they finally reached their headquarters.

No doubt, you will understand how the canyon earned its reputation as you make the long, steep climb to Long Lake some 2.5 miles from Buchanan Creek. Fishing in the lake is good and Mt. Irving Hale, which rises 1,500 feet, provides a magnificent setting. You may be tempted to make this your destination, but you will find it worthwhile to continue on beyond Long Lake. The terrain becomes less steep (but remains challenging) and the trail becomes a rough

Monarch Lake. U.S. Forest Service photo.

foot path, as Forest Service maintenance is provided only to Long Lake. Crawford Lake, .5 mile farther up the canyon, is worth pushing on for, set as it is in a large and unexpected meadow. The terrain beyond becomes very interesting as you approach Stone Lake and timberline. Boulders as large as houses dot the landscape, and trees give way to grasses and shrubs.

From Stone Lake you climb a final 600 feet to the saddle that is your destination. A sign marking the southern boundary of Rocky Mountain National Park indicates the top of Hell Canyon. Travel north takes you into the park and Paradise Park. After enjoying this beautiful area, return as you came.
—*Doug Crocker*

HIKE 70 *ST. VRAIN MOUNTAIN*

General description: A day hike to the summit of St. Vrain Mountain in the Indian Peaks Wilderness Area at the southern edge of Rocky Mountain National Park.

General location: About 1.5 miles south of Allens Park; about twenty miles northwest of Boulder.

Maps: Allens Park USGS quad; Roosevelt National Forest Map, Trails Illustrated Rocky Mountain National Park.

Degree of difficulty: Moderate.

Length: 9.8 miles round trip.

Elevations: 8,800 to 12,126 feet.

Special attractions: Panoramic views of Rocky Mountain National Park, the Indian Peaks Wilderness, the foothills and the eastern plains.

Best season: Summer and fall.

For more information: Roosevelt National Forest, Boulder Ranger District, 2995 Baseline Rd., Room 110, Boulder, CO 80303; (303) 444-6001.

The hike: This hike takes you into the edge of the beautiful Indian Peaks Wilderness Area and to the summit of St. Vrain Mountain, with its panoramic view in all directions.

To reach the trailhead, take Colorado Highway 7 south from Estes Park or west and north from Lyons to Allens park. At Allens park take the dirt road leading south to the Rock Creek Ski Area. About 1.5 miles along, turn right at the Forest Service sign pointing to Meadow Mountain and the St. Vrain Glaciers. From the sign it is .5 mile to the trailhead and parking area.

The trail begins through stands of lodgepole pine and aspen and climbs gradually along a lateral glacial moraine until it breaks into a large opening— an old forest fire area. It then climbs more steeply across the top of a bowl that once held a minor valley glacier.

About two hours of hiking brings you to a saddle south of Meadow Mountain. For those wishing a shorter hike with a good view, it is only about .25 mile due north to the top of the mountain. Here you'll have a magnificent view of Mt. Meeker, Longs Peak, Pagoda Mountain, and the peaks ringing Wild Basin in southern Rocky Mountain National Park. From the saddle continue about .7 mile south along the trail through a small stand of trees and back into the open. Then head due west up St. Vrain Mountain by any route you wish. The view from the peak is a 360 degree panorama of the Great Plains, Longs Peak, Wild Basin, the St. Vrain Glaciers, and the northern Indian Peaks.

This part of the Front Range is heavily glaciated and includes some of the last moving bodies of ice in Colorado. Some of the most spectacular remnants of the Great Ice Age are the St. Vrain Glaciers directly west of you at the head of Middle St. Vrain Canyon. All of the landmarks with the name St. Vrain, including the glaciers, the rivers, and the mountain are named for Ceran St. Vrain, an early trader in the area.

On your return from St. Vrain Mountain, two additional trail routes are possible when you reach the trail. To the right (south) the trail continues on and descends into the middle St. Vrain drainage where you can connect with other trails going into the Indian Peaks Wilderness. In addition, an old trail

HIKE 70 *ST. VRAIN MOUNTAIN*

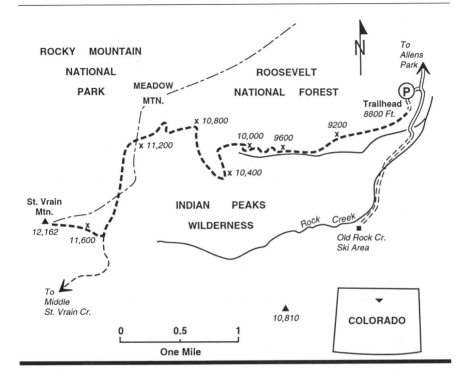

ROCKY MOUNTAIN

NATIONAL

PARK

MEADOW
MTN.

ROOSEVELT

NATIONAL FOREST

Trailhead
8800 Ft.

To
Allens
Park

N

x 10,800

10,000 9600

9200
x

x 11,200

x 10,400

St. Vrain
Mtn.

▲
12,162

x

11,600

INDIAN PEAKS

WILDERNESS

Rock Creek

Old Rock Cr.
Ski Area

To
Middle
St. Vrain Cr.

▲
10,810

COLORADO

0   0.5   1

One Mile

leads down Rock Creek directly to the east of St. Vrain Mountain. It has largely disappeared from lack of use but eventually intersects with old roads constructed to build the defunct Rock Creek Ski Area. These connect back to the road to Allens park. You won't get lost on this route as long as you stay in the Rock Creek drainage.

Portions of the St. Vrain Mountain hike traverse the southern edge of Rocky Mountain National Park, the boundary of which has been extended to the drainage divide connecting Meadow Mountain and St. Vrain Mountain. Therefore, you should be prepared to follow park regulations and register for any overnight trips in this area. Be sure to take plenty of water with you on your hike and enjoy the view.—*Norm Nielsen*

HIKE 71 *LION GULCH TRAIL*

General description: An easily accessible day hike to Homestead Meadows, a beautiful area of historical interest.
General location: Thirteen miles northwest of Lyons.
Maps: Panorama Peak USGS quad; Roosevelt National Forest and Homestead Meadows Trail System maps.

Degree of difficulty: Easy.

Length: Five miles round trip.

Elevations: 7,360 to 8,400 feet.

Special attractions: Easily accessible; pretty wildflowers and meadows; historic Homestead Meadows is your destination.

Best Season: Late spring through late fall.

For more information: Roosevelt National Forest, Estes-Poudre Ranger District, 148 Remington St., Fort Collins, CO 80524; (303) 482-3822.

The hike: The Lion Gulch Trail takes you through stands of lodgepole pine, ponderosa pine and Douglas fir to Homestead Meadows. There you will find the remains of many old homesteads as well as a multitude of wildflowers and scenic views.

To reach the trailhead, take Colorado Highway 36, thirteen miles northwest of Lyons or seven miles southeast of Estes Park. Look for the Lion Gulch Trail on the west side of the road—it is clearly marked and a parking area is provided.

Begin your hike through a forest of lodgepole pines. Chiming bells grow in abundance on the forest floor and the whir of hummingbird wings is in the air. Stop at the trail register to sign in.

At first the trail winds gently down to a footbridge crossing the Little Thompson River, then bears right after the bridge and heads back into the pines. Soon the trail drops again and crosses another footbridge over Lion

---

HIKE 71 *LION GULCH TRAIL*

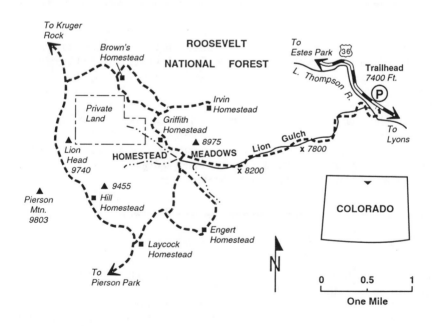

Lion Gulch.

Gulch at its mouth. From this point, the trail will ascend Lion Gulch while crossing the stream several more times as it follows both the north and south sides of the canyon. This provides an excellent opportunity to observe the distinct differences in moisture conditions and vegetation between the two canyon slopes. As you climb steeply up the north (south-facing) slope of the canyon during the first part of the trail, the intense Colorado sun may provide you with the first clue to this difference. This slope receives the greatest amount of solar radiation during the year and is consequently much drier and more open. It is characterized by grasses and mountain brush species interspersed with ponderosa pines, Douglas firs and junipers. The stand of dead trees you encounter along the way are ponderosa pines killed by pine bark beetles.

After dropping down and crossing another footbridge, you follow along the canyon bottom for about one mile. During this section, the trail crosses the stream several times, but without the benefit of footbridges. Due to the small size of the stream, however, these crossings should not present any problems, except perhaps during spring runoff. Along the canyon bottom you will encounter several beautiful stands of aspen, riparian vegetation such as willows and alder, and a mixture of plants representative of both north and south-facing slopes. This combination of vegetation types provides an outstanding variety of wildflowers which, combined with the occasional small waterfalls along the way, make for some excellent picture taking opportunities. You may also want to keep your eyes open for wild strawberries along this stretch of the trail.

As you make progress along Lion Gulch, the trail slowly steepens and eventually begins to climb steeply along the south (north-facing) slope of the canyon. This is the best place along the hike to observe the moist conditions and dense vegetation found on steep, shaded north-facing slopes. There are lodgepole pines, Englemann spruce and a profusion of mosses covering the ground. The cool air along this section of the trail compensates for its steepness and the many small waterfalls below you provide good excuses to stop and rest.

After crossing the stream once again, the trail leads out and enters into a long, open meadow. Another .5 mile brings you to an upland park surrounded by forested mountains. This is Homestead Meadows. At this point, a sign indicates several trails leading to the many homesteads in the area. The closest structures are of Griffith Homestead, about .25 mile straight ahead. The weathered remains of cabins, corrals, and ranch buildings provide for many photographic possibilities, and one could easily spend several days exploring this historic area. In doing so, please do not remove artifacts or disturb any of these historic sites.

A brochure prepared by Jo Ireland for the Arapaho-Roosevelt National Forest entitled "A Valley In Transition: Hunters, Homesteaders, and Hikers" provides insight into the history of Homestead Meadows. After taking time to explore the old homesteads (and keeping an eye out for deer and elk) return as you came.—*Caryn, Peter and Crystal Boddie*

HIKE 72 *GREYROCK TRAIL*

General description: A day hike taking you to Greyrock Mountain and back through Greyrock Meadow.
General location: Seventeen miles west of Fort Collins.
Maps: Poudre Park USGS quad; Roosevelt National Forest Map.
Degree of difficulty: Moderate.
Length: Approximately seven miles round trip.
Elevations: 5,560 to 7,600 feet.
Special attractions: Panoramic views of northern Colorado plains and mountains; beautiful meadows.
Best season: Year round.
For more information: Roosevelt National Forest, Redfeather Ranger

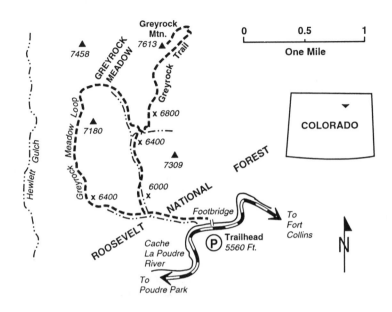

District, 220 E. Olive Fort Collins, CO 80524; (303) 498-1375.

The hike: The Greyrock National Recreation Trail takes you from the canyon of the Cache la Poudre River through beautiful foothills to the summit of Greyrock Mountain, a unique landmark of the northern Front Range. This popular trail was built in the 1930s by the Civilian Conservation Corps, and a loop trail, taking you through a pristine meadow, was added in 1978.

This hike can be done in any season (provided there is no snow) but is best in spring and fall when temperatures are milder and the rattlesnakes are hiding. Be sure to take plenty of water.

To reach the trailhead, drive seventeen miles west of Fort Collins on Colorado Highway 14 through Poudre Canyon and look for the trailhead parking on the left (south) side of the road.

To begin your hike, find the trail (on the opposite side of the highway) and the footbridge across the Cache la Poudre River. Once across the river, you begin to climb along a small foothills gulch going west. During the storm that caused the deadly Big Thompson Canyon flood of 1976, the water in this small, usually dry gully was more than 100 feet wide where it entered the Poudre River. The river itself crested the footbridge and took out the railing. The footbridge was reconstructed in 1988 using the old stone foundation. As you walk along the edge of the Poudre River and then along this foothills stream, look for evidence of this flash flood in the form of boulders, gravel bars, logs and other debris. Although much of this evidence is now hidden by new vegetation, you can still get an idea of the power of summer flash floods.

About .5 mile into the hike you will encounter a fork in the trail. A left here will take you along a 2.3-mile loop through Greyrock Meadow and back to the main trail. This route offers great views of Hewlett Gulch and Poudre Canyon as it climbs to a spectacular saddle at the edge of the meadow. The right fork is the main trail to the summit of Greyrock Mountain. As it climbs the gulch, you pass through stands of ponderosa pine and Douglas fir. (Please do not cut across switchbacks. This causes erosion.) After a good steady climb the trail intersects again with the meadow loop and then levels off somewhat.

Through the trees you can see the domelike summit of Greyrock Mountain, an intrusive dome of granitie, igneous rock which was forced upward and then cooled while still beneath the earth's surface. After the region uplifted, exposing this dome, the release of pressure from the overlying rocks caused it to slowly exfoliate (expand and crack) dividing into great slabs that split and then slid from its sides.

Continue on climbing steeply to the base of the mountain and then follow its southeastern slope until the trail turns and ascends the east side. Once on the dome hike southwest (the trail climbs gently through intermingled rock, grass and forest) to the barren high point at the southwest end which is the summit. Along the way you will pass an unexpected, small, rain-fed lake trapped in the granite.

From the top of Greyrock Mountain you have a spectacular view of the plains, the foothills and the peaks of the northern Front Range. To the southeast is Fort Collins. To the west are the Medicine Bow Mountains and the Rawah Wilderness. To the southwest you can make out the prone shape of The Mummy (giving its name to the Mummy Range at the northern end of Rocky Mountain National Park) and the Comanche Peak Wilderness. Below you lies Greyrock Meadow. On your return, you might want to follow the loop trail through this beautiful meadow.—*Caryn, Peter and Crystal Boddie*

HIKE 73 *McINTYRE CREEK TRAIL*

General description: A day hike or overnighter into the Shipman Park Area and the Rawah Wilderness.
General location: Approximately fifty miles west of Fort Collins.
Maps: Glendevey and Shipman Mountain USGS quads; Roosevelt National Forest Map, Trails Illustrated Cowdrey and Red Feather Lakes.
Degree of difficulty: Moderate.
Length: Seven miles one way.
Elevations: 8,400 to 9,600 feet.
Special attractions: A hike along two beautiful mountain streams to an upland park; prime elk habitat; numerous beaver ponds with trout.
Best season: Summer and fall.
For more information: Roosevelt National Forest, Redfeather Ranger District, 220 E. Olive, Fort Collins, CO 80524; (303) 498-1375.

The hike: This hike to Shipman Park takes you up the McIntyre Creek Trail from the junction of McIntyre Creek and Jinks Creek into a series of upland parks and follows McIntyre and then Housmer Creek, two beautiful mountain streams. The fourteen-mile round trip from the trailhead to Shipman Park along steep terrain makes a strenuous two-day hike, the trail gaining 1,200 feet in elevation along the way. Figure on five to seven hours in and three to five out. As an alternative, you can camp the first night in Shipman Park and then hike another two miles the next day to Ute Pass. At this point, the trail joins the Medicine Bow Trail and ties into the major trail network in the Rawah Wilderness Area. Therefore, several alternative hikes of varying lengths and difficulty can be added.

To reach the McIntyre Creek trailhead, drive west from Fort Collins on Colorado Highway 14 for fifty-nine miles. Turn right (north) on the Laramie River Road and follow it seventeen miles to the Glendevey turnoff, which is well-marked. Turn left (west) on Glendevey Road and travel approximately three miles to the parking lot provided for the trailhead.

The trailhead has been relocated from the Hooligan Roost Camp Group as it is shown on the USGS Glendevey quad to a joint trailhead with the Link Trail, approximately .75 mile east of the old location. At the trailhead, follow the trail sign for McIntyre Creek Trail along the powerline cut for approximately .5 mile to the junction with the old trail. At this point, there is a registry box for the wilderness area. After you register, follow the trail winding downward among the ponderosa pines to cross McIntyre Creek.

For the next four miles, the trail will follow the north side of McIntyre Creek in a steep canyon where occasional side canyons enter. In this section you will climb gradually (sometimes steeply) through ponderosa pines, aspen, Englemann spruce and subalpine fir. Willows are also present along the creek.

After about four miles you will enter Housmer Park, a narrow upland park about one mile in length where there is a pretty meadow and good campsites for those not interested in continuing on to Shipman Park. The creek through Housmer Park is dammed by beavers in several locations, creating small ponds that look potentially good for fishing.

After exiting the north end of Housmer Park, the trail climbs up about .25 mile to a divide. An unmapped trail joins the main trail at this point. Be sure to continue to your left. The trail then drops another .25 mile to the edge of Shipman Park. This end of the park is boggy and it may be necessary to wade through some standing water. However, as you move northward and westward, the ground rises and becomes drier.

Shipman Park is an upland meadow approximately 4.5 miles long and as much as a mile wide at its widest point. A fun day hike from a base camp takes you to fishing at several small ponds. In addition, the area is frequented by deer and elk, most often seen at dusk and dawn.

Several possibilities exist for a continued hike. As noted, the trail goes on to Ute Pass. At the pass there is a spectacular view into North Park, as well as a junction with the Medicine Bow Trail, from which much of the Rawah Wilderness Area, with its numerous alpine lakes, can be explored.—*New Hope Community Church High School Youth Group*

HIKE 73 *McINTYRE CREEK TRAIL*

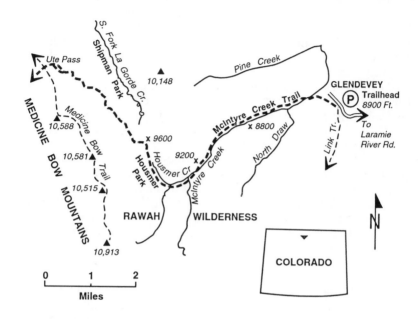

HIKE 74 *MONTGOMERY PASS TRAIL*

General description: This lightly used trail takes you on a short hike through subalpine forest to above timberline where you'll have good views of the mountains of northern Colorado.

General location: About sixty-five miles west of Fort Collins.

Maps: USGS Rawah Lakes Quad; Trails Illustrated Poudre River map; Roosevelt National Forest Map.

Length: About two miles round trip.

Degree of difficulty: Easy.

Elevations: 10,040 to 11,000 feet.

Special attractions: An excellent trail for a short day hike to and above timberline. You will have beautiful views of the northern Colorado mountains, including the Neota Flat Tops Wilderness and access to longer treks above timberline. Because the trail is lightly used, you will have it mostly to yourself.

Best season: Summer through early fall.

For more information: Arapaho and Roosevelt National Forest, Redfeather Ranger District, 210 East Olive, Fort Collins, CO 80524, (303) 498-1375.

The hike: This moderate day hike takes you through thick subalpine forest

The ridge south to Diamond Peaks from Montgomery Pass.

to timberline in short order. It leads into the Colorado State Forest and to Montgomery Pass from which you'll have nice views of the mountains of northern Colorado.

To reach the trailhead, drive sixty-five miles west from Fort Collins on Colorado Highway 14 until you reach Joe Wright Reservoir. (You can also come east over Cameron Pass on Highway 14 to the reservoir.) Parking for the Montgomery Pass Trail is in the Zimmerman Lake parking lot—the first lot west of the reservoir.

The Montgomery Pass Trail begins on the north side of the highway a short ways to the east. It skirts the forest for a short distance before entering the timber. You will see a cairn and the trail going off into the trees.

Begin your hike on the old jeep trail. It's well-maintained and easy to see. Fairly steep at the start, the trail heads directly up toward the pass after an initial wide switchback.

You will hike through dense spruce-fir forest and, after you've hiked for a ways and have gained altitude, you will pass an old log cabin that is making its way back into the earth. Now the trail becomes a bit difficult to discern. Look for the green arrows on the trees that mark the way. Soon you will reach timberline and the characteristic krummholz forest here and there, where trees and shrubs are twisted and dwarfed by harsh conditions. Keep heading up and you will reach Montgomery Pass at 11,000 feet.

The rolling terrain at Montgomery Pass, the beautiful view, and the gentle ridges extending north and south beckon you to hike on and on; to see more and more. From the pass you will see the Flat Top Mountain in the Neota Flat Tops Wilderness to the south; Bald Mountain to the southeast; Cameron Peak to the north; and the eastern edge of North Michigan Reservoir to the west.

Climb the ridge to the south and you will reach Diamond Peaks, which rise

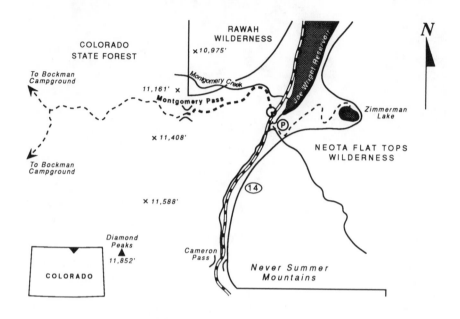

about 800 feet above Montgomery Pass. From there you will look down on Cameron Pass, the beautiful Never Summer Mountains, and more of the Neota Flat Tops Wilderness to the south.

Climb the ridge to the north and you will reach Clark Peak from which you will see more the Rawah Mountains and the Rawah Wilderness to the northeast.

On this short day hike you may want to check out the lay of the land and plan a longer trip for the future. The trail continues west from Montgomery Pass down to Bockman Campground and North Michigan Reservoir. West of the pass, the trail is open to vehicles. A hike over the pass to the campground to meet a friend with a car could be a fun trip.—*Caryn and Robin Boddie*

HIKE 75 *MIRROR LAKE*

General description: A long day hike, overnighter, or part of an extended backpacking trip through the high country of Rocky Mountain National Park and the adjacent Comanche Peak Wilderness Area.

General location: Thirty miles west of Fort Collins.

Maps: Chambers lake and Comanche Peak USGS quads; Rocky Mountain National Park map; Roosevelt National Forest map; Trails Illustrated Poudre River and Rocky Mountain National Park maps.

Degree of difficulty: Moderate.

Length: Six miles one way.

Elevations: Starts at 10,070 feet, drops to 9,760 feet, then rises to 11,025 feet at Mirror Lake.

Special Attractions: Views across montane meadows to Rowe and Hagues Peaks; wildflowers in spring and early summer; wildlife; fishing; destination a magnificent cirque lake.

Best season: Late spring through early fall.

For more information: Rocky Mountain National Park, Estes Park, CO 80517, (303) 586-2371 and Roosevelt National Forest, Redfeather District Office, 210 E. Olive, Fort Collins, CO 80524, (303) 498-1375.

The hike: This high country hike leads you through a variety of attractions —montane meadows, montane and subalpine forests, glacial features, streamside hiking, and a beautiful lake. It also gets you into a less-visited part of Rocky Mountain National Park as well as the Comanche Peak Wilderness Area of Roosevelt National Forest.

To reach the trailhead, take Colorado Highway 14 from either Walden on the west or Fort Collins on the east towards Cameron Pass. The turnoff onto Long Draw Road, which is Larimer County Road 156, is 4.7 miles east of the pass. Continue towards Long Draw Reservoir, but turn left into the small Corral Creek trailhead parking area after 8.5 miles. The parking area is right across the road from the joint NPS-USFS Corral Creek Information Station, which is only open in the summer. Long Draw Campground (USFS) is located just 0.2 mile farther along Long Draw Road which, by the way, is not plowed in the winter.

The signs at the trailhead explain the regulations that apply in the wilderness and the park, so take a moment to read the notices. If you make this more than a day hike and plan to camp in the park's backcountry, you must have a permit. The trail is easy to follow and well-signed at intersections.

A delightful aspect of the first third of this hike is the nearness of streams and fishing opportunities. The streams include Corral Creek, Cache la Poudre ("hide the powder") River, and Hague Creek. These water courses provide many places to cool off if it is a hot summer day. You will find yourself alternately at streamside, in lodgepole pine forest, and in open meadows. You may see gray jays and Stellar's jays, should see and hear mountain chickadees and gray-headed juncos, and might startle a red-shafted flicker as it forages for ants along the trail.

A grand view of Rowe Mountain (13,184 feet), Rowe Peak (13,380 feet), and Hagues Peak (13,560 feet), from left to right, across a willow-dominated

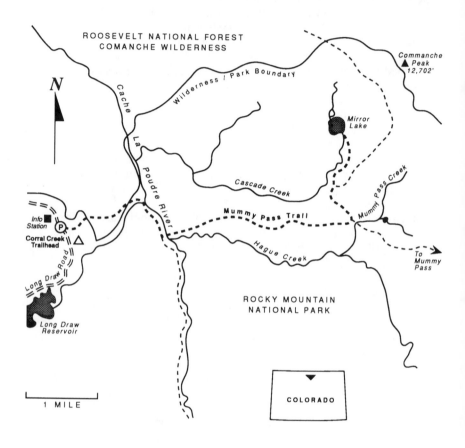

ROOSEVELT NATIONAL FOREST
COMANCHE WILDERNESS

N

Cache La Poudre River

Wilderness / Park Boundary

Commanche
▲ Peak
12,702'

Mirror
Lake

Cascade Creek

Mummy Pass Creek

Mummy Pass Trail

Info ■
Station
P

Corral Creek △
Trailhead

Long Draw Road

Hague Creek

To
Mummy
Pass

Long Draw
Reservoir

ROCKY MOUNTAIN
NATIONAL PARK

1 MILE

▼
COLORADO

meadow, opens up after a short steep climb over a glacial moraine. The sign at this point indicates that Mirror Lake is 4.1 miles ahead. While enjoying the view from one of the nearby streamside boulders (to the right and just beyond the sign), note the upper climatic limit of tree growth straight ahead on Rowe Mountain, the stunted "krummholz" growth form of the trees approaching Flint Pass, and the steep, glacially-steepened slopes of Hagues Peak.

Here, at the boundary of a lodgepole pine forest, you are at the edge of a chickaree's home territory, so don't be surprised to be scolded as an intruder. When you continue towards the lake, watch for the piles of discarded cone scales (called middens) of this small tree squirrel. If you are hiking in autumn, look for holes in the middens where the chickaree's winter supply of cones is being stored. This forest is good chickaree habitat. Lodgepole pines, unlike most conifers, produce a good cone crop every year and each chickaree here is actively protecting a patch of forest from one-half to two acres in size. They prefer older cones, because they are easier to open, even though younger cones contain more edible seeds. If it is autumn, you will be scolded frequently, because that's when they are busy harvesting cones for their winter cache and when the youngsters are searching for habitat in which to establish new territories.

As you approach the lake, you will pass through subalpine forest comprised of Engelmann spruce and subalpine fir. I was once lucky enough to see a pine marten here, and you may very well see Clark's nutcrackers and white-crowned sparrows. These sparrows have been known to live to more than thirteen years of age. In late spring and early summer many subalpine plants will be in flower.

Upon arrival at Mirror lake take time, if a summer storm is not threatening, to enjoy the ice-sculptured landscape before you. This area and the steep slopes of the Mummy Range peaks to the southeast were source areas for glaciers that once flowed downslope and filled the valleys below. On your hike back to the trailhead notice the impressive glacial moraines and huge boulders that were transported by the ice from these high peaks. In fact, the ridge separating Cascade and Hague creeks which the trail follows for approximately two miles is actually a large side moraine of the glacier which filled the valley of Hague Creek.—*Mark Noble* (Mark Noble is a naturalist who provides guided natural history hikes. For information and reservations, contact him at: Reflections of the Rockies, P.O. Box 73, Estes Park, CO 80517-0073, (303) 586-8924.)

HIKE 76 *BAKER GULCH*

General description: A day hike or backpack beginning in Rocky Mountain National Park and following Baker Gulch to Baker Pass in the Never Summer Range and Never Summer Wilderness.
General location: Approximately six miles from the west entrance in Rocky Mountain National Park.
Maps: Bowen Mountain and Mount Richthofen USGS quads; Arapaho National Forest Map, Trails Illustrated Rocky Mountain National Park.
Degree of difficulty: Moderate.
Length: Six miles one way.
Elevations: 8,940 to 11,250 feet.
Special attractions: Moderately-used, undeveloped area; beautiful views from Baker Pass; good fishing in Baker Gulch Creek; lots of wildlife, including bighorn sheep and blue grouse, Never Summer Wilderness.
Best season: Summer and fall.
For more information: Arapaho National Forest, Sulphur Ranger District; 62429 US Highway 40, P.O. Box 10, Granby, CO 80446-9212; (303) 887-3331.

The hike: The Baker Gulch Trail takes you from Rocky Mountain National Park into the Arapaho National Forest and up to Baker Pass, where you'll have beautiful views in all directions.

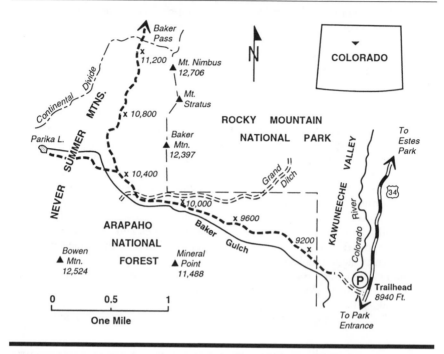

To reach the trailhead, enter Rocky Mountain National Park at the west entrance and follow Trail Ridge Road for 6.4 miles to the trailhead. Park in the picnic area parking lot and hike up the dirt road .5 mile to the "Baker Trailhead" sign. Go right at the fork.

Rising from the Kawuneeche Valley through lodgepole pine, the trail follows Baker Gulch at a moderate grade. Up the trail 1.3 miles, a worn spot to the right indicates the way to a large beaver pond fishermen will find inviting. The trail then continues through an area of deadfall and follows several switchbacks (where you'll want to stop for raspberries) before leveling off to cross a boulder field. As you cross the boulders, look for the small mammals that make this boulder field their home. The marmots shouldn't be too difficult to spot, but not so for those little, squeaky picas. You will also pass the Grand Ditch road carved into the steep south-facing slope above the trail. The ditch, built in the 1890s, provides the eastern plains with runoff water for irrigation.

After switching back through stands of aspen, the trail passes through a lush meadow alive with wildflowers, particularly columbine and the unusual American bistort. Look for Longs Peak to the east here and for the cliffs of Bowen Mountain above Baker Gulch to the southwest. You can also see the green of the Kawuneeche Valley below.

Shortly after leaving the meadow, the trail crosses the Grand Ditch service road. There is then a wooden bridge across the ditch itself, and you enter

Looking northeast from the summit of Parkview Mountain to the Never Summer Range.

a forest of Engelmann spruce and subalpine fir. Four miles from the trailhead you will meet a stream which becomes difficult to cross during spring runoff. On the opposite bank is a sign marking the Parika Lake turnoff. Follow the Baker Gulch Trail which continues north and to the right, crossing several small streams and meadows where deer and elk can frequently be seen grazing. The large barren mountain to the right is Baker Mountain (elevation 12,397 feet). Rock cairns mark the last .5 mile of the hike, which follows a gentle slope through marshy alpine meadows (a fragile environment) to the saddle of Baker Pass.

To the east are the "cloud mountains" of the Never Summer Range, which form the boundary between the Routt National Forest and Rocky Mountain National Park. The southernmost of these is Mount Stratus, named after low altitude horizontal clouds. Looking north of Mount Stratus is Mount Nimbus. Farther to the north is Mount Cumulus. Mount Cirrus, named after high altitude clouds, is the highest of the cloud mountains with a summit of 12,797 feet. Between Cirrus and Cumulus is Howard Mountain, said to have been named after Luke Howard, the man who first classified cloud forms. North of the cloud mountains is Mount Richthofen, at 12,940 feet, the highest mountain in the Never Summer Range.

Another trail from Baker Pass leads southwest, traversing the slope just below the Continental Divide to Parika Lake. You can also continue on into the Routt National Forest along the Michigan River Trail and the Jack Creek Trail, known as Baker Pass Trail. Otherwise, return as you came once you have enjoyed this beautiful view. Be sure to watch for wildlife including bighorn sheep and blue grouse as you return.—*U.S. Forest Service.*

HIKE 77 *PARKVIEW MOUNTAIN*

General description: A day hike to the summit of Parkview Mountain, the high point of the Rabbit Ears Range.
General location: About thirty-five miles southwest of Walden and twenty miles northwest of Granby.
Maps: Parkview Mountain and Radial Mountain USGS quads; Arapaho National Forest Map, Trails Illustrated Rand Map.
Degree of difficulty: Moderate.
Length: Five miles one way.
Elevations: 9,500 to 12,296 feet.
Special attractions: Beautiful views of North and Middle parks and the mountains of northern Colorado; wildflowers; big game.
Best season: Summer.
For more information: Arapaho National Forest, Sulphur Ranger District, 62429 US Highway 40, Box 10, Granby, CO 80446-9212; (303) 887-3331.

The hike: An imposing and aptly named landmark in northern Colorado, Parkview Mountain is the high point of the Rabbit Ears Range, which separates North and Middle parks. A hike to its summit offers beautiful alpine wildflowers, herds of elk and spectacular views of the surrounding mountains and mountain parks.

Drive south from Walden (or north from Granby) on Colorado Highway 125 to the summit of Willow Creek Pass. Proceed south over the pass for about .6 mile to the second timber road on your right. You can park or drive on, but the road becomes increasingly rough and steep as you proceed, and it may not be suitable for passenger cars. Your hike will be longer if you park here, but the walking is easy up this old road.

Begin your hike by crossing a small stream and make a right and then a

HIKE 77 *PARKVIEW MOUNTAIN*

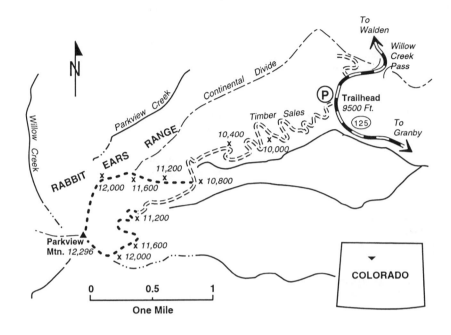

left turn at two forks encountered as the road climbs in the first .25 mile. From here keep to what is obviously the main road, as it switches back many times for about two miles through old timber sales on the lower slopes of Parkview Mountain.

This area was once clearcut and has since been reseeded. As you climb, you can use this opportunity to observe the reestablishment of a new forest. At the upper end of the timber sale the road steepens and switches back several times more until it crosses a steep bowl and avalanche chute below timberline. Just past this point, the road reenters forest as it rounds the end of a ridge. At this point, you have a choice of two routes leading to the summit.

One possibility (and the easier of the two) is to climb to your right directly up the ridge from the road. This route climbs steadily through scattered timber to timberline. From here it is a short, but steep, climb to the long ridge leading west and then south to the summit. This route provides beautiful views of North Park along its length. Look for elk on the broad grassy slopes on the north sides of the mountain.

An alternate route begins another .5 mile along where the road ends in a beautiful glacial cirque below the peak. From this point you can see the small lookout shelter on the summit. Set out around the cirque and intersect the ridge on the south side. Take time to notice the wildflowers here: American bistort, columbine, Indian paintbrush, and many more. The climb is very steep here to the summit ridge, but the last quarter-mile is nearly level. Keep an eye out for the tiny alpine flowers which thrive in this harsh environment, including blue forget-me-nots.

Once at the summit, sign the register and enjoy the view. To the north is the beautiful green expanse of North Park, bordered on the west by the Park Range and the Mount Zirkel Wilderness Area and on the east by the Medicine Bow Mountains and the Rawah Wilderness Area. On a clear day you should be able to discern the outline of the sand dunes of North Park, which lie at the base of the Medicine Bow Mountains, a much smaller version of those found at Great Sand Dunes National Monument. To the east is the Never Summer Range, and beyond it, to the southeast, are Longs Peak, the Indian Peaks, and Berthoud Pass. To the south lies Middle Park and to the southwest are the Gore Range and the Flat Tops. To the west you may be able to discern the distinct shape of Rabbit Ears Peak, marking the end of the Rabbit Ears Range at Rabbit Ears Pass. From this one point you can see most of the course of the Continental Divide throughout northern Colorado.—*Caryn, Peter and Crystal Boddie.*

HIKE 78 *RED CANYON*

General description: A day hike or overnighter along the spectacular Red Canyon to Lost Ranger Peak in the Mount Zirkel Wilderness.
General location: Fifteen miles west of Walden.
Maps: Pitchpine Mountain and Mount Ethel USGS quads; Routt National Forest map; Trails Illustrated Steamboat Springs North map.
Degree of difficulty: Difficult.
Length: Three miles to the mouth of Red Canyon, 9 miles one way to the summit of Lost Ranger Peak.
Elevations: 8,400 to 11,900 feet with loss of 600 feet.
Special Attractions: Lesser used route into the Mount Zirkel Wilderness; spectacular falls and glacially carved 2,000-foot-deep Red Canyon; panoramic view from summit of Lost Ranger Peak; possibility of seeing moose, elk, and other wildlife.
Best season: Summer.
For more information: Routt National Forest, North Park Ranger District, 612 Fifth St., P.O. Box 158, Walden, CO 80480; (303) 723-4707.

The Hike: This hike takes you along a steep, rough trail through the grand Mt. Zirkel Wilderness. It would probably be best to plan an overnighter so that you can take your time and enjoy this hike. You will view rugged Red Canyon at many points along the way and hike to Red Canyon Saddle, a summer range for elk along the Continental Divide. If you choose you can ascend to the summit of Lost Ranger Peak and extend your hike along the Continental Divide or make a loop to include some of the high country lakes in the Mount Zirkel Wilderness.

Driving to the trailhead you see North Park mountain country at its best: traveling west from Walden you'll cross the open expanses of the park ranchlands with a perfect view of the Park Range and your destination, the

HIKE 78 *RED CANYON*

Mount Zirkel Wilderness.

To reach the trailhead drive west from Walden on County Road 12W about nine miles (continuing west at the fork with County Road 18 in about five miles). Turn right (north) where the pavement ends on County Rd 5 to Delaney Butte Lakes. Go west on County Rd 20 from Delaney Butte Lakes to the National Forest boundary. The Pitchpine Trailhead is just west of the boundary and there is ample parking. You will take the Grizzly-Helena Trail (#1126) to meet the Lost Ranger Trail (#1131) at Red Canyon Reservoir.

You do have an alternative route to the reservoir and the Lost Ranger Trail, which is to take County Road 12W west from Highway 125-14 just west of

Walden to County Road 16, which will take you directly through the Lone Pine Ranch. Follow this road to the National Forest boundary and continue west about one mile to the trailhead, which is on the south side of the trail. You will then cross Lone Pine Creek and hike south about two miles to meet the Lost Ranger Trail on the west side of Red Canyon Reservoir. It may be a good idea to check with the Ranger District office in Walden before taking this route, because gates on the Lone Pine Ranch may be locked at times to through traffic.

From the Pitchpine Trailhead the trail leads you northeast initially, through open aspen groves. After a half mile you enter a dense forest of lodgepole pine and continue in heavy timber, descending to and then crossing Sunday Creek in about one mile. After crossing Sunday Creek the trail descends through timber to irrigated meadows along the Roaring Fork of the North Platte River. About two miles after crossing Sunday Creek you will come to the mouth of Red Canyon Reservoir and the falls of the Roaring Fork. Please note that the hay meadows, the reservoir, and the falls are all on private land and there is no camping or fishing allowed there. You will view sharply rising formations to the west as you walk—the southeastern walls of Red Canyon— and North Park to the east. After crossing the Roaring Fork the Grizzly Helena Trail meets the Lost Ranger Trail.

The Lost Ranger Trail now takes you into Red Canyon along the Roaring Fork to where it meets Red Canyon Creek, which begins at the head of the canyon in the cliffs and Roxy Ann Lake to the west.

After entering the canyon and crossing the Mount Zirkel Wilderness boundary, the trail enters an area where hundreds of trees blew down during an ice storm in 1977. A makeshift trail winds through the debris, although recent downfall may continue to block the trail in places.

Spectacular is the word for the views within Red Canyon, with its towering red walls! Continuing along the steep north canyon wall is a steep, rough climb, which culminates in an ascent to Red Canyon Saddle before the Continental Divide by way of a number of switchbacks. Take time to enjoy the views of Red Canyon as you climb. On top you may see elk in their summer range, if you're lucky. The trail winds through meadows of sedge and wildflowers interspersed with stands of spruce-fir.

Right at the divide you will come to the Wyoming Trail (#1101). Climb south to the summit of Lost Ranger Peak and you will be sitting atop the Continental Divide at 11,932 ft. with a panoramic view of the Park Range (Mt. Ethel to the south; Mt. Zirkel far to the north) and the Mount Zirkel Wilderness with its many small lakes and creeks, and vast North Park to the east.

You can return as you came or you have a number of options of continuing north or south in the wilderness area. One possible loop route would be to continue south from Lost Ranger Peak on the Wyoming Trail (#1101) about one mile to the intersection with the Rainbow Lake Trail (#1130), which takes you southeast past a trail that leads to Roxy Ann Lake and past Slide Lakes and Rainbow Lakes to an intersection with the Grizzly-Helena Trail (#1126) about three miles south of the Pitchpine Trailhead. Although this route provides access to Roxy Ann Lake, but a return descent down Red Canyon from the lake is discouraged because of heavy and downed timber and steep cliffs.

Enjoy this beautiful wilderness!—*Gib Frye*

HIKE 79 _LONG LAKE_

General description: Long day hike or overnighter to a large alpine lake near the Continental Divide in the Park Range. Shorter day hikes are also possible. Paved trails in recreation area.

General location: About three miles southeast of Steamboat Springs.

Maps: Routt National Forest map; USGS Mt. Werner and Steamboat Springs quads.; Trails Illustrated Steamboat Springs South map.

Degree of difficulty: Moderate.

Length: About six miles one way.

Elevations: 7,600 to 9,800 ft.

Special attractions: A range of hiking opportunities for all members of the family, including disabled members; beautiful falls, well-maintained trail, interesting geologic features, wildflowers, pristine alpine lake near the Continental Divide; opportunities to extend hike.

Best season: Summer and early fall.

For more information: Routt National Forest, Hahns Peak Ranger District, 57 10th St., P.O. Box 771212, Steamboat Springs, CO 80477; (303) 879-1870.

The hike: The trail to Long Lake in the Park Range near Steamboat Springs begins in the heavily used, but well-maintained, Fish Creek Falls Recreation Area. It offers excellent outdoor opportunities for families—especially families who have young children or family members with disabilities. Everyone can spend time in the outdoors together on a short hike on a paved trail to Fish Creek Falls and picnic together, then send members who'd like to make a longer hike off toward Long Lake, an alpine lake near the Continental Divide. (The trailhead is close to the town of Steamboat, so it would be easy for the rest of the family to go back to town and come back for hikers doing a longer day hike or overnighter.)

It would also be possible to plan to pick hikers up at Fish Creek Reservoir and Granite Campground north of Long Lake. You might also shuttle cars to do this. Contact the Forest Service about conditions of forest routes.

Don't be put off by the numbers of cars in the parking area or the numbers of people on the paved trails. Soon you will climb up and away to solitude and a beautiful alpine lake. Although, you should keep an eye out and ear open for mountain bikers who can really come upon you quickly on parts of the trail.

It would probably be best to do this hike as an overnighter if you are planning on going to Long Lake, because it is a long trek and you will want to spend some time at the lake enjoying the scenery, exploring, and fishing. Then you can enjoy your hike out the next day.

To reach the trailhead drive to the eastern edge of the town of Steamboat Springs, which is on US Highway 40. Turn north on Third St. for one block. Turn east on Fish Creek Falls Road (County Road 320). Drive four miles to Fish Creek Falls Recreation Area. You'll see signs for parking; first a sign for overnight parking, then a sign for day use parking.

Follow the signs to the base of Fish Creek Falls. The surrounding cliffs were formed of volcanic rock that metamorphosed into gneiss, amphibolite, and schist. During the Ice Age, glaciers created both the hanging valley over which

Taking a breather at Upper Fish Creek Falls.

Fish Creek falls, and the hundreds of feet of elevation change to the creekbed below. Hike up to your right, as you're facing the falls, and away from their base.

You will begin to switchback through a forest of Douglas fir, Utah juniper, serviceberry, gamble oak, mountain ash, and Rocky Mountain maple. You may want to notice the understory in the forest: thimbleberry grows there—a plant with big leaves that almost look like maple leaves—along with skunk cabbage, willow, ferns, kinnickinick, and wild roses.

You soon head into aspen groves. Unfortunately, this being a very popular area, the aspen have been marked with the names of some who've passed by, and rocks have been painted with peoples' "signatures"; blemishes that can't ever be removed.

As you hike, notice the huge boulders with lichens and moss growing on their north sides. You might also like to see how many shades of green you can find in one part of the forest. Decorating it all, like jewelry, are the bright

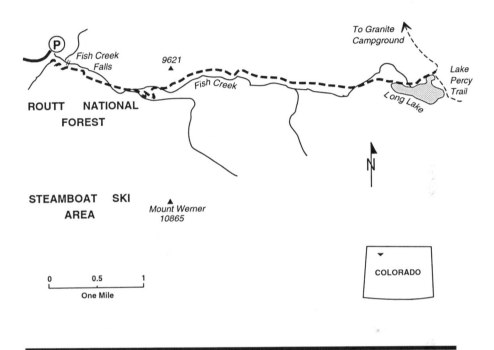

orange serviceberries. Watch also for Richardson's ground squirrels (often mistaken for chipmunks), which are common here. And, listen for the chick-a-dee-dee-dee of the chick-a-dee.

In August the only flowers still blooming were white mountain asters, purple clover, golden composite flowers, and fireweed—the last bloomer of the summer. Look for other species on your hike.

Soon you will climb out of the aspen grove and find yourself in the hanging valley over which Fish Creek makes its plunge. If you look toward the creek from the trail you will see the mark of the glaciers on the rock face; it has been smoothed and grooved. Also notice the blue spruce along the river. Englemann spruce and Douglas fir also grow along this part of the trail.

You will go around a little falls, come to a big boulder field, and cross a bridge over Fish Creek. The trail then switches back from the bridge a couple of times, climbing moderately up the opposite slope. You will go in and out of more aspen and evergreens, then come to another boulder field, and go along a cliff. Around the cliff the trail breaks out into the open and climbs away from the creek.

As you climb, notice how Englemann spruce and Douglas fir grow less densely and how spruce, in particular, have been twisted and sculpted by the wind. Also take a moment to look back down valley at the Steamboat Springs area—a good view.

After switching back some more you will come to Upper Fish Creek Falls. You may want to take the side trail down to the falls and have a snack there, then continue up and around on the trail which is to your left as you are facing the falls. This would also be a good place to head back.

To head up to Long Lake switchback on the trail up and around the falls. The bittersweet smell of sage is in the air. The trail skirts the river and then comes close to it as you walk along the smooth face of a gneiss rock wall.

You will climb from the hot, dry slope into a bit of forest, again. Wildflowers and beautiful butterflies are plentiful. The trail becomes smaller, but still easy to follow as it nears the creek again and as you walk through meadows and then an area carpeted with golden mountain asters. Patches of "krummholz," with its twisted subalpine fir stand here and there.

After quite a walk through this subalpine area, you come into an open meadow and walk through tall skunk cabbage. Skirt the meadow on the left and follow the gentle trail until you get into some heavy-duty willows.

Notice the extensive glacial moraine on the hillside as you walk along. Keep hiking and cross Fish Creek—much smaller now—two times, go over some little hills, and then you will arrive at Long Lake.

Long Lake is, indeed, long, and pretty and quiet. You come upon the lake on its northwestern edge where wildflowers and grasses dominate. The opposite shore is defined by a wall of evergreens.

If you are going to stay overnight, be sure to camp well away from the lake.

You may want to return as you came next day. You can also take the Lake Percy Trail, which connects with the Fish Creek Falls Trail at the northeastern edge of the lake in the timber, to the east over the Continental Divide to Round Lake, Lake Percy, and Lake Elmo, among others.

You can also hike north from Long Lake on the Lake Percy Trail for about one mile to Fish Creek Reservoir and Granite Campground.—*Caryn Boddie*

HIKE 80 *SERVICE CREEK*

General description: A backpack along Service Creek in the northern part of the Gore Range.

General location: Approximately fifteen miles east of Yampa.

Maps: Blacktail Mtn., Walton Peak, and Lake Agnes USGS quads; Routt National Forest Map, Trails Illustrated Steamboat Springs South.

Degree of difficulty: Moderate.

Length: About twelve miles one way.

Elevations: 7,000 to 9,240 feet.

Special attractions: Very primitive area; historic log flumes and homesteads present; opportunity to view elk and deer.

Best season: Summer.

For more information: Routt National Forest, Yampa Ranger District, 300 Roselawn, P.O. Box 7, Yampa, CO 80483; (303) 638-4516.

The hike: This hike following Service Creek (originally named Sarvis Creek after the Sarvis Timber company's logging operations in the area), takes you through a very primitive area in the Gore Range, one which has been recommended for wilderness designation.

To reach the trailhead drive north on State Highway 131 from Yampa for eight miles to County Road 14. Follow County Road 14 east four miles to County Road 18A. Follow County Road 18A east .6 mile to County Road 18. Follow County Road 18 for 3.2 miles past Stagecoach Reservoir and dam. Below the dam look for the State Wildlife Area sign on the right and then cross the Yampa River to the trailhead.

To shuttle a vehicle to your ending point at the east end of the trail (at Buffalo Park) or to begin there, follow Colorado Highway 131 9.5 miles south from Yampa to Colorado Highway 134. Follow Highway 134 east eleven miles to Forest Route 250. Follow Forest Route 250 north nine miles to Forest Route 100, then take Forest Route 100, 8.5 miles to the trailhead at the north end of Buffalo Park.

Beginning at the west end, the trail leaves the parking area and rises through stands of spruce into Service Creek Canyon on the western side of the Gore Range, a faulted anticline with Precambrian rocks at its core. Further

HIKE 80 *SERVICE CREEK*

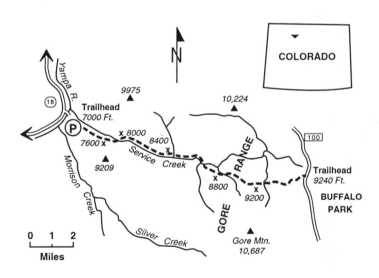

upstream, where the valley widens, there is evidence of glaciation (apparent as you look at your topographic map, an essential on this hike).

Although this portion of the Gore Range is below timberline, during glacial periods it received sufficient snowfall for small glaciers to form in the many tributary drainages to Service Creek. The small glaciers then combined to form a larger valley glacier. From the landforms evident on the topographic maps, this valley glacier terminated before reaching the main valley of the Yampa River. As you climb the Service Creek Canyon, you may want to look for glacial boulder and moraine deposits, indicating the terminus point. Continuing southeast, the trail enters a small mountain park. Notice the Douglas fir at the far end of the park on the steep slopes of the canyon. From this point, you pass through stands of aspen and finally enter dense spruce-fir forest at an elevation of 7,800 feet. For the next .9 mile the trail remains fairly level until it crosses a bridge over the creek.

Now, on the north side of the creek, you will notice that the creek disappears for several hundred yards. In another .3 mile the trail crosses a small open park. Remains of the Sarvis Timber Company's logging operations still exist here in the form of logging flumes built around 1913. Not long after, the company folded.

At mile post 4.5 the remains of an old homesteading cabin are visible on the other side of the river. Then the trail enters a series of small parks along the creek's edge: a good spot to camp, provided you can stay at least 200 feet back from the creek and the trail. At mile 6.5 you will enter a small lot of private land—the cabin and lodge are used for guided hunting and fishing trips—then, after another .8 mile, the trail leaves the main drainage, crosses through stands of lodgepole pine and connects with an old road. A short way along this road you come into Buffalo Park—an alpine meadow that once served as range for buffalo—and then connect with Forest Route 100, your destination if you are meeting a vehicle here. You have several options from this point. You might want to camp in Buffalo Park and then return the way you came.

Another option would be to walk south on Forest Route 100 about five miles to the Silver Creek Trail which will take you back to County Road 18A some seven miles southeast of the junction of County Roads 18A and 18, and about ten miles southeast of the Service Creek trailhead. If this is what you plan to do, you will want to shuttle a vehicle to the Silver Creek Trailhead before you start out on your hike.

While you are hiking this area keep your eyes open for big game animals, and be sure to wear blaze orange in the fall. This is a popular hunting area. Other denizens that may be seen in the Routt National Forest are bear, bighorn sheep, mountain lion, coyote, beaver, marmot, ptarmigan, and various raptors. Fishing is considered excellent in the upper part of Service Creek in Buffalo Park for small brook trout. The lower part is heavily fished.—*U.S. Forest Service.*

HIKE 81 _ENCAMPMENT RIVER LOOP_

General description: A two- to three-day backback along two forks of the Encampment River in the northern end of the Mount Zirkel Wilderness Area.
General location: Approximately thirty miles northwest of Walden. Maps: USGS West Fork Lake, Davis Peak and Mt. Zirkel quads; Routt National Forest Map.
Degree of difficulty: Moderate.
Length: Seventeen miles round trip.
Elevations: 8,500 to 9,800 feet.
Special attractions: Two beautiful glaciated valleys leading into the Mount Zirkel Wilderness; great fishing; opportunities to see big game; pretty alpine lake in a spectacular setting.
Best season: Summer and fall.
For more information: Routt National Forest, North Park Ranger District, 612 5th St., P.O. Box 158, Walden, CO 80480; (303) 723-4707.

The hike: The Encampment River is one of the most pristine rivers in northern Colorado and has been suggested for inclusion in the National Wild and Scenic Rivers System. With its headwaters in the Mount Zirkel Wilderness Area, this river provides excellent fishing and hiking opportunities. One enjoyable route combines trails along the Main and West Forks of the river, forming a loop of about seventeen miles. This loop makes for an excellent two- or three-day backpack which can be extended by following connecting trails into the wilderness area.

To reach the trailhead for the Encampment River Loop, take Colorado Highway 125 north from Walden about nine miles to Cowdrey. Turn left on County Road 6W and follow it for about twenty miles, past Pearl. Then turn left on County Road 6B toward Hog Park Reservoir. Continue west on this road, past the forest boundary, about fifteen miles to Commissary Park. Turn left just past the bridge over the Encampment River and follow this small road south. Park just past the Hog Park Guard Station. From this point, the trailhead for the West Fork Trail is one mile straight ahead and the trailhead for the Main Fork Trail is two miles. However, parking at this spot is recommended: the jeep roads are rough and boggy and the wet meadows ahead especially fragile. (Note: The Forest Service is planning to change the location of the trailhead soon. You may want to call the district office before you go.)

This meadow area, Commissary Park, was named for the town of Commissary located just north of the guard station in the early 1890s. The town was a supply depot for the tie hacks, those hardy souls who cut railroad ties and floated them down the Encampment River to the railroad in Wyoming.

As you begin your hike, the jeep road will fork. To the right is the Ellis Trail, which continues on towards the town of Columbine. To the left is the road which leads to the trailheads. Go left, and after fording the West Fork, you will come to another branch in the road. Another left turn leads to the Main Fork trailhead after fording the Main Fork of the Encampment River. A right turn takes you to the West Fork Trail.

If you take the West Fork Trail it is about six miles to West Fork Lake and another mile to the intersection with the Main Fork Trail. As you hike along

HIKE 81 ENCAMPMENT RIVER LOOP

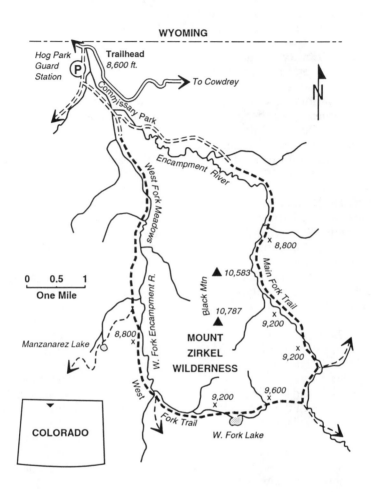

what was once a popular jeep trail you head out of stands of lodgepole pine, cross the West Fork again (there is good fishing here for brook and brown trout) and come into West Fork Meadows. To the east looms Black Mountain, a recent addition to the Mount Zirkel Wilderness. Follow the trail marker posts across the meadow and into forest again. There is then practically no grade for several miles and the wide trail is easy to follow.

You will reach the boundary of the Mount Zirkel Wilderness Area just before you begin the steep climb to West Fork Lake, blessed with a spectacular setting and good fishing. Several beaten out campsites along the north shore attest to past years of heavy use. In order to protect this overused area, please camp well way from both the lake and trail (at least 200 feet).

Next day, after making sure you've left no trace of your presence at your campsite, follow the West Fork Trail another mile through open stands of lodgepole pine and over the broad saddle to the Main Fork Trail. At this point you can go south (right) for a more extended backpack to Encampment Meadows, Gem Lake, or beyond into the Mount Zirkel Wilderness. Or you can go north (left) and down the Main Fork of the Encampment River to your vehicle in about eight miles.

As you follow the Main Fork downstream, you will notice that the meadows become smaller and the Encampment River ever larger, growing from a gently meandering brook to a boulder strewn rushing stream. Watch for mule deer and elk in the high meadows—good habitat in summer and fall.—*U.S. Forest Service*

Columbine.

The Plateaus

West of Colorado's highest mountains lies the plateau country. To the uninitiated it is hot, dry and humdrum. But to hikers who have explored there it is an enchanted land. Nowhere else in Colorado have natural forces produced a greater variety of landscapes and life zones, from the tundra and glacial lakes of the highest plateaus to the meandering desert canyons cut by the West's great rivers.

The following hikes will take you through the various terrains of plateau country. We hope you enjoy them.

HIKE 82 *LIMESTONE RIDGE*

General description: An overnight hike to the high point at the eastern edge of the O-wi-yu-kuts Plateau.

General location: Approximately eighty miles northwest of Craig.

Maps: Irish Canyon and Big Joe Basin USGS quads.

Degree of difficulty: Moderate.

Length: Twelve to fourteen miles one way.

Elevations: 6,200 to 8,636 feet.

Special attractions: Views of Irish Canyon, the Vermillion Creek Basin, and Brown's Park—highly colorful examples of various geologic phenomena; a remarkable standing burnt pinyon forest; various archeological sites; a profusion of wildlife.

Best season: Spring, winter and fall, excluding hunting season.

For more information: Bureau of Land Management, Craig District Office, 455 Emerson, P.O. Box 248, Craig, CO 81626; (303) 824-8261.

The hike: Limestone Ridge offers a unique opportunity to experience an area largely ignored by hikers. It is characterized by pinyon-juniper forests, sage and grass parks, and windswept ridges that command sweeping views of a fascinating area. The twelve to fourteen-mile round trip described here could be made in a day, but a night out helps to fully absorb the experience.

From US 40 at Maybell, take Colorado Highway 318 northwest for approximately 41.5 miles to Moffat County Road 10N. Go north on County Road 10 about four miles. Turn left (west) onto a small dirt track passable, barring deep snow or mud, in any vehicle, 1.5 miles to a good camping spot (minus water). Park off the main gravel road; all of this land is administered by the Bureau of Land Management.

A wide trail, built for cattle drives, leads from the parking area northwest through thick juniper stands that open up .6 mile on, where you pass through an old gate. Around 1970 a fire burnt this area, leaving the curious and haunting skeletons of pinyons and junipers and exposing the succeeding benches of red sandstone which build toward the ridges. The fire also made for easy off trail walking, at a northeast bearing, from the gate toward the top of the high bench rising 500 feet. This climb is the most demanding part of the hike,

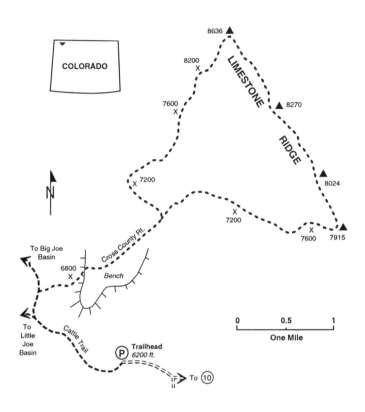

but it is fun. Exertion can be minimized by careful inspection and route selection. The edge of this bench is a good place to camp and provides an excellent view of Brown's Park and the Green River as it cuts into the eastern-most finger of the Uinta Range, forming Lodore Canyon in Dinosaur National Monument.

If you left your car before 9:00 A.M., you'll probably want to leave most of your gear here and head on with day packs to the top of the ridge to your east. If you gain the ridge directly from your camp and head for the southern end first you can largely avoid the down and up of another drainage. In addition you'll have an excellent view of dramatic Irish Canyon, which displays twelve different geologic outcroppings and is noteworthy in that it was formed by two parallel faults rather than the cutting action of water.

The length of the ridge is an easy walk, climbing gradually to the north and offering excellent views in all directions. To the northeast the badlands of the Vermilion Creek drainage display their colors and to the north is rugged Wyoming rangeland above which, on a very clear day, the snowcapped peaks of the Wind River Range are visible. To the northwest and west the O-wi-yu-kuts Plateau stretches into the high Uintas. South of Cold Springs Mountain, at the end of the plateau, Brown's Park stretches west towards Red Canyon, flooded to form Flaming Gorge Reservoir. Southeast and east are the Flat Top Mountains and the Continental Divide.

The ridgetop provides a good vantage point from which to observe golden and bald eagles, vultures, and an occasional peregrine falcon. Elk are numerous, with herds of over 200 grazing at times along the parks just below the ridge. You may be lucky enough to see mountain lion or moose, too, but are more likely to spot antelope, deer, coyote, or fox.

You can also select your route back to camp from the ridge or perhaps satisfy your curiousity with a detour into Big Joe Basin or Little Joe Basin. Be on the alert for pictographs or petroglyphs, as there is much evidence of earlier cultures throughout the region.

This area was dropped from the BLM wilderness inventory largely because of the extent of roads and stockpond improvements. Still under consideration is an area approximately seven miles to the west (extending into Utah) called Cold Springs Mountain. It deserves our support. Hiking here in winter is recommended for several reasons. Summer means heat, rattlesnakes, and no snow to melt for safe drinking water.

Remember that this arid ecosystem is fragile and slow to regenerate when disturbed. The magic of the area would be diminished by clumsy camping, so please use a campstove, walk lightly, and let your spirit soar with the raptors of the area.

If you have a spare minute on your drive home, you will want to stop at the southern mouth of Irish Canyon and view the petroglyphs.—*John Randolph*

HIKE 83 *CROSS MOUNTAIN*

General description: A day hike or backpack along Cross Mountain in northwestern Colorado.

General location: Approximately forty-five miles west of Craig.

Maps: Lone Mountain and Cross Mountain Canyon, Twelve-mile Mesa, and Peck Mesa USGS quads; Canyon of Lodore and Rangley BLM color quads.

Degree of difficulty: Moderate to difficult.

Length: Two to eight miles one way.

Elevations: 5,600 to 7,800 feet.

Special attractions: Cross Mountain Canyon; wildlife including bighorn sheep and raptors; panoramic views of surrounding semi-arid country and Dinosaur National Monument. Recommended for wilderness designation.

Best season: Late spring and fall.

For more information: Bureau of Land Management, 455 Emerson Street, Craig, CO 81625; (303) 824-8261.

The hike: Cross Mountain is a beautiful and unique hiking experience in Colorado's northwestern plateau country. This Bureau of Land Management Wilderness Study Area features deep Cross Mountain Canyon on the Yampa River, several archeological sites, bighorn sheep, and raptors such as bald eagles and peregrine falcons.

Cross Mountain is considered to be the eastern-most extension of the Uinta Mountains, an oblong, flat-topped mountain that trends ten miles north to south and rises 2,200 feet above the floodplain of the Yampa River (on the east) and the Little Snake River (on the west). It is an easily distinguishable landmark, approximately four miles wide with the highest point (7,804 feet) in the north. There are no developed hiking trails but many good hiking routes traverse the side canyons and ridges, and this is an area where you are on your own.

One of the easiest routes into this spectacular area can be reached by taking US Highway 40 to the Deerlodge Park Road about sixteen miles west of Maybell. Follow Deerlodge Road along the west side of Cross Mountain to the turnout for the National Park Service parking area at the mouth of the Cross Mountain Canyon.

From the Park Service parking lot, by taking the first drainage to the south, you may begin a five- to six-mile round trip day hike along the south rim of the canyon up to the top of Cross Mountain and back to the rim. The terrain is at times steep and rocky but does not require any special climbing skills. Once on the rim, walking is easy through pinyon-juniper woodlands and you have a good view into the canyon while the roar of the river echoes below you.

The Yampa River has cut 1,200-foot-deep Cross Mountain Canyon through the south end of the mountain, an example of a superimposed westward flowing stream on the Cross Mountain anticline. It has entrenched the resistant Mesozoic and Paleozoic rock layers, all sedimentary, to form incised

Bighorn Lambs.

HIKE 83 CROSS MOUNTAIN

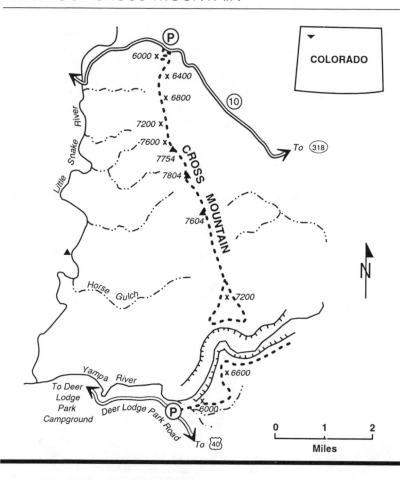

meanders within the canyon. Watch for turkey vultures, golden eagles (or bald eagles, when they migrate in winter), and prairie falcons soaring above the Yampa. Peregrine falcons nest in nearby canyons and in Dinosaur National Monument and may be seen here, also. Continued protection of the cliffs where these raptors nest and maintenance of undisturbed roosting and hunting areas is critical to their survival, so do not harrass or disturb any nest or nesting area you come upon. The river itself has been the target of much controversy. The proposed Juniper-Cross Mountain hydroelectric project, tabled for now because of economic reasons, would flood the canyon to a depth of 200 feet.

Other hikes are possible on the north end of the mountain, where there are many colorful wildflowers in late spring and early summer. This cross country route might follow the ridge that is the backbone of Cross Mountain to its highest point and beyond. Vehicle access around the mountain is generally good from Moffat County Road 10 when it is dry. Most of the mountain is covered with pinyon-juniper woodlands and vast sagebrush openings.

The top is open, flat, and covered with grasses, allowing for panoramic views in all directions. On a clear day, you can see eighty to ninety miles eastward to the Continental Divide or westward over Dinosaur National Monument and into Utah.

Interesting geologic features along this route include colorful formations, up to a billion years old, exposed on the mountain. The Madison limestone, Pennsylvanian age Morgan and Chinle formations containing fossils and petrified wood, outcrop on the mountain and in the canyon. Minor outcrops of the Morrison formation also occur (the same formation containing the dinosaur bones found in Dinosaur National Monument to the west).

Be sure to watch for wildlife while hiking Cross Mountain. There are elk, deer, antelope, mountain lion, coyote, small mammals, bats and bighorn sheep.

The bighorns, reintroduced here in 1977 by the Colorado Division of Wildlife and the BLM, inhabit upper slopes and grassy areas. They use the Yampa River as a water source and the north canyon rim as a lambing area. Maintenance of solitude, water sources, and grassland/mountain shrub vegetation is vital to their survival—another case for the establishment of a wilderness area here.

While I was hiking here in mid-canyon in October of 1983, I stumbled upon a young ram snoozing behind the boulder on which I was standing. We were not more than three feet apart. I quickly sat down out of sight to get my camera ready when he suddenly and quietly jumped upon the rock right beside me. We looked each other straight in the eye, then he turned and ran down the canyon before I could snap a picture.

Keep your eyes open for archaeological sites as you hike. It is believed that the diversity of topography and life zones on Cross Mountain attracted prehistoric peoples throughout the last 12,000 years. You may come upon rock art (petroglyphs and pictographs), granaries, campsites with lithic scatter from stone tool manufacture, and rock shelters and caves. Please remember that all archaeologic sites and artifacts are protected by federal law and may not be disturbed or collected.

Remember these few things to have a safe and enjoyable hike on Cross Mountain:

- Carry all your drinking water.
- Watch for rattlesnakes.
- Use a stove if you're backpacking.
- If you're hiking during October and November, wear the requisite blaze orange and be very careful. There are many deer and elk hunters in the area during that time.
- Follow the minimum impact rules discussed at the beginning of this book.—*Dave Cooper*

HIKE 84 *K-CREEK*

General description: A day hike into the edge of the BLM Bull Canyon Wilderness Study Area with camping possibilities and great views.
General location: Just south of Dinosaur National Monument.
Maps: Plug Hat Rock and Snake John Reef USGS quads.
Degree of difficulty: Easy to difficult, depending on route.

Length: 5.5 miles round trip.

Elevations: 6,850 to 7,529 feet.

Special attractions: Good views; lots of wildlife, colorful geologic formations.

Best season: Early summer.

For more information: Bureau of Land Management, White River Resource Area, 73455 Highway 64, P.O. Box 928, Meeker, CO 81641; (303) 878-3601

The hike: A half-day hike that offers spectacular desert vistas, K-Creek is located at the edge of the Bureau of Land Management (BLM) Bull Canyon Wilderness Study Area, very near Dinosaur National Monument. You'll be hiking along a southern slope where it can be very hot, so the best times to visit are during the spring and fall. However, tenacious cedar gnats are numerous in the spring and hunters are in the area in the fall, so perhaps early summer would be best. If you do go in the spring take lots of insect repellent. If you go in the fall, be sure to wear blaze orange. Be sure to take plenty of water on your hike. You won't find any in the area except at the expedition site where there is a flowing well. And, please respect private property and leave any artifacts you find.

To reach the area, drive east from the town of Dinosaur on US Highway 40 for one mile to the Dinosaur National Monument turnoff. Travel up the park road (Harper's Corner Road) 11.6 miles. To the left is a graded dirt road named Miner's Draw Road. Although there is no sign, the road is obvious and there is a cattle guard across it. Drive down this road about .25 mile and park where you see a steep jeep road drop off to the left.

There are several sandstone finger canyons to explore in this little-visited Wilderness Study Area, including Middle Creek, Richardson Draw, Buckwater Draw and Bull Canyon. Together they form a very scenic canyonland. Cottonwoods line the drainages, while pinyon and juniper make up the remainder of the dominant vegetation. An extended backpack here would be a dfficult trip over rough terrain.

Eventually all drainages converge at the lush K Ranch (private property that should be respected), built on a campsite of the Escalante Expedition of 1776. Remember that you are on BLM land and that cattle are grazed on the upper elevations during the summer, so if you open a gate, be sure to close it again.

Your hike begins as you walk down the jeep trail past some springs to the trail's end, climb a fence, and continue downhill along the creek, where you will encounter another road. Follow it west and downhill along the creek. Many small roads wander about in this area; just stay on the one that follows closest to the creek. After about a mile, cross the creek and follow it on the trail to your right. You will come to yet another road and an open area. Head in a southwesterly direction across this plateau. You will go through an ancient juniper stand to the plateau's edge. There are many rock outcrops from which to enjoy the spectacular views of the desert beyond and the canyons below. To the west are the impressive geologic folds of Blue Mountain. At the mouth of the canyon is the K Ranch. To the south are the other canyons making up this canyon land.

You'll encounter a variety of wildlife in K-Creek, including deer and predatory birds. We also encountered an unusual phenomenon while hiking in late July: migration of Mormon crickets, the large, wingless grasshoppers common in the arid West. When migrating, they move across the countryside

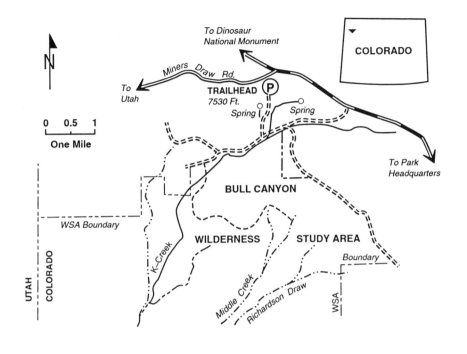

by the millions, completely covering the ground in some areas. They are harmless—at least to hikers—and the migration is an astonishing thing to see.

K-Creek becomes brushy below the plateau, but for those who don't mind bushwhacking, there are Indian petroglyphs to be found in the lower canyons. Otherwise, return from the plateau by the same route.—*Mary Menconi and Rich Boddie*

HIKE 85 *EAST FORK TRAIL*

General description: A backpack along a beautiful valley in the northern end of the Flat Tops Wilderness.

General location: Fifteen miles southwest of Yampa.

Maps: Devils Causeway and Dunckley Pass USGS quads; Trails Illustrated Flat Tops NE map.

Degree of difficulty: Moderate.

Length: Up to fourteen miles one way.

Elevations: 8,400 to 11,600 feet.

Special attractions: Varied terrain; beautiful views; fair to good fishing.

Best season: Summer and fall.

For more information: Routt National Forest, Yampa Ranger District, 300 Roselawn, P.O. Box 7, Yampa, CO 80483; (303) 638-4516.

The hike: This hike takes you across a narrow saddle in the Flat Tops at the base of the Devils Causeway and into the East Fork of the Williams Fork River valley, all within the Flat Tops Wilderness. Along the way the trail traverses a variety of terrain (from tundra to thick forest) and passes alpine lakes. This hike can be a short day hike to the Devils Causeway or a fourteen-mile trip for the length of the trail, which requires a car shuttle. Side trips to numerous lakes in the area are also possible.

To reach the trailhead, turn west on the road along the Bear River at the south end of the town of Yampa. Follow it as it becomes Forest Route 900 and leads to Stillwater Reservoir and a common trailhead for several trails. Begin your hike at the west end of the parking lot at the trail registration station where there is a map of the area.

If you plan on following the East Fork Trail to its end at the Pyramid Guard Station you will want to shuttle a vehicle to that point. To do so, turn west at the north end of Yampa on the Dunckley Pass Road, which becomes Forest

Pronghorn antelope. Colorado Division of Wildlife photo.

HIKE 85 *EAST FORK TRAIL*

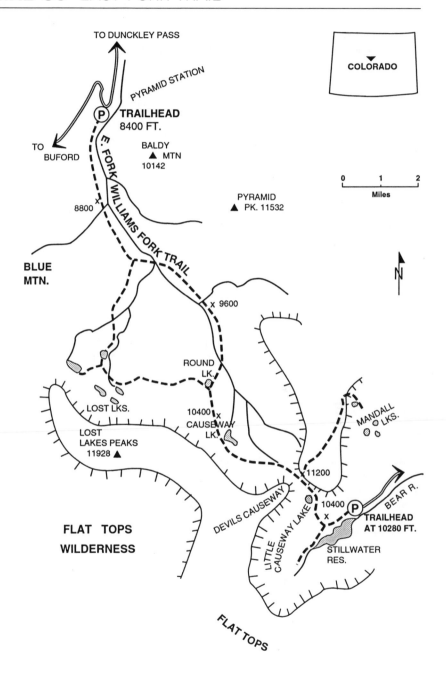

TO DUNCKLEY PASS

PYRAMID STATION

Ⓟ **TRAILHEAD**
8400 FT.

TO BUFORD

BALDY
▲ MTN
10142

E. FORK WILLIAMS FORK TRAIL

8800 ×

PYRAMID
▲ PK. 11532

BLUE MTN.

× 9600

ROUND LK.

LOST LKS.

10400 ×
CAUSEWAY
LK.

LOST LAKES PEAKS
11928 ▲

MANDALL LKS.

×11200

DEVILS CAUSEWAY

FLAT TOPS
WILDERNESS

LITTLE CAUSEWAY LAKE

10400
×

Ⓟ **TRAILHEAD**
AT 10280 FT.

BEAR R.

STILLWATER RES.

FLAT TOPS

COLORADO

0   1   2
Miles

N

Route 16. Follow this road northwest over Dunckley Pass and continue south, where the road forks, and on to Pyramid Station. Park in the area provided north of the Forest Route.

For the first .8 mile the trail takes you along the north shore of Stillwater Reservoir and then it turns north at the junction with the Bear River Trail. The East Fork Trail then climbs slowly through scattered stands of spruce and fir, crosses the wilderness boundary at 1.2 miles from the trailhead and follows the talus slopes of the adjacent plateau. To the west, a short distance off the trail, is Little Causeway Lake with fair fishing for brook trout.

For the next .4 mile, the trail climbs steeply to a saddle at 11,600 feet on the ridge dividing the Bear River and Williams Fork drainages. There are beautiful views of the alpine environment of the Flat Tops from here.

If you would like to view the Devils Causeway, ascend the ridge to the southwest, a short climb of 200 feet that is well worth the effort. Here the plateau is only four feet wide and drops some 1,500 feet to the valley below.

Crossing into the Williams Fork Valley, you will pass the junction with the Mandall Lakes Trail and head down into thick stands of spruce, fir and aspen, dotted with alpine lakes. Legend has it that this valley was named after Old Bill Williams, a scout and trapper who explored Colorado's mountains in the 1830s.

You will descend slowly, coming to Causeway Lake at mile 5.2 and then, in another 1.2 miles, to Round Lake and the Lost Lakes Trail, which heads off to your left. These lakes are deep, offer good fishing, and make a good side trip or alternative hiking destination.

This part of the valley was burned by a forest fire around the turn of the century and has still not recovered. A lightning strike is believed to have been the cause. Continuing in a northerly direction, East Fork Trail crosses the East Fork of the Williams Fork River, which offers fair to good fishing for brook, cutthroat and rainbow trout, and then meets the Black Mountain Trail, which follows Black Mountain Creek. The East Fork Trail goes straight ahead towards the Blue Mountain Slide.

At mile 10.2 you cross the river once again, climb a small hill via a series of switchbacks and meet the looping Lost Lakes Trail again. This crossing can be dangerous during high water.

For the next 3.6 miles the trail continues towards its destination at the Guard Ranger Station, meeting the Transfer Trail as it does, which heads off to the left. After continuing straight on from this junction and leaving the wilderness, the trail ends at some Forest Service buildings. Please, do not enter the buildings.

A short walk takes you to the parking area just north of Forest Route 16, where you should have a vehicle waiting for you, unless you are planning to return as you came. You can, of course, expand your backpack by exploring any of the trails you came into contact with as you followed the East Fork Trail.—*U.S. Forest Service.*

HIKE 86 *HOOPER LAKE*

General description: A day hike or overnighter to a beautiful alpine lake at the base of the Flat Tops.

General location: Fifteen miles southwest of Yampa.

Maps: Orno Peak and Dome Peak USGS quads; Routt and White River National Forest Maps, Trails Illustrated Flat Tops NE.

Degree of difficulty: Easy.

Length: Six miles round trip.

Elevations: 10,300 to 11,300 feet.

Special attractions: Scenic view of the impressive basalt cliffs that rim the Flat Tops; good fishing.

Best season: Summer through early fall.

For more information: Routt National Forest, Yampa Ranger District, 300 Roselawn, P.O. Box 7, Yampa, CO 80483; (303) 638-4516.

The hike: The trail to Hooper Lake takes you into the Flat Tops Wilderness Area where you will find interesting geology, beautiful scenery and good fishing.

To reach the trailhead, drive thirty miles south of Steamboat Springs or forty-two miles north of Wolcott on Colorado Highway 131 to the town of Yampa. Leave the highway and go into town. In the southwest corner of town near the Antlers Bar there is a paved road which follows the Bear River and leads to the trailhead. Follow this road to its end at Stillwater Reservoir. It is about fifteen miles or so and you can't get lost.

There is a relatively large parking area at the end of the road and it's likely to be packed with cars. Don't worry, this is the take-off point for numerous fishermen who are out for the day, as well as for other hikers heading off in many different directions. There is a sign pointing the way to Hooper and Keener Lakes near the end of the parking lot. Take a left turn and walk along the dam that impounds Sweetwater Reservoir. After about .25 mile or so (near the end of the dam) look for the Hooper Lake Trail to the left. It isn't marked but is easy to pick out. There are no other forks from here to the lake.

You will travel through open country for several hundred yards after you leave the dam, then enter forest and begin to climb at a moderate grade. About .5 mile after entering the forest, the trail levels off and then bends to the right, passing a few small ponds. It then turns left and climbs along a small stream. The climb steepens considerably when it leaves this stream, but the views get better and better as you approach the divide which separates Sweetwater Reservoir from Hooper Lake. You reach the divide after one last short, steep climb.

This is a good spot to pause, rest and enjoy the panoramic views of the Sweetwater Lake area, the Flat Tops to the northwest, and Derby Creek valley to the south. To the east is Flat Top Mountain whose broad grassy slopes make for an easy climb and an even more spectacular view. The basalt cliffs to the west of the divide are impressive, but cannot be ascended without technical climbing gear. This area is on the northeastern end of the Flat Tops Wilderness Area, one of the earlier wilderness areas to be established in Colorado.

The Flat Tops area is the most uplifted part of the White River Plateau and

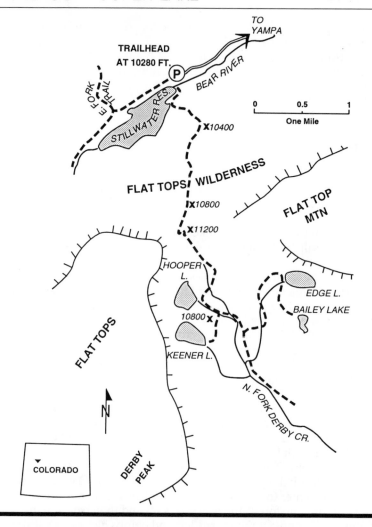

includes extensive areas above timberline. Hooper Lake, like most of the lakes in the Flat Tops, was sculpted by glaciers which formed in the depressions or cirques along the rim of this high plateau. The spectacular cliffs which extend for many miles in all directions are formed by resistant basalt capping the top of the plateau. The trail continues south from the divide, winding through gently sloping meadows. It becomes a bit obscure in places, but within a few hundred yards of the divide you can see Hooper Lake, sporadically good fishing for rainbow trout to fourteen inches. There are good camping areas along the north and east sides of the lake; the south and west sides are rather rugged. Be sure to camp 200 feet from the lake itself, though. And one word of caution on selecting your campsite: many of the trees surrounding the lake are dead and may be blown over by strong winds. Our party didn't worry about it much when we camped here until about two o'clock in the morning when a storm blew through. Next day, we noticed some freshly-downed trees nearby.

The main trail continues past the lower end of Hooper Lake. Several hundred yards past Hooper Lake there is a right turn to Keener Lake. The main trail winds down along the North Fork of Derby Creek to a very scenic meadow about .5 mile below. A trail to the left in this meadow leads you to Edge and Bailey Lakes.—*Bill Bath*

HIKE 87 *GRIZZLY CREEK*

General description: An easily accessible day hike along Grizzly Creek, a fast-moving tributary of the Colorado River, which forms a deep canyon in the White River Plateau.
General location: Six miles east of Glenwood Springs.
Maps: Glenwood Springs, Carbonate USGS quads; White River National Forest Map, Trails Illustrated Flat Tops SE map.
Degree of difficulty: Moderate.
Length: Six miles one way.
Elevations: 6,000 to 8,000 feet.
Special attractions: Towering Grizzly Creek Canyon; good views of lower Grizzly Creek toward Glenwood Canyon and Glenwood Springs; excellent, though difficult, fishing.
Best season: Summer and fall.
For more information: White River National Forest, Rifle Ranger District, 0094 County Road 244, Rifle, CO 81650; (303) 625-2371.

The hike: This is a well-traveled trail due to its accessibility from Interstate 70. Yet, because of the dense foliage, there is little sense of overcrowding.

To reach the trailhead, drive east from Glenwood Springs about five miles on I-70 to the Grizzly Creek exit. Take the road on the east side of the creek approximately .5 mile to Grizzly Creek Picnic Ground and the trailhead.

Grizzly Creek is a large creek that has sliced through the White River Plateau to drain south into the muddy Colorado. The White River Plateau is composed of sedimentary rocks that fold downward sharply along its south and west edges for 135 miles. The creek, starting high in the snows atop the plateau, runs clear and fast through the limestone canyon it has cut. It offers excellent but difficult fishing (big boulders and the narrow canyon hinder casting efforts) for ten-inch brook trout in the upper reaches and twelve to fourteen-inch whitefish along the lower stretches when they run from the Colorado River in mid-October.

The Grizzly Creek Trail primarily follows Grizzly Creek through the narrow and very rocky (watch your footing) canyon. It begins in dense foliage, which obscures your views except of the river and the rims of the canyon overhead. As you hike, keep a lookout for some of the limestone solution caves along the cliffs. Water is available along the entire trail (you'll have to purify it, though).

After the first mile, the trail climbs at a steeper grade on the hillside, then descends again to the creek before rising sharply from 6,000 feet to the upper reaches of the canyon.

At points, the trail opens up briefly to offer views of mountain ridges ahead, and at about the three mile point, you'll have excellent views of lower Grizzly Creek and of Glenwood Canyon with its deep-cut gorges. At 8,000 feet, from higher ridges, you'll have a more extensive view down the canyon all of the way to Glenwood Springs.

HIKE 87 *GRIZZLY CREEK*

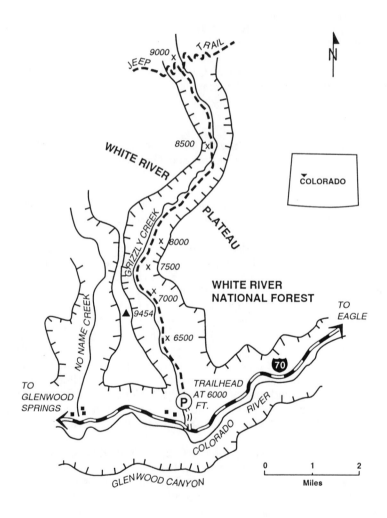

Grizzly Creek. Gilbert Frye photo.

At no point along the six-mile trail is the grade particularly severe, though the narrow tread and loose rocks do make footing treacherous. Good shoes are in order.

Your day hike can extend to a backpack to the top of the plateau. Simply continue on the Grizzly Creek Trail for about six miles and camp in the upper reaches of the canyon where it is more open. In another three miles you will connect with a jeep trail that will take you to the top of the plateau. Return as you came.

If you've marvelled at the colors and cut of Glenwood Canyon while driving I-70 to Glenwood Springs, then you'll find some special rewards in the canyon of Grizzly Creek, with its rushing water, towering walls, and evergreen forests.—*Gib and Liz Frye*

HIKE 88 *THREE FORKS TRAIL*

General description: A day hike or short overnight hike in a forested canyon at the western edge of the White River Plateau.
General location: About fifteen miles north of Rifle.
Maps: Triangle Park quad; White River National Forest map; Trails Illustrated Flat Tops SW map.
Degree of difficulty: Moderate.
Length: 5.5 miles one way.
Elevations: 7,600 to 9,300 feet.

Special attractions: Mid-elevation forests and meadows in canyon and plateau terrain; numerous deer and elk; and unique disappearing stream.
Best season: Summer and fall.
For more information: White River National Forest, Rifle Ranger District, 0094 County Road 244, Rifle, CO 81650; (303) 625-2371.

The Hike: The Three Forks Trail north of Rifle provides an easily accessible introduction to the forested plateau and canyon country of the White River Plateau, an extensive uplift which rises gradually from the Grand Hogback on the southwest and west, and culminates in the high peaks and mesas of the Flat Tops to the north and northeast.

To reach the Three Forks Trail, take Colorado Highway 13 north from Rifle and turn onto Colorado Highway 325 at the sign for Rifle Gap Reservoir. Follow this route to the reservoir, across the dam, and on past the Rifle Falls State Park, the Rifle Falls Fish Hatchery, and the City of Rifle Mountain Park, to the Three Forks Campground. Once you reach the campground, continue on to the parking area at the north end and look for the trail taking off along the left (west) side.

The Three Forks Trail follows the west side of the valley for the first .3 mile and then enters a long meadow where there is a bridge across Three Forks Creek. There are a number of good fishing spots along the creek both upstream and downstream of the bridge and people staying at the campground often do not continue beyond this point.

Cross over the bridge and follow the east bank of the creek. Notice the lupine, mountain aster, and penstamen, and the big spruce (some of them blue spruce) down along the river.

The first side stream you come to is called Stump Gulch. Cross over and continue on a short distance to a fork in the trail. You may take either trail, because they meet again at a little saddle in the distance; the trail to the right stays up high on the edge of the meadow, the left goes straight up the meadow.

About one and one-half miles along the trail through aspen forests mingled with spruce and even big old narrowleaf cottonwoods you'll come to a junction with another trail. A side trail goes up Garden Gulch to the northeast. The Three Forks Trail (Trail 2150) goes down to your left and up the main valley; follow it.

About .25 mile past the trail junction, you come to GV Creek, which comes down from Irish Gulch. Bear to the left and look for the sign marked 2150. A short way above GV Creek, the trail crosses over Three Forks Creek and meets the trail to Coulter Lake. It looks as if horseback riders use this as a loop route down to the campground and up again. Before this point there is series of springs and the stream above the spring is dry most of the year (at least it was in July). Look carefully for the trail sign saying 2150 to show you where the Three Forks Trail turns upstream through an aspen forest decorated with lots of monkshood flowers. Cross the creek again in about .1 mile (still dry) and climb .3 mile from the junction with the Coulter Lake Trail through a steep aspen forest and to a meadow to find running water again. Look at the end of the meadow before the channel drops steeply down a gully and through the aspen forest; you'll find that the stream doesn't go down the gully but disappears into a sink hole about fifteen feet deep and twenty feet around instead. Probably the presence of limestone beneath your feet made this interesting phenomenon possible.

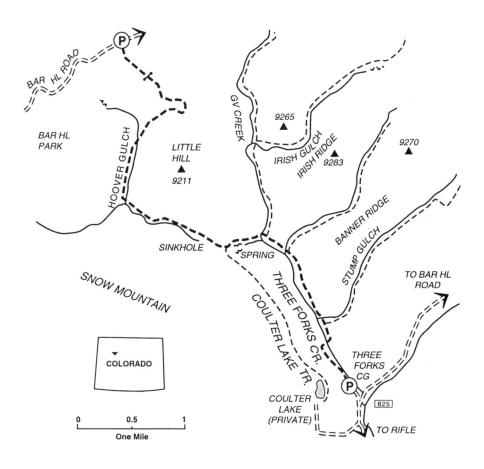

Continue on to the upper meadows where the trail takes off and up a side gulch and out the top to the Bar HL Road, where you can end your hike if you shuttled a car. Otherwise, return as you came.

This would be a nice hike to take in the fall with all the aspen. It's generally an enjoyable and interesting hike with changing ecosystems, waterfalls, the sinkhole, and active beaver dams. You might want to camp in the campground at the bottom and go fishing in the early evening.—*Peter Boddie*

HIKE 89 *SPRING CANYON*

General description: A long day hike or overnighter into the canyons of the Little Book Cliffs Wild Horse Area.

General location: Ten miles northeast of Grand Junction.

Maps: Cameo and Round Mountain USGS quads.

Degree of difficulty: Moderate to difficult.

Length: Nine miles one way.

Elevations: 5,000 to 7,000 feet.

Special attractions: Spectacular canyons; desert and semi-arid flora; intricate rock formations; opportunity to spot wild horses.

Best season: Spring.

For more information: Bureau of Land Management, Grand Junction Resource Area, 764 Horizon Drive, Grand Junction, CO 81506; (303) 243-6552.

The hike: A hike into Spring Canyon in the Little Book Cliffs Wild Horse area provides an opportunity to spot some of Colorado's rare wild horses, as well as to explore a seldom-visited canyon. The length of this hike can be varied according to the time available and the hiker's ability, with the hike increasing in difficulty as you go along. If you choose to backpack, you could easily spend several days exploring the many canyons and rolling upland areas of this BLM Wilderness Study Area.

The Little Book Cliffs Wild Horse Area includes several deep (1,000 feet) canyons which dissect a gently sloping plateau. This plateau is bordered on the west by the spectacular Book Cliffs, a 1,500-foot escarpment that extends for many miles into Utah. The lower canyons are semi-desert with vegetation consisting primarily of sagebrush, rabbitbrush and fourwinged saltbrush. The upland areas include pinyon-juniper woodlands interspersed with sage and grass meadows. A hike along the length of Spring Canyon will take you through this entire range of topography and vegetation, culminating in a spectacular view from the top of the Book Cliffs. The chance to see wild horses along the way adds to the intriguing nature of this hike.

To reach Spring Canyon, take Interstate 70 east from Grand Junction or west from DeBeque to the Cameo exit. Follow the paved road alongside the highway and across the bridge over the Colorado River to the electrical generating plant. Continue straight past the plant, across an irrigation ditch and on up the dirt road into the canyon ahead. There are several service roads associated with the nearby coal mining and power plant operations, but it is easy to determine which road continues on into the canyon. This road becomes progressively smaller and more rugged as it makes several crossings of the Coal Canyon streambed. However, when dry, it should be accessible to most passenger cars. Should you find it necessary to park somewhere along the way, it is only about 1.5 miles from the power plant to the take-off point for the Spring Canyon hike.

The take-off point is reached where you see a road climbing to the right and over a low saddle. Just ahead on the main road are a cattle guard and a BLM boundary sign. Park at the base of the side road and begin hiking up to the saddle. At the top there is a locked gate, which you will have to climb over or around, and below you is Main Canyon which drains the wilderness study area.

HIKE 89 *SPRING CANYON*

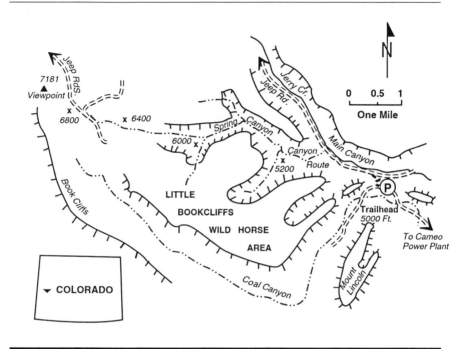

Descend from the saddle along the road to the canyon bottom. After crossing the often dry streambed of Jerry Creek, follow the jeep road up Main Canyon while crossing the creek several more times. This stretch of the trail along Main Canyon is notable for the inspiring views it provides many miles up the canyon to the headwaters of the creek on the plateau above. When these upland areas are cloaked in clouds and the canyons resound with thunder, be prepared for the dry streambed of Jerry Creek and its many side canyons to quickly change into a raging torrent of water, mud, rocks and logs. Because of its width, Main Canyon can be an excellent place to observe one of these flash floods, provided you stay well away from the streambed and are prepared to add several hours to your trip while you wait for the waters to recede. Should these same conditions occur while you are hiking in one of the smaller canyons, immediately seek the safety of higher ground and wait out the storm. Under no circumstances should you set up camp in a narrow canyon or near a creekbed.

Continue along Main Canyon for about 1.5 miles, past a small side canyon on the left, until you reach a much larger canyon. This is Spring Canyon. At this point, you will leave the jeep road and follow the streambed of Spring Canyon and occasional horse trails for the remainder of your hike. Spring Canyon provides an amazing variety of exploration possibilities—each bend reveals some new geologic features or plant type and there is always the chance of glimpsing one of the area's wild horses before it spots you.

Shortly after entering Spring Canyon, you will encounter an area of spectacular rock pedestals. These pedestals are formed when resistant blocks of sandstone, which have fallen from the cliffs above, form a cap, preventing erosion of the soft, underlying materials. As you continue, the canyon slowly steepens until you encounter sandstone ledges which block your way. These obstacles can all be overcome with a few minutes of effort by backtracking to a point where you can climb up and around on one of the canyon slopes. In many cases, you may find a horse trail indicating the best route.

About two miles along in Spring Canyon, after passing a couple of side canyons on the left, you will come to a fork. The right fork takes you into a box canyon with some spectacular falls, a good destination for a day hike. The left fork follows Spring Canyon for another four miles to the top of the plateau. This route becomes progressively more rugged for some distance as you ascend the canyon and, in places, is quite overgrown with vegetation. However, these difficult spots are separated by enough easy stretches to make the hike enjoyable. You will be rewarded for your efforts by the continuing changes in vegetation and geologic formations and the appearance of water. You will also hear the cries of many types of raptors that nest in the upper canyons.

One particularly interesting spot is reached about .5 mile above the fork in the canyon. Here, where a side canyon enters, there is a stand of Douglas fir clinging to the shaded north-facing slope. A little farther along, if you are hiking during late spring, you may come across an equally surprising find—a few red columbines growing where water reappears in the streambed.

During the next couple of miles the canyon gradually opens into an upland area of pinyon and juniper-covered hills, benches and gullies. Go straight ahead and along the main channel until you reach a sage area and an old jeep road. You are now at the top of Spring Canyon. The ridge to the west of you can be followed in a northwesterly direction to a high point at the edge of the Book Cliffs. From here you have a spectacular view of the Grand Valley and Grand Junction below you. Southwest is Colorado National Monument and the Uncompahgre Plateau extending for many miles. To the south towers Grand Mesa and to the north are the extensive cliffs and plateaus which contain Colorado's vast deposits of oil shale. Directly below you to the south (paralleling Spring Canyon) is Coal Canyon, at whose bottom you left your car. From the high point you can return as you came or by way of Coal Canyon.

If, instead, you choose to take an alternate and longer route back or to spend an extended period exploring this fascinating area, you will need to remember a few important points. Always ascend and descend from the upland areas by way of the larger canyons near their headwaters; many of the smaller canyons end in steep drop-offs. Carry enough water for your planned trip and treat any water you may find in the canyons. The best and safest camping spots are in Main Canyon and on the upland benches. The best season to hike here is spring, when the flowers are blooming and water is available. Fall and winter are also enjoyable, but summer is too hot with too many rattlesnakes. A good topo map is essential for making an extended hike in this area.—*Peter Boddie*

HIKE 90 *NO THOROUGHFARE CANYON*

General description: A long day hike or overnighter through a beautiful canyon in Colorado National Monument.

General location: Colorado National Monument, five miles west of Grand Junction.

Maps: Colorado National Monument and Glade Park USGS quads; Park Service and Trails Illustrated Colorado National Monument maps.

Degree of difficulty: Moderate.

Length: 8.5 miles round trip.

Elevations: 5,000 to 6,800 feet.

Special attractions: Two ephemeral waterfalls; spectacular Wingate sandstone cliffs and canyons and many other interesting geologic features; semiarid desert flora and fauna.

Best season: Spring.

For more information: Colorado National Monument, Fruita, CO 81521; (303) 858-3617.

The hike: Colorado National Monument was established in 1911 in recognition of its unique geological features. The red cliffs, canyons, and monoliths of this desert area are strikingly beautiful against the green pinyon-juniper forest, and the quiet solitude of these canyons gives one ample chance to "get away from it all."

There are a number of maintained trails throughout the Monument, as well as many canyon drainages and mesas which are very hikeable, particularly from October to April. (Summer temperatures, as well as swarms of "noseeums," those irritating clouds of insects you never see cause many to avoid canyon hiking at that time.) One especially interesting unmarked trail follows the drainage of No Thoroughfare Canyon for 8.5 miles on the eastern edge of the Monument.

One access to No Thoroughfare Canyon is found at Devil's Kitchen Trail near the east entrance to the Monument, five miles west of Grand Junction. The other access is at the upper end of the canyon on Little Park Road where there is a sign and pullout. If you hike the entire canyon, you will need to shuttle a vehicle from one point to the other.

To begin your hike at the lower end of the canyon, park at the Devil's Kitchen Trailhead, follow the Devil's Kitchen Trail for about .5 mile until the trail intersects the No Thoroughfare Canyon streambed. Turn upstream and follow the drainage.

Along the streambed, dry except during spring runoff and after summer thunderstorms, there are two waterfalls that flow over the Precambrian rock of the area. The first you will come to is about 1.5 miles along and is 100 feet high. A primitive trail is seen on the right side of the canyon going up and around the waterfall. Follow this, keeping in mind that footing is hazardous in places. After reaching the top of the falls, follow the streambed again until you come to a side canyon in less than .25 mile. Take the time to explore. There is an old sheepherder's cabin immediately after the fork in the streambed and you'll discover many interesting rock formations within this extensive side canyon. There are numerous smaller waterfalls you'll need to climb

HIKE 90 *NO THOROUGHFARE CANYON*

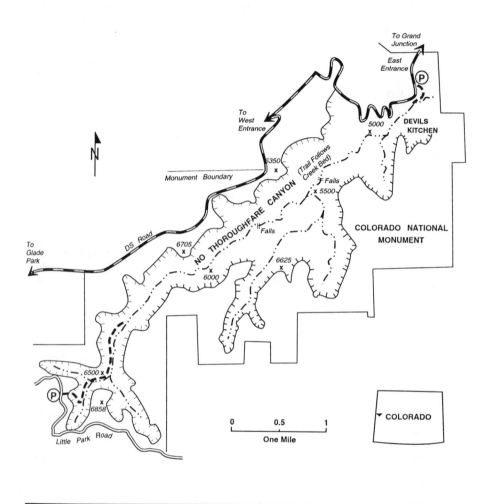

around in order to get into the upper reaches of the canyons. In the upper reaches of one of these canyons is the Monument's only stand of Douglas fir.

Back in the main drainage, you proceed about .75 mile on until you reach the 200-foot cascade. This is one of the most impressive sites in the canyon, especially when the water is really flowing. If you are day hiking, you may want to turn around here. Otherwise, you will need to backtrack until an easy slope is found (try the right side of the canyon) to climb up and around the waterfall (again, be careful of footing) and continue upstream for about two miles.

At this point, it is best to climb to the bench on the right above the stream to avoid the thick-tangled growth along the canyon bottom. The bench has waist-high (and later, in places, head-high) sagebrush and can be tick-infested during spring months.

Keep an eye out for deer in this area. A small side canyon cuts through the bench at about mile eight. Here you will need to carefully descend the eighty-foot dirt slope and climb up the other side. Further on, there is a very rough, but passable, trail that leads you out of the canyon to the trailhead on Little Park Road.

All along your hike, keep an eye on the intriguing geology surrounding you and watch for the wildlife typical of this semi-arid environment.

The hard, black crystalline metamorphic and igneous, erosion-resistant rock of the lower canyon bottom dates to the Precambrian age some 1.7 billion years ago. Towering 300 to 400 feet above this resistant layer are the Wingate sandstone cliffs, formed of windblown sand about 170 million years ago. They have weathered and continue to weather into fantastic shapes, including many alcoves and monoliths.

The reptile, animal and birdlife in the canyon is intriguing and varied: watch the stream drainage for lizards (the yellow-headed, collared lizard is most common); watch the skies for birds such as canyon wrens, rock wrens, broad-tailed and black-chinned hummingbirds, rufous-sided towhees, bushtits, titmice, blue-gray gnatcatchers, white-throated swifts, and violet-green swallows. There is a pair of golden eagles that nest in the vicinity, so you may have the opportunity to see one of them, as well. Watch also for rock squirrels, desert cotton-tails, ground squirrels, chipmunks, and mule deer, and keep an eye out for bobcat tracks.

During the spring, a profusion of wildflowers brings splashes of color to view. Three types of cactus grow here: fishhook, prickly pear, and claret cup. And sego lily, pepperweed, wild columbine, buttercup, Indian paintbrush, goldenweed, twin bladderpod, buckwheat, and many flowering shrubs bloom at nearly the same time. In the fall, the yellow flowers of rabbitbrush and broom snakeweed mixed with ocean spray, yucca and brickelia add their color to the scene.

Colorado National Monument is a little known hiking area and you will rarely meet other hikers. The beauty of the area, coupled with this solitude, will make your trip a special one. To preserve this special area and to have a safe trip, follow all Park Service regulations. Of special importance: you should register and pick up a backcountry permit (free) at the Visitor Center near the west entrance to the Monument if you'll be backpacking or if you're day hiking alone (try to avoid it); wood fires are not allowed in the Monument so you'll need a stove for backpacking; you'll also need to carry all your water.—*Beth Kaeding*

HIKE 91 *POLLOCK CANYON*

General description: A desert canyon hike in the Black Ridge Canyons Wilderness Study Area.
General location: Thirteen miles northwest of Grand Junction.
Maps: USGS Mack quad; Mesa County Map, sheet one of six.
Degree of difficulty: Moderate to difficult.

Length: Seven miles one way.

Elevations: 4,600 to 5,700 feet.

Special attractions: Varied and spectacular canyon desert country including geologic faulting and numerous arches in Rattlesnake Canyon. Wildlife including desert bighorn sheep, mountain lions, and raptors.

Best season: Spring or fall.

For more information: Bureau of Land Management, Grand Junction District Office, 764 Horizon Drive, Grand Junction, CO 81506, (303) 243-6552.

The hike: For hikers whose appetites for canyon country have been whetted through exploration of nearby Colorado National Monument, the Pollock Canyon Trail provides a glimpse of the wilderness that lies beyond the monument. Located within the Black Ridge Canyons Wilderness Study Area, an area containing six major and three minor canyon systems, some of which are only accessible from above by a steep climb down or by boat along the Colorado River below, the Pollock Canyon Trail leads you to the world's second greatest concentration of natural arches. This trail is the most accessible of all those in the Black Ridge Canyons Wilderness Study Area.

To reach the trailhead drive west from Grand Junction on Interstate 70 to the Fruita exit. Turn south on Highway 340 toward Colorado National Monument, and just after crossing the Colorado River, turn right on King's View Road. After the subdivision, bear left where the road forks and follow the signs for Pollock Canyon. In about three miles the road dips steeply down into a gully (Flume Creek) just before reaching the Colorado River. Turn left and follow this road about .3 mile up to the trailhead.

From the trailhead the Pollock Canyon Trail follows an old jeep road approximately one mile to a bench between Pollock Canyon and Flume Canyon. This part of the trail offers spectacular views of Flume Canyon and the Wingate Sandstone cliffs of Devil's Canyon near the northwest corner of Colorado National Monument.

Once on the bench, the trail intersects with another old jeep road that continues on up the bench. Stay right (west) and just past a small stock pond look for the trail as it turns north and descends a cleft in the sandstone cliffs. Below these cliffs the trail again turns west and descends in .7 mile into Pollock Canyon. From this point you have several choices. You can follow Pollock Canyon upstream and explore either the East Fork or the West Fork. In the upper part of either canyon, the streams have cut a short distance through the sedimentary rocks and into the harder Precambrian rocks. This sequence is abruptly altered where the canyons intersect an east/west fault.

Another option is to continue up Pollock Canyon only about .2 mile to where the trail climbs out to a bench on the west side. In about .7 mile the trail intersects with the Old Ute Indian Trail. Go left on this old jeep road and as you start out look for the small "Rifle Sight Arch" on the cliffs above. When this trail heads west again it climbs over a saddle, which marks the same fault encountered in upper Pollock Canyon. From this vantage point it is easy to recognize the trace of the fault to the southeast into Colorado National Monument or to the west toward Rattlesnake Canyon where it changes from faulted to folded strata.

Above the fault the trail switches back steeply to an upper bench between the Wingate Sandstone and the Entrada Sandstone formations. Look for a trail intersection just before the trail climbs the upper cliffs. From this junction

Folded and faulted strata west of Pollock Canyon.

you can head west along this bench and around the west end of the cliffs to reach the Rattlesnake Arches from below. Many good camping spots can be found along this route. Nine of the eleven arches in Rattlesnake Canyon are along the Entrada Sandstone cliffs above this bench.

If you climb up the switchbacks, you will intersect the Upper Rattlesnake Arches Trail and the Rattlesnake Arches trailhead at the end of the Black Ridge Hunter Access Road. If you have a four-wheel drive vehicle, the Black Ridge Road offers an alternative access to the Rattlesnake Canyon arches and the upper end of the Pollock Canyon Trail. The total distance between the lower Pollock Canyon trailhead and the Black Ridge trailhead is about seven miles.

As you hike, notice the pinyon-juniper about you, and watch for wildlife: deer, mountain lion, black bear in the real backcountry, lizards, golden eagles, Peregrine falcon, and other raptors.—*Peter Boddie*

HIKE 91 *POLLOCK CANYON*

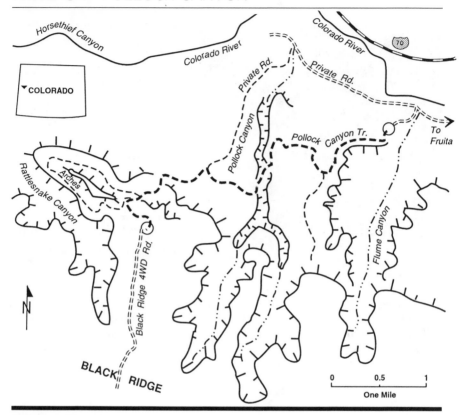

HIKE 92 *DOMINGUEZ CANYON*

General description: Off-trail day hiking or backpacking in the Dominguez Canyon Wilderness Study Area on the Uncompahgre Plateau.

General location: About twenty miles south of Grand Junction.

Maps: Bureau of Land Management Delta map; Uncompahgre National Forest Map; USGS Dominguez, Escalante Forks, Good Point, Jacks Canyon, Keith Creek, and Triangle Mesa quads.

Degree of difficulty: Moderate to difficult, depending on length of hike and route.

Length: Varies—from four to more than twenty miles possible.

Elevations: 4,800 to 8,200 feet, depending on route.

Special attractions: Extensive wilderness canyons with vegetation varying from desert to forest; interesting geology and inner canyon pools and small falls; possibility of seeing wildlife including deer, mountain lion, bobcat, and coyotes.

Best season: Spring and fall.

For more information: Bureau of Land Management, Grand Junction District Office, 764 Horizon Drive, Grand Junction, CO 81506; (303) 243-6552.

The hike: A hike into Dominguez Canyon takes you into one of the largest BLM Wilderness Study Areas in Colorado: tens of thousands of acres of mesa and dry canyon country including Big and Little Dominguez Creeks. With this extensive area, a variety of vegetation types ranging from desert to forest, and several canyon routes to explore, you could easily spend several days here.

There are three different access points into the Dominguez Canyons; Cactus Park, Dominguez Campground and Bridgeport. For day hiking and easy access, the Cactus Park trailhead would be the best choice. From that point you can easily explore either Big Dominguez or Little Dominguez Canyons. To reach the Cactus Park trailhead, drive south on US Highway 50 from Grand Junction nine miles and turn west onto Colorado Highway 141 towards Gateway and Naturita. In 9.5 miles look for a sign on the left that says Cactus Park. Turn onto that road and bear left at all forks to stay on the east side of Cactus Park. In four miles you will come to a junction. There is a sign that says Dominguez Canyon Trail. Bear right here. In another .3 mile turn left, there should be another sign for the trail here. In 1.5 miles you will reach the WSA boundary. It is two more miles to the trailhead from this point, the last 1.5 miles of which is pretty rough and may require a 4WD or high clearance vehicle.

For longer hikes or a trip along the length of Big Dominguez Canyon, you could make a car shuttle between the Bridgeport and Dominguez Campground trailheads. To reach the Dominguez Campground, take Highway 141 west and instead of turning at Cactus Park, continue on to the Divide Road. Follow southwest on the Divide Road for eight miles, then turn left on the Dominguez Conservation Area road. It is six miles on this road to the campground and the trail begins on the north side of Big Dominguez Creek. To reach the Bridgeport trailhead, take US Highway 50 south from the Grand Junction another twelve miles past the Highway 141 junction to Deer Creek Road. Take this road five miles to Bridgeport and the Gunnison River. Please note that at this writing, the Bridgeport trailhead was accessible only by boat across the

Big Dominquez Canyon from the Cactus Park trailhead.

HIKE 92 *DOMINGUEZ CANYON*

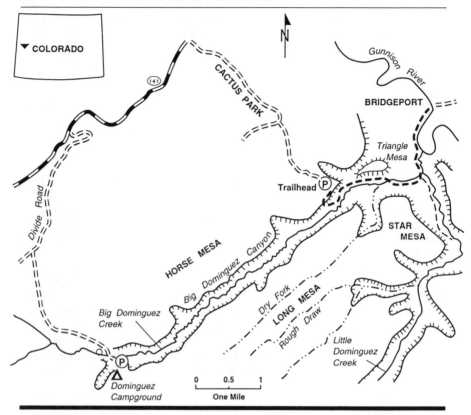

Gunnison River and then a short hike upstream to the mouth of Big Dominguez Canyon. The old bridge has been condemned and for liability reasons, the property owner does not let anyone use it, even on foot. The BLM is exploring ways to alleviate this access problem, possibly by constructing a new foot bridge or by purchasing the property and improving the existing bridge for hikers. It may be best to inquire about the status of the Bridgeport trailhead with the BLM in Grand Junction before attempting this route.

The best times to hike here are in the spring and fall to avoid the heat. Be sure to take lots of water with you along with a hat, sunscreen, and insect repellent. It would also be a good idea to take topo maps—either USGS quads or the BLM map.

From the Cactus Park trailhead, a trail goes west along the canyon rim about .8 mile before dropping some 800 feet into the canyon. At the bottom of the canyon you can go west (upstream) three to four miles to the Dominguez Campground. A good place for a rendezvous.

If you choose to go downstream in the canyon bottom, in .3 mile you will come to an old mine with a mine shaft (be sure to stay away from it for safety's safe) and a shelter in the rocks. From the mine there is a remnant of a jeep road that you can follow all the way out of the canyon to where Dry Fork and

Little Dominguez creeks join Big Dominguez Creek to flow on down to the Gunnison River at Bridgeport.

The main canyon walls along Big and Little Dominguez creeks are of Wingate sandstone while Precambrian gneiss and schist are exposed in places to form a small inner gorge. Within this inner canyon the Precambrian rocks have been eroded and polished to form lots of pools, small waterfalls and amazing rock formations.

The rims of the canyons and mesas of the area are covered with pinyon and juniper, while cottonwods and other riparian vegetation grows in the canyon bottoms. Watch for lots of wildlife in the area: deer, mountain lion, bobcat, coyotes—and many more species.

The Dominguez Canyon Wilderness Study Area is a pristine and primitive area. Hopefully, this area will be protected as wilderness. Enjoy your canyon adventure!—*Peter Boddie & Steve Adams*

HIKE 93 *INDIAN POINT*

General description: A long day hike for the ambitious hiker or an excellent overnight to the top of Grand Mesa at Indian Point.
General location: Fifteen miles southeast of Grand Junction.
Maps: Indian Point USGS quad, Trails Illustrated Grand Mesa.
Degree of difficulty: Moderate to difficult.
Length: Fifteen miles round trip.
Elevations: 6,200 to 9,996 feet.
Special attractions: Many viewpoints of the west side of the Grand Mesa, southwest Mesa County, Northwest Delta County; beautiful wildflowers and mountain meadows.
Best season: Late spring to early fall.
For more information: Grand Mesa National Forest, Collbran Ranger District, 216 High St., P.O. Box 338, Collbran, CO 81624; (303) 487-3249.

The hike: This fifteen-mile round trip along the Indian Point Trail on Grand Mesa takes you from 6,200 feet at the trailhead to the lookout point at 9,996 feet, a gain in elevation of 3,796 feet. Figure on eight to nine hours minimum walking time for the round trip.

As an alternative to such a long day hike, you can camp in the aspen groves or meadows which occupy the bench just below the rim of Grand Mesa, then, next morning, walk the remaining two miles to the point, and finally in the afternoon, make the full return trip, downhill all the way. To reach the trailhead, go thirteen miles southeast of Grand Junction on State Highways 6 and 50 to County Road #F.S. (unmarked at present). Look for the Kannah Creek Wildlife Park marker at the entrance of the road. From here, following the Kannah Creek sign where the road splits, go approximately eleven miles northeast to Kannah Creek gaging station where the Spring Camp trailhead parking lot is just beyond the bridge. This trail takes you to the start of the Indian Point Trail, approximately five miles out.

The trail quickly climbs above Kannah Creek, heading into a pine forest (with nice cool morning shade) that gradually becomes scrub oak terrain. For three miles along open hillsides (on a very gradual slope) the trail overlooks

HIKE 93 *INDIAN POINT*

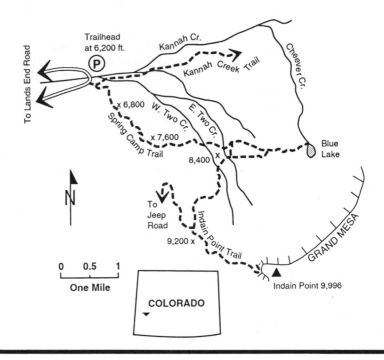

scattered meadows, the Kannah Creek Valley below, and Lands End Point above. It then goes through two separate aspen groves and crosses East Two Creeks and West Two Creeks, about .5 mile apart. As the trail goes through the second aspen grove it winds around a series of beaver ponds. A short distance from here it splits—south to the Indian Point Trail, or straight ahead (two miles) to Blue Lake.

A short distance from the forks, the trail comes into open meadows with a beautiful variety of wildflowers from early summer to early fall. If you are quiet and alert early in the morning, you may see mule deer and elk here.

There is another fork in the trail here; stay to your right and look for trail markers as you cross the meadows and through the scattered aspen groves.

Another trail merges with the Indian Point Trail about two miles along. From this point things get confusing, with forks at various points. At the first fork stay to your left, then at the second to your right over a short hill. From the top you can see the Mesa's rim where it curves around to Indian Point. Just follow the trail up to the point. From here you can enjoy a spectacular view of the Colorado and Gunnison Valleys, the Uncompahgre Plateau and the San Juan Mountains to the south.—*Steve Adams*

HIKE 94 *CRAG CREST NATIONAL RECREATION TRAIL*

General description: A day hike along a narrow, rocky ridge overlooking Grand Mesa.

General location: Atop Grand Mesa thirty miles east of Grand Junction.

Maps: Grand Mesa USGS quad (trail information not current); Grand Mesa National Forest Map, Trails Illustrated Grand Mesa.

Degree of difficulty: Moderate.

Length: A ten-mile circular loop with possibilities for shorter outings.

Elevations: 10,150 to 11,189 feet.

Special attractions: A spectacular ridgetop trail overlooking Grand Mesa, one of the largest flat top mountains in the world, and beautiful views of other mountain ranges and nearby lakes.

Best season: Late summer through early fall.

For more information: Grand Mesa National Forest, Collbran Ranger District, 216 High St., P.O. Box 338, Collbran, CO 81624; (303) 487-3249.

The hike: The Crag Crest National Recreation Trail takes you on a spectacular hike along a ridgetop from which you can view Grand Mesa, the San Juans and parts of many other mountain ranges.

There are two points of access to the trail: one at Island Lake, the other at Eggleston Lake. There are also three options with regard to the length of your hike: a ten-mile circular trip; a 6.5-mile trip from one end of the trail to the other; and a short hike in from either end after which you retrace your steps to your starting point.

To reach the Island Lake trailhead, turn off Interstate 70 and go south on Colorado Highway 65 (the junction is about twelve miles west of the exit to Debeque or seven miles east of Palisade) to Island Lake, about eight miles southeast of Mesa Lakes Resort. Watch for the sign indicating the Crag Crest parking lot just past Grand Mesa Lodge.

To reach the Eggleston Lake trailhead, continue past Island Lake and turn left on Forest Route 121 toward Ward and Alexander Lakes. Bear left at the junction you'll encounter some two miles along, continuing on toward Trickle Park and Collbran. After about one mile, look for the Crag Crest parking lot on the right. It's on the shore of Eggleston Lake a short distance past Eggleston Campground.

Although the trail occasionally crosses small streams, it is recommended that you carry water with you. In the summer you can fill your bottles at the many nearby campgrounds before setting out.

Beginning at the east end of Eggleston Lake, you will start climbing gradually through the woods to Bullfinch Lake. You will come upon a junction with another trail on the left about a hundred yards from the trailhead. This is a 3.5-mile-long connection between Island and Eggleston Lakes, and makes possible a swifter return to your starting point than would retracing your steps.

After you reach Bullfinch Lake you will go up several long switchbacks on a fairly open hillside that overlooks the lake. As you climb, more and more lakes become visible in the distance (there are hundreds of them on the mesa). Just before you reach the actual crest you will cross an open boulder field of volcanic rock from the ancient lava flow that created the cap forming the

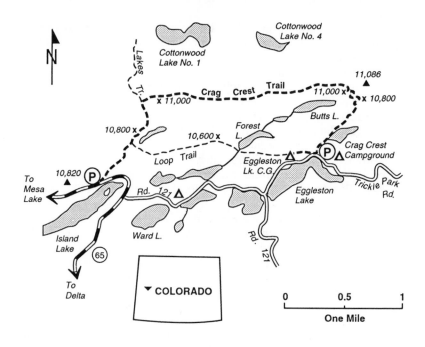

top of the mesa. From here the trail traverses a narrow ridge for over a mile with spectacular drop-offs on each side. Be sure to notice the columbines here; they seem to thrive in rocky areas.

Looking off to the north, you will see the Cottonwood Lakes area and, in the distance, the Book and Roan Cliffs and Battlement Mesa. On the south side you will see long, narrow Butts Lake just below you and the San Juan and West Elk Mountains in the distance. To the west beyond the Uncompahgre Plateau, you may be able to see the La Sal Mountains in eastern Utah.

After dropping down off the crest the trail continues through the dense spruce-fir forest for about a mile before going through an open meadow, then joins the Cottonwood Lakes Trail. The next mile to the junction with the Crag Crest Loop Trail is mostly through the forest, except for an open area on the lower switchbacks that overlooks Wolverine Lake. Upon reaching the junction with the loop trail you can either continue straight for another .5 mile to the Crag Crest parking lot above Island Lake or turn left for the 3.5 mile return trip over rolling terrain to your starting point at Eggleston Lake. This lower trail goes through woods and open hillsides from which you can see some of the lakes to the south. It joins the main trail just above the Crag Crest Campground, about 100 yards from the trailhead.

Be prepared for cool temperatures at higher elevations and stay off the crest if thunderstorms are a possibility. If you backpack, be sure to camp at least 200 feet off the trail and away from water. The fishing is good in the many lakes, which, however, are easily accessible and receive a lot of use.—*Andy Berry*

HIKE 95 *DILLON PINNACLES*

General description: An easily accessible day hike to some very interesting geologic formations in the Curecanti National Recreation Area.

General location: Twenty-one miles west of Gunnison; forty-four miles east of Montrose.

Maps: Sapinero USGS quad; Curecanti National Recreation Area Map.

Degree of difficuilty: Easy.

Length: Four miles round trip.

Elevations: 7,500 to 7,850 feet.

Special attractions: Intriguing geologic formations; beautiful views of Blue Mesa Reservoir; vegetation typical of West Slope Upper Sonoran Transition Zone.

Best season: Spring and fall.

For more information: Curecanti National Recreation Area, Box 1040, Gunnison, CO 81230; (303) 641-0407.

The hike: This easily accessible hike leads you through the sagebrush country of the Upper Sonoran Transition Zone (typical of western Colorado's plateaus) to the eroded, volcanic Dillon Pinnacles.

To reach the trailhead, drive west from Gunnison 21.3 miles on Colorado Highway 50 to the parking area and sign for the Dillon Pinnacles trailhead, located at the north end of the bridge crossing Blue Mesa Reservoir.

Begin your hike by following the well-marked trail along the northern shore of Blue Mesa Lake, the largest of three man-made lakes that make up the Curecanti National Recreation Area. Fishing in the lake is good for Kokanee salmon, rainbow, brown and Mackinaw trout. Browns and Mackinaw are especially large and catchable in May and June. You may also see shore and water birds along the lake in spring.

As you head away from the lake you will climb across open country covered with sagebrush, then drop across Dillon Gulch. Notice the vegetation change at the gulch. Cotton woods, willows, juniper and scrub oak grow near this water source.

While climbing again on the trail, take time to stop and read the signs provided at viewpoints and notice the big old Douglas firs and ponderosa pines that dot the landscape. The rocks of the Dillon Pinnacles were formed almost thirty-five million years ago during a period of volcanic activity which also formed the West Elk and San Juan mountains. Lava, mud flows and rocks from exploding volcanoes formed the breccia, a conglomerate of sharp fragments of rock cemented together, then eroded to form pinnacles.

As you near these formations you will come to a fork with a jeep road heading up Dillon Gulch. Follow the trail to the left, paralleling the pinnacles to a lookout point whith great views of these intriguing formations and the reservoir. Watch for golden and bald eagles, for red-tailed hawks, ravens

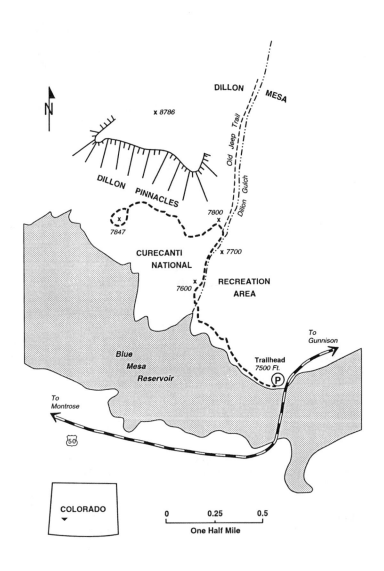

N

DILLON MESA

x *8786*

Old Jeep Trail

Dillon Gulch

DILLON PINNACLES

7800 x

x *7847*

x *7700*

CURECANTI NATIONAL

x *7600*

RECREATION AREA

To Gunnison

Blue Mesa Reservoir

Trailhead 7500 Ft.

P

To Montrose

50

COLORADO

0   0.25   0.5

One Half Mile

Dillon Pinnacles.

and magpies as you rest here. Near the lake you may spot eared grebes, seagulls, or great blue herons.

Winter brings the elk down into this country, but you are more likely to see small mammals such as chipmunks, goldenmantled ground squirrels, cottontail rabbits, marmots and prairie dogs. And it is very unlikely that you will see the bear, short-tailed weasels, coyotes, and bobcats said to live here. Try to identify the many wildflowers you'll come upon spring through fall, including Indian paintbrush, bright yellow rabbitbrush (a favorite of butterflies) and others. Be sure to take plenty of water with you on this short but interesting hike.—*Caryn, Peter, and Crystal Boddie*

HIKE 96 *CRYSTAL CREEK TRAIL*

General description: A day hike to a point overlooking Crystal Lake and the Black Canyon of the Gunnison in the Curecanti Recreation Area.
General location: Approximately sixty miles west-northwest of Gunnison.
Maps: Cimarron USGS quad; Curecanti National Recreation Area Map.
Degree of difficulty: Easy.
Length: five miles round trip.
Elevations: 8,510 to 8,894 feet.
Special attractions: Scenic views of Uncompahgre Peak, the West Elk Mountains, Poverty Mesa, Crystal Lake, and the Black Canyon of the Gunnison.
Best season: Summer and fall.
For more information: Curecanti National Recreation Area, Box 1040, Gunnison, CO 81230; (303) 641-0407.

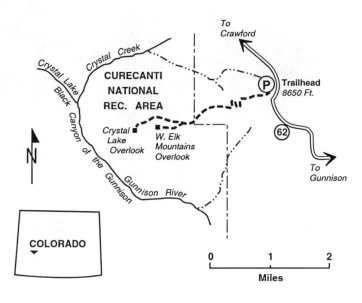

The hike: The Crystal Creek Trail, located on the western end of the Curecanti National Recreation Area, is a fairly level path through wildflowers and stands of fir and aspen to a Crystal Lake overlook on the edge of the Black Canyon of the Gunnison.

To reach the trailhead drive west from Gunnison on Colorado Highway 50 for twenty-eight miles to the junction with Colorado Highway 92. Turn right (north) on Highway 92 and follow it for 24.1 miles to the parking area and sign for the Crystal Creek Trail.

The trail starts out through an open landscape of scrub oak and sagebrush. Stroll along at a comfortable pace and frequently scan the panorama as you criss-cross back and forth with each switchback. Benches at the base of some of these switchbacks are reminders to slow down and enjoy the distant views. As you move on down the trail you will soon enter a shady tunnel of juniper and Douglas fir ascending into scrub oak, sagebrush, and the showy purple aster. You will find a stand of aspen a short distance ahead as you travel downgrade. You may see deer, coyotes, blue grouse and the golden eagle.

As you continue you'll have to overcome a fairly steep incline, but there is a breathtaking view at the end. Bear to the left where the trail splits and head towards the scenic view of the volcanic West Elk Mountains to the north. This is one of two overlooks.

Backtrack and take the right fork of the trail to the Crystal Lake overlook. On the way you will pass through an area ravaged in 1974 by a forest fire that destroyed over seventy acres. The trail ends with a bird's eye view of

Crystal Lake fifteen hundred feet below and rock spires in the upper Black Canyon of the Gunnison.

This portion of the Black Canyon was surveyed as early as 1880 in the hopes of finding a railroad route from Cimarron through the canyon. Although the route was infeasible, interest in the canyon remained high when the possibility arose to divert water through a tunnel to the Uncompahgre Valley. Such efforts set the stage for the Gunison River Diversion Project and tunnel of 1905, one of the most dramatic engineering feats of the time.

After enjoying the views, return to your starting point as you came. You may want to take advantage of the many other trails in the curecanti National Recreation Area. They are easily accessible and relatively short, and well-suited to travelers with little time and a desire to get to know this beautiful area. (See Dillon Pinnacles.)—*Elizabeth Richards*

HIKE 97 *TRANSFER TRAIL*

General description: A day hike along the Uncompahgre Plateau with access to Roubideau Canyon.
General location: Approximately fifteen miles west of Montrose.
Maps: Davis Point USGS quad; Uncompahgre National Forest Map.
Degree of difficulty: Moderate to difficult.
Length: About six miles one way.
Elevations: 7,300 to 8,600 feet.
Special attractions: Beautiful forest and meadows along the plateau; good access to Roubideau Canyon.
Best season: Spring and fall.
For more information: Uncompahgre National Forest, Ouray Ranger District, 2505 S. Townsend, Montrose, CO 81401; (303) 249-3711.

The hike: Transfer and Coal Bank Trails form a loop which traverses alternating canyons and benches on the eastern slope of the Uncompahgre Plateau. Along the way you will travel through meadows, oakbrush, aspen, spruce, fir and pine, with occasional views to the east of the canyons which dissect this plateau. From this route, you can also descend into Roubideau Canyon for a more lengthy and primitive hiking experience.

To reach the trailhead, take the Jay Jay Road west from US Highway 50 between Delta and Montrose. It becomes the Deadman's Drive. Turn right on Coal Creek Drive and, at the Coal Creek School, take a left onto Jasmine Road and then a right onto Hillside which winds around and becomes Holly. Finally turn left onto the Transfer Road and drive seven miles to the national forest boundary, then four miles farther to Oak Hill. A carved trailhead sign for the Transfer Trail stands on the right (west) side of the road in some bushes. Look carefully for it.

You will need a topographic map for this hike, which will test your orienteering abilities. This is cattle country and numerous stock trails crisscross the Transfer Trail, which begins with switchbacks into Roubideau Canyon, down the bench that was your beginning. The path is wide and free of overgrowth.

Roubideau Canyon was named after Joseph Roubideau, who explored the

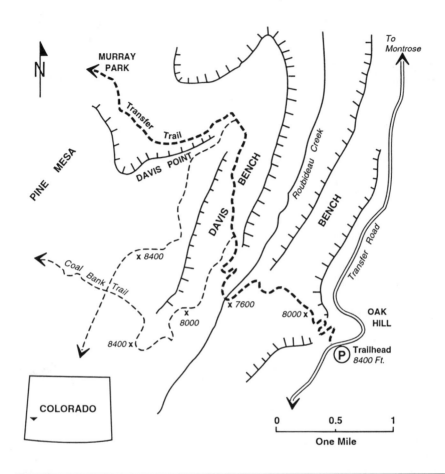

area in the early 1800s looking for beaver. Looking up and down the canyon from here, you have a full view of the surrounding area. The vegetation becomes lusher and greener upstream, close to the headwaters of Roubideau Creek. Atop the plateau flat areas of sage and grass mingle with stands of aspen, pine, fir and spruce. Downstream, the greenery gives way to exposed rocky cliffs and pinyon-juniper. Other mountain shrubbery in the area includes scrub oak, cliff rose, and many other species. In the spring many wildflowers are in bloom, starting with the delicate cactus flower and sego lilies and ending in the fall with the hardy gold rabbitbrush.

Roubideau Creek, with its headwaters near the Divide Road and Darling Lake, drains nearly straight northeast to the Gunnison River. It has sculpted this canyon, cutting through the hard caprock of Dakota sandstone atop the high plateau and down through brilliant red rock near Monitor Creek, north of the national forest boundary. Roubideau Canyon could provide a separate hike in itself, an exploration of its entire twenty-five-mile length. The deepest part of the canyon occurs about five miles downstream from the Transfer Trail. In the lower levels significant archeological finds have been made.

After entering the canyon you'll reach another bench. Stagnant water pools dot the area. The trail then develops offshoots that test your attention. The trail is vague in this area but marked by blazed posts. Keep to the right after crossing a small creek and the trail will lead you directly to Roubideau Creek. There is no bridge at the crossing but it should be no problem, except during spring runoff.

After crossing, proceed on switchbacks up the opposite side of the canyon. The trail curves to the left and becomes better defined. Here cow paths can be confusing. Maintain a northern course.

Looking ahead to your left (northwest) you will see Davis Point. Hike toward it. You will come across a refrigerator filled with salt blocks along the way—a confirmation that this is cattle country. Soon after, the trail becomes rocky and brings you through an open meadow, then through brush, and down to a small clearing with faint jeep tracks. Go left through this clearing and continue west toward the bottom of Davis Point. The jeep trail becomes more evident and rises to the top of the point as a steep and rocky road.

Here you will have a good view and find another refrigerator filled with salt blocks. The jeep trail continues through a forest of ponderosa pine, green meadows, and munching cattle. Look for the small cache of fallen logs on your left, just off the trail. There is a fresh water spring among the trunks: a good place to rest. The jeep trail continues another .25 mile to another meadow surrounded by aspen and intersects the Coal Bank Trail. The trail goes southeast through stands of aspen, then curves right to forests of juniper, pinyon and ponderosa pine.

Cattle trails once again make your way confusing, so watch for the old Coal Bank Trail signs. They are rusty and in disrepair, if even still standing, so be sure to read them correctly. Soon you will turn left off your present trail. If you go straight, you will come to a ledge with no marked trail down; to the right are only cattle trails. The main trail will skirt a swamp on the right and bring you back to the first refrigerator you discovered. You will then find your original jeep trail. Now refresh yourself and head home up the canyon; across the bench; and back up the clear, wide, rocky switchbacks to your car.

The best camping spots in this area are in Murray Park and on the flat area between the Transfer Road and Roubideau Creek. Wear blaze orange if hiking during hunting season: deer are numerous on this end of the Uncompahgre Plateau.—*Jeanne Vallez*

HIKE 98 *GUNNISON GORGE*

General description: A day hike or overnighter into the lower gorge of the Black Canyon of the Gunnison River by way of the Ute Trail.
General location: Ten miles north of Montrose.
Maps: USGS Black Ridge quad; BLM Paonia 30 x 60 minute quad; and BLM Gunnison Gorge River map.
Degree of difficulty: Easy to moderate.

Length: 4.5 miles one way.

Elevations: 6,540 to 5,300 (1,200 ft. drop).

Special attractions: Spectacular canyon and geology, camping opportunities, and gold-medal trout stream.

Best season: Spring, summer, and fall.

For more information: Bureau of Land Management, Uncompahgre Basin Resource Area, 2505 S. Townsend Ave., Montrose, CO 81401; (303) 249-7791.

The hike: The Ute Trail into the Gunnison Gorge provides for a spectacular introduction to a canyon wilderness. It has been reconstructed recently to accommodate both foot and horse travel. The Gunnison Gorge includes the lower portion of the Black Canyon of the Gunnison River below the Black Canyon of the Gunnison National Monument. This area has been proposed for Wild and Scenic River status, as a BLM Wilderness Study Area and for possible inclusion in the National Monument. The Gunnison River in this area is listed as a gold-medal trout stream and is popular for rafting and kayaking despite the fact that people must portage their crafts down to the river.

The Ute Trail descends into the canyon to Ute Park—a traditional place for Ute Indians to ford the Gunnison River and a good area to camp and fish. Although longer than some of the other access routes into the canyon, the Ute Trail has been constructed at an easier grade and provides access to a much longer stretch of the canyon bottom and adjacent bench areas.

To get to the Ute Trail, take US Highway 50 south from Delta approximately eight miles or north from Olathe approximately three miles to Carnation Road, a paved county road. Take Carnation Road east to its end at County Road 62. Turn left and follow this road north and northeast as it winds its way through the badlands located at the base of the Dakota Hogback. At the end of County Road 62 bear left on Peach Valley Road for .4 mile, and look for the sign for the Ute Trail road on the right. From this point, it is 2.5 miles on this jeep road to the trailhead at the top of the ridge. Depending on road conditions, passenger cars should be able to make it at least half that distance before drivers will need to pull off and park. With a 4WD or high clearance vehicle, you could make it all the way to the trailhead.

At the trailhead there are picnic tables and spectacular views both to the west across the Uncompahgre Valley and to the east into the Gunnison Gorge. This hogback ridge was formed by the resistant sandstone of the Dakota formation, which dips back to the west below the Uncompahgre Valley and reappears to form the broad slope of the Uncompahgre Plateau.

From the trailhead the Ute Trail descends at a gentle grade into a large amphitheater formed in the softer shales and sandstones that lie below the Dakota Sandstone. At the bottom of this amphitheater, the trail opens out onto a narrow bench separating the sandstone and shale slopes above from a precipitous drop into the gorge. This narrow bench is formed on the top of the highly resistant Precambrian rocks that give the Black Canyon its name. At one point where the trail trends north along this bench it skirts a steep gully, which drops away through the cliffs to another bench below. This is a spectacular illustration of the Ute Indian fault; the same thin veneer of Entrada sandstone on which you stand appears again about 500 to 600 feet below indicating the amount of displacement that has occurred along the fault.

After following north, the trail then turns east and descends via numerous switchbacks to the lower bench. As you begin the descent of the cliff, you

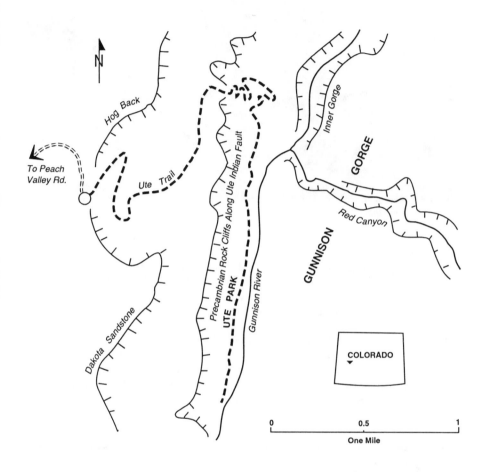

are actually crossing the Ute Indian Fault and you can easily see its north-south trace through the canyon. To the south, the steep cliffs mark the fault line to the end of Ute Park, where it crosses the Gunnison River. Beyond the river, the fault changes to the folded sedimentary rocks of a monocline. To the east the gentle dip and sequence of sedimentary rock strata are repeated and to the north the river reenters the Precambrian rocks of the lower bench to form an inner gorge.

After the trail descends to the lower bench, it turns north to Ute Park. From this point a very extensive reach of the Gunnison River is accessible for hiking, fishing and camping. It is also possible to follow the lower bench for several

Hikers descend the Ute Trail into Gunnison Gorge.

miles to the south, and even along the inner gorge for some distance, particularly at times of low flow.

At Ute Park the BLM has established three camping sites for river rafters, so that backpackers may want to look for less crowded sites back from the river or along one of the benches. If you are fishing, be sure and note the regulations and bag limits for the gold-medal trout stream which are posted at the trailhead.

Depending on river flow, it is also possible to ford the river at Ute Park (as the Utes did) and access the country on the east side of the gorge. Red Canyon looks like a particularly inviting but rugged area to explore. You may want to inquire at the BLM office in Montrose about current river conditions and upstream reservoir releases before attempting a crossing of the river.
—*Peter Boddie*

HIKE 99 *CROSS CANYON*

General description: A day hike or overnighter up cottonwood-lined Cross Canyon to explore its unique ecosystem and archaeology.

General location: Near the Utah/Colorado border in southwestern Colorado about thirty miles northwest of Cortez.

Maps: Ruin Point (showing start of hike and much of the access route into the primitive trailhead), Papoose Canyon, Ruin Canyon, and Champagne Spring USGS quads. BLM Bluff, Cortez, and Dove Creek 30x60 minute quads.

Degree of difficulty: Easy to moderate. (This trail follows an old jeep road for some distance. Then you will be on your own to orient yourself and complete your hike; so good topographic map-reading skills and orienteering skills are recommended.)

Length: Four to thirteen miles one way.

Elevations: 5,200 to 6,600 feet.

Special attractions: A unique hike accessible during dry weather year round. The hike follows a cottonwood/willow riparian area along the bottom of Cross Canyon in plateau country. During normal seasons, Cross Creek flows year round. Small cliff dwellings and ruined pueblos of the 12th and 13th century Anasazi Indians can be explored. Desert wildflowers can be found in late spring and early summer.

Best season: Early spring, late summer, and fall are best. Avoid May and June due to cedar gnats. Accessible in winter, depending on weather.

For more information: Bureau of Land Management, San Juan Resource Area, 701 Camino del Rio, Durango, CO 81301, (303) 247-4082.

The hike: This hike will give you a unique opportunity to explore the archaeology and plateau country of the Cross Canyon Wilderness Study Area in southwestern Colorado, at the northern perimeter of what was once the home of the prehistoric Anasazi Indians.

Before you go you may want to gather books on the archaeology of the Anasazi that are available in bookstores in Cortez and Durango. Also, you may want to plan to stop at the Anasazi Heritage Center museum in Dolores on your way to the trailhead and perhaps at the Lowry Ruin or Hovenweep developed interpretive sites. All will add to your appreciation of Cross Canyon.

You have a few options in terms of the length of your hike. A day hike up the canyon and back will enable you to view several archaeological sites and give you the general flavor of the canyon. You could also plan to really explore the canyon by dropping into it from the head of Cross or Ruin canyons and hiking back to the trailhead. This would require two to three days and moderate bushwhacking. It is four miles one-way from the trailhead to the confluence with Ruin Canyon; twelve miles one-way to the confluence with Cahone Canyon; and thirteen miles to the confluence with Alkalai Canyon. With added miles you can hike out Cross Canyon, Cahone Canyon, or Alkalai Canyon to US Highway 666. You will have to shuttle cars to the end of your hike (Cahone is nearby) if that is your plan.

The trailhead from which you'll start out is in a remote spot, but access by 2WD is available during most of the year. It might be more comfortable to go in a pickup or four-wheel drive.

To reach the trailhead, drive southeast from Monticello, Utah or northwest from Dolores, Colorado to Pleasant View, Colorado. Turn west on County Road CC (Pleasant Valley Road) near the radio tower. A sign here directs you to Lowry Ruin. Follow this road 5.5 miles to an intersection. Turn left here following a sign directin you to Hovenweep. (If you choose to visit Lowry Ruin before your hike, continue straight for three more miles, then backtrack to this road.) Drive twenty-four miles on the county road to the point where a small brown sign on the right side of the road directs you to "Cross Canyon" (If you choose to visit Hovenweep before your hike, continue straight for three more miles to the Ranger Station, then backtrack to this point.) Turn right and follow a seasonally-maintained road down into Cross Canyon. It is seven miles from here to the trailhead area. You are now in Utah.

Cross the creek (shallow crossing with good bottom except during flash floods) and bear right. Go up the canyon about four miles on the main road to the point where you pass through a wire gate by a sign that says "Welcome to

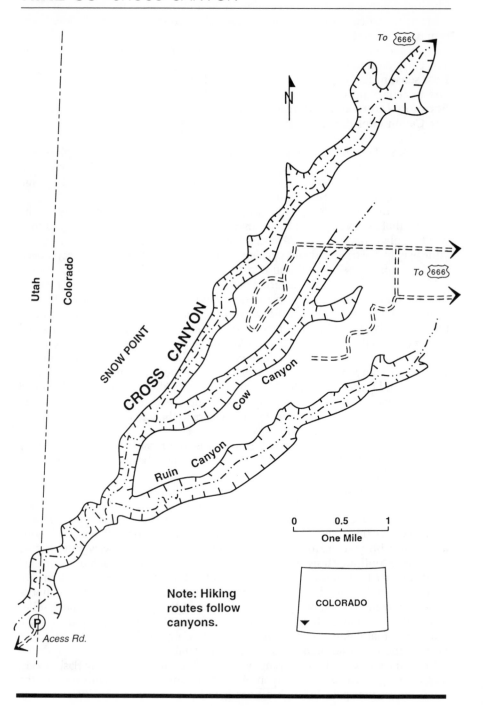

To ⟨666⟩

N

Utah

Colorado

SNOW POINT

CROSS CANYON

To ⟨666⟩

Cow Canyon

Ruin Canyon

0   0.5   1
One Mile

**Note: Hiking
routes follow
canyons.**

COLORADO

Ⓟ

Acess Rd.

Foxtail grass.

the San Juan Resource Area." Continue on beyond this sign about .5 mile to the wilderness study area boundary. Begin your hike here where a vehicle closure sign designates the WSA boundary. An old jeep trail crosses Cross Creek here and travels into Utah for a short distance before returning to Colorado.

A ruined Anasazi pueblo lies just northeast of the creek along a section of rimrock on a low ridge here. A large boulder bears several spiral petroglyphs (designs pecked into the stone surface) at this site.

Please note: The Cross Canyon Wilderness Study Area was awaiting a congressional decision as to wilderness designation at the time of this writing (1990). It was not recommended for wilderness status by the Bureau of Land Management but wilderness restrictions applied during the interim. As of this writing, camping is restricted only in archaeological or historic sites, and fires can be built if fire rings are dismantled after use.

Dead-and-down and driftwood firewood is abundant. Please use care when visiting archaeological and historic sites in this area. Feel free to pick up and look at the artifacts but put them back where you found them. Also, please report any vandalism to the BLM in Durango. Areas such as Cross Canyon are becoming more and more accessible and the BLM must rely on recreationalists as key protectors of the valuable archaeological and natural resources here.

You may continue up the canyon using the jeep route as your trail or begin exploring the canyon slopes and ridges. Binoculars are useful in spotting small cliff dwellings or granaries (walled-up areas used by the Anasazi for food storage). If you are planning overnighters you may want to hike in a couple of miles and set up a base camp, take your time, and do day hikes to visit archaeological sites and explore the canyon more closely.

Ruined pueblos can be found as sage-covered rubble mounds on the canyon floor, at the base of the canyon slopes, or on low ridges extending into the canyon from its sides. Pottery can be found at these sites and its abundance is often indicative of the length of time the Anasazi lived there. Rock art in the form of pictographs (paintings) and petroglyphs is common and can be found on cliff faces of large fall rocks low on the canyon slopes.

Beavers have set up housekeeping along Cross Creek and water is usually available year round. Be sure to purify water you use.

The trail up the lower part of Cross Canyon crosses the creek several times and wading may be necessary (an extra pair of shoes or sandals and socks may come in handy). You may notice as you walk along the creek that brush and dead vegetation can be found six to eight feet up in the cottonwood trees. It was deposited by flash flooding common in the late summer and early fall from violent thunderstorms. Watch out for flash floods when hiking and climb to safety if necessary.

If you hike to the confluence of Ruin and Cross canyons, a short hike (about .75 mile) up Ruin Canyon will enable you to visit a standing wall ruin structure just up off the canyon bottom to your right (south) where a small drainage comes down. This is a fairly massive structure and well worth the hike. If you continue up Cross Canyon past its confluence with Ruin Canyon, the canyon gets narrower and you must make your own way as there is no longer a good trail. Archaeological sites can still be found, but the farther up the canyon you go, the brushier and rockier it becomes. You can now return as you came or continue bushwhacking for nine miles up Cross Canyon and hike out Alkali Canyon about three miles to US Highway 666 about .75 mile northwest of Cahone, Colorado. Or continue up Cross Canyon to the top end onto BLM land about 2.5 miles west of Cahone. You should shuttle cars to Cahone in these cases.

Hikers who have explored Cross Canyon keep coming back—and bring their friends. You will enjoy the solitude of a lesser-known area and the sense of discovery that comes with exploring its archaeology on your own. If you are interested in making a personal contribution to the long-term protection of archaeological sites in the Cross Canyon area or other areas on BLM lands in southwestern Colorado, you may adopt an area to visit on a regular basis. Please contact the BLM in Durango and let them know you'd like to help.—*Kristie Arrington*

HIKE 100 *SAND CANYON*

General description: A day hike into sandstone canyons containing Anasazi ruins.

General location: About ten miles west of Cortez.

Maps: USGS Battle Rock and Woods Canyon quads; BLM Cortez 30 X 60 minute map.

Degree of difficulty: Easy to moderate.

Length: From one to five miles one way depending on route.

Elevations: 5,500 to 6,800 feet.

Special attractions: Spectacular sandstone canyons and slickrock with many hidden Anasazi cliff dwellings; opportunities to see wildlife; good views.

Best season: Spring and fall.

For more information: Bureau of Land Management, San Juan Resource Area, 701 Camino del Rio, Durango, CO 81301 (303) 247-4082.

The hike: Sand Canyon, west of Cortez, offers a unique opportunity to explore sandstone canyons containing many hidden Anasazi cliff dwellings. Potential routes range from easy hikes along the lower bench in Sand Canyon to more rugged excursions along the inner canyon or to the top of the mesa. Along any of the routes you can experience the intricate landscape of rocks, sand and desert vegetation little changed from the time of the Anasazi.

To reach the area go south from Cortez on US Highway 666 about 2.5 miles until you come to McElmo Canyon Road (County Road G) and signs for the airport and Hovenweep National Monument. Turn right (west). The paved road will eventually follow McElmo Canyon, which divides an area with Sleeping Ute Mountain on the south and a smaller plateau on the north into which Sand Canyon cuts. After twelve miles on McElmo Canyon Road and about 100 yards after the pavement ends, you will cross McElmo Creek. About .5 mile past that you will come to a parking area for the Sand and East Rock Canyon BLM access on the right.

From the parking area start up the bare rock to the left of a small rock outcrop or pinnacle and look for the start of an old jeep road. After you go behind the rock outcrop and cross another slickrock ledge, the old jeep trail continues to the northeast on the bench below a small sandstone cliff and enters Sand Canyon. As you hike in you may hear loud engine noises—pumps on carbon dioxide wells across Sand Canyon (The BLM expects to put mufflers on them).

From the bench at the entrance to Sand Canyon, you have several hiking options. The old jeep road which you start out on follows along the bench for about one mile and then disappears. You can continue along the bench or descend into the inner canyon, exploring the slickrock and canyon bottom in either direction, being sure to return by way of the bench (the lower canyon exits onto private land). It is also possible to hike all the way up Sand Canyon and out onto the mesa top to County Road N, a route which requires some rock scrambling. From this vantage point the panoramic view is fabulous: The Abajo Mountains to the northwest; the LaSal Mountains to the north; Lone Cone showing above the Glade Plateau to the northeast; the La Plata Mountains to the east; Point Lookout and Mesa Verde to the southeast; Sleeping Ute mountain to the south; the Chuska Mountain Range to the southwest; and Comb Ridge to the west.

Also at the top of Sand Canyon is the Sand Canyon Pueblo, one of the major archaeological sites in the area, where the Crow Canyon Archaeological Center is performing an excavation in conjunction with the BLM. For those interested in learning more about the Anasazi culture and participating in an excavation, the Crow Canyon Center offers programs. Contact: Crow Canyon Archaeological Center, 23390 County Road K, Cortez, CO 81321, (303) 565-8975.

Within Sand Canyon you will be hiking through a colorful Mesozoic cliff sequence of sandstones, shales, conglomerates of the Entrada, Summerville, Morrison, and Dakota formations. Pinon-juniper and an understory of sagebrush and grama grass on the benches and lower slopes add greens and browns to the beautiful colors of the rugged geology. Besides looking for ruins as you hike, keep an eye open for lizards, snakes, cottontail rabbits, deer, coyote, small birds and rodents, and raptors.

It should be easy for you to imagine the ancient Anasazi living in this environ-

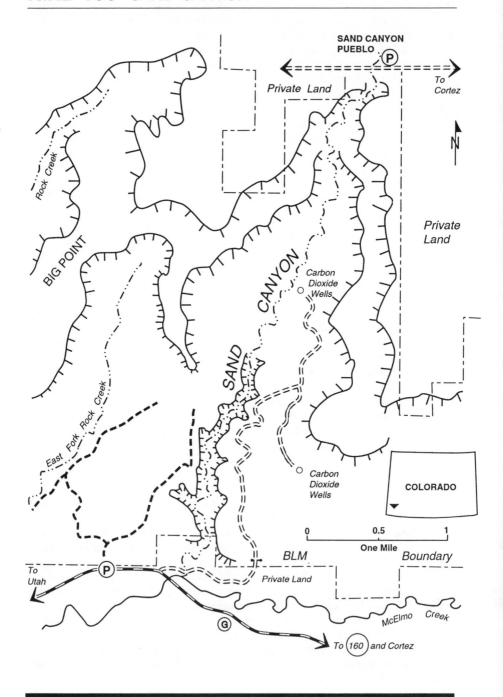

SAND CANYON PUEBLO

Private Land

To Cortez

N

Private Land

Rock Creek

BIG POINT

SAND CANYON

Carbon Dioxide Wells

East Fork Rock Creek

Carbon Dioxide Wells

COLORADO

0   0.5   1

One Mile

BLM   Boundary

Private Land

To Utah

McElmo Creek

To 160 and Cortez

Anasazi ruins in Sand Canyon.

ment. Studies have confirmed that they lived here at the same time they occupied Mesa Verde to the southeast. Indeed, Sand Canyon was a central "cradle" for the Anasazi culture in southwest Colorado throughout its development.

"Evidence of this ancient farming culture includes their physical remains, homes, kivas, towers, weapons, clothing, and utensils," according to the BLM. Recorded site data indicates that the Anasazi were in the Sand Canyon and East Rock Canyon area from what is called the Basketmaker II-Basketmaker III period (300 BC to 500 AD) during which they lived by basic horticulture and agriculture and dwelled in semi-permanent pit dwellings, through the Pueblo III period (1150 AD to 1300 AD) when the people used cliff dwellings, pottery, water control and distribution, had centralized group religious activities, and "canyonhead complexes" where larger groups of people lived. The majority of sites in Sand Canyon are of the latter period.

When visiting any of the ruins in Sand Canyon, please be aware of how fragile the structures are. Do not climb even on the rubble below the structures—that can weaken the foundations—and definitely do not climb on the walls.

It's O.K. to pick up and look at the scattered artifacts, such as pottery shards, but please replace everything just where you find it. Digging and taking home artifacts is illegal. Even changing the position of artifacts can minimize or ruin their scientific value and impair archaeologists' ability to reconstruct the prehistory of the site. In addition, please report any motor vehicles in the area, pot hunting or vandalism of sites to the county sheriff or BLM.

This is a precious area with unique and inestimable prehistoric value. The BLM has opened it to the public so that we can have a more primitive experience of the environment in which the Anasazi lived. Please protect it.—*Peter and Caryn Boddie*

APPENDIX I

Local Hiking Clubs and Conservation Organizations

Colorado Environmental Coalition
777 Grant St., Suite 606
Denver, CO 80203
(303) 837-8701

The Colorado Mountain Club
2530 West Alameda Ave.
Denver, CO 80219
(303) 922-8315

Colorado Native Plant Society (CNPS)
Eleanor Von Bargen
P.O. Box 200
Fort Collins, CO 80522
(303) 756-1400

Colorado Outward Bound School (COBS)
945 Pennsylvania St.
Denver, CO 80203
(303) 837-0880

Colorado Wildlife Federation
1560 Broadway, Suite 895
Denver, CO 80202
(303) 830-2557

Earth First! CSU
Box 708 LSC
Colorado State University
Fort Collins, CO 80523
(303) 484-8991

Environmental Defense Fund
1405 Arapahoe
Boulder, CO 80302
(303) 440-4901

High Country Citizens Alliance (HCCA)
Box 1066
Crested Butte, CO 81224
(303) 349-7104

Jefferson County Open Space Division
18301 W. 10th Ave.
Suite 100
Golden, CO 80401
(303) 278-5925

National Audubon Society
Rocky Mtn. Regional Office
4150 Darley Ave.
Boulder, CO 80303
(303) 449-0219

National Audubon Society chapters are
found in these Colorado cities, as well:

Boulder, Coaldale, Colorado Springs,
Denver, Durango, Evergreen, Fort
Collins, Glenwood Springs, Grand
Junction, Greeley, Pueblo

Nature Conservancy
1244 Pine St.
Boulder, CO 80302
(303) 444-2950

Sierra Club
Rocky Mtn. Chapter
777 Grant St. #606
Denver, CO 80203
(303) 861-8819

Sierra Club Chapters are found in
these cities, as well:

Boulder, Colorado Springs, Denver,
Dillon, Durango, Evergreen, Grand
Junction, Greeley, Parker

Volunteers for Outdoor Colorado
(VOC)
1410 Grant
Denver, CO 80203
(303) 830-7792

Wilderness Society
777 Grant St. #606
Denver, CO 80203
(303) 989-1175

APPENDIX II

Federal Land Management Agencies

Bureau of Land Management (BLM)

Colorado State Office
2850 Youngfield St.
Lakewood, CO 80215
(303) 236-1721

Canon City District Office
3170 E. Main Street
P.O. Box 311
Canon City, CO 81212
(719) 275-0631

Northeast Resource Area
Denver Federal Center
Bldg. 41, Room 129
Denver, CO 80225
(303) 236-4399

Royal Gorge Resource Area
3170 E. Main St.
P.O. Box 311
Canon City, CO 80212
(719) 275-0631

San Luis Resource Area
1921 State Street
Alamosa, CO 81101
(719) 589-4975

Craig District Office
455 Emerson, P.O. Box 248
Craig, CO 81625
(303) 824-8261

Kremmling Resource Area
1116 Park Avenue
P.O. Box 68
Kremmling, CO 80459
(303) 724-3437

Little Snake Resource Area
1280 Industrial Ave.
Craig, CO 81625
(303) 824-4441

White River Resource Area
73455 Highway 64
P.O. Box 928
Meeker, CO 81641
(303) 878-3601

Grand Junction District Office
Grand Junction Resource Area
764 Horizon Drive
Grand Junction, CO 81506
(303) 243-6552

Glenwood Springs Resource Area
P.O. Box 1009
(50629 Highways 6 & 24)
Glenwood Springs, CO 81602
(303) 945-2341

Montrose District Office
2465 South Townsend
P.O. Box 1269
Montrose, CO 81401
(303) 249-7791

Gunnison Resource Area
216 North Colorado
Gunnison, CO 81230
(303) 641-0471

San Juan Resource Area
Federal Buidling
701 Camino Del Rio
Durango, CO 81301
(303) 247-4082

Uncompahgre Resource Area
2505 S. Townsend
Montrose, CO 81401
(303) 249-7791

US Forest Service (USFS)

Rocky Mountain Region
Regional Office
11177 W. 8th Ave., P.O. Box 25127
Lakewood, CO 80225
(303) 236-9431

Arapaho and Roosevelt National Forests
Headquarters
240 West Prospect Rd.
Fort Collins, CO 80526-2098
(303) 498-1100

Boulder Ranger District
(Roosevelt)
2995 Baseline Rd., Room 110
Boulder, CO 80303
(303) 444-6001

Estes-Poudre Ranger District
(Roosevelt)
148 Remington St.
Fort Collins, CO 80524-2834
(303) 482-3822

Pawnee National Grassland
(Roosevelt)
660 "O" Street, Suite A
Greeley, CO 80631-3033
(303) 353-5004

Redfeather Ranger District
(Roosevelt)
220 East Olive
Fort Collins, CO 80524
(303) 498-1375

Clear Creek Ranger District
(Arapaho)
101 Chicago Creek
P.O. Box 3307
Idaho Springs, CO 80452
(303) 567-2901
(303) 460-0325
(Denver Metro Phone)

Dillion Ranger District
(administered by White River
    National Forest)
135 Colorado Highway 9
P.O. Box 620
Silverthorne, CO 80498
(303) 468-5400

Middle Park Ranger District
(Administered by Routt National
    Forest)
210 South 6th, P.O. Box 278
Kremmling, CO 80459-0278
(303) 724-3244

Sulphur Ranger District
(Arapaho)
62429 US Highway 40
P.O. Box 10
Granby, CO 80446-9212
(303) 887-3331

*Grand Mesa, Uncompahgre and
    Gunnison National Forests*
Headquarters
2250 Highway 50
Delta, CO 81416-8723
(303) 874-7691

Cebolla Ranger District
(Gunnison)
216 N. Colorado
Gunnison, CO 81230
(303) 641-0471

Collbran Ranger District
(Grand Mesa)
216 High St., P.O. Box 338
Collbran, CO 81624
(303) 487-3249

Grand Junction Ranger District
764 Horizon Dr.
Room 115
Grand Junction, CO 81506
(303) 242-8211

Norwood Ranger District
(Uncompahgre)
1760 East Grand Ave., P.O. Box 388
Norwood, CO 81423
(303) 327-4261

Ouray Ranger District
(Uncompahgre)
2505 S. Townsend
Montrose, CO 81401
(303) 249-3711

Paonia Ranger District
(Gunnison)
North Rio Grande St., Box 1030
Paonia, CO 81428
(303) 527-4131

Taylor Ranger District
(Gunnison)
216 N. Colorado
Gunnison, CO 81230
(303) 641-0471

Pike and San Isabel National Forests
Headquarters
1920 Valley Dr.
Pueblo, CO 81008
(719) 545-8737

Comanche National Grassland
Comanche Ranger District
(San Isabel)
27162 Highway 287, Box 127
Springfield, CO 81073
(719) 523-6591

Leadville Ranger District
(San Isabel)
2015 N. Poplar
Leadville, CO 80461
(719) 486-0752

Pikes Peak Ranger District
(Pike)
601 S. Weber St.
Colorado Springs, CO 80903
(719) 636-1602

Salida Ranger District
(San Isabel)
230 W. 16th
Salida, CO 81201
(719) 539-3591

South Park Ranger District
(Pike)
P.O. Box 218
Fairplay, CO 80440
(303) 836-2031

South Platte Ranger District
(Pike)
11177 W. 8th Ave, Box 25127
Lakewood, CO 80225
(303) 236-7386

Rio Grande National Forest
Headquarters
1803 W. Highway 160
Monte Vista, CO 81144
(719) 852-5941

Conejos Peak Ranger District
21461 State Highway 285
La Jara, CO 81140
(719) 274-5193

Creede Ranger District
3rd and Creede Ave., P.O. Box 270
Creede, CO 81130
(719) 658-2556

Del Norte Ranger District
13308 W. Highway 160
Box 40
Del Norte, CO 81132
(719) 657-3321

Sagauche Ranger District
626 Gunnison Ave.
Saguache, CO 81149
(719) 655-2553

Routt National Forest
Headquarters
29587 W. US 40
Suite 20
Steamboat Springs, CO 80487
(719) 879-1722

Bears Ears Ranger District
356 Ranney St.
Graig, CO 81625
(303) 824-9438

Hahns Peak Ranger District
57-10th St., P.O. Box 771212
Steamboat Springs, CO 80477
(303) 879-1870

North Park Ranger District
612-5th St., P.O. Box 158
Walden, CO 80480
(303) 723-4707

Yampa Ranger District
300 Roselawn, P.O. Box 7
Yampa, CO 80483
(303) 638-4516

San Juan National Forest
Headquarters
701 Camino del Rio, Room 301
Durango, CO 81301
(303) 247-4874

Animas Ranger District
110 W. 11th St.
Durango, CO 81301
(303) 247-4874

Dolores Ranger District
100 N. 6th, P.O. Box 210
Dolores, CO 81323
(303) 882-7296

Mancos Ranger District
41595 E. Highway 160, Box 330
Mancos, CO 81328
(303) 533-7716

Pagosa Ranger District
P.O. Box 310
Pagosa Springs, CO 81147
(303) 264-2268

Pine Ranger District
367 Pearl St., P.O. Box 439
Bayfield, CO 81122
(303) 884-2512

White River National Forest
Headquarters
Old Federal Bldg., 9th and Grand
P.O. Box 948
Glenwood Springs, CO 81602
(303) 945-2521

Aspen Ranger District
806 W. Hallam
Aspen, CO 81611
(303) 925-3445

Blanco Ranger District
361-7th St., P.O. Box 358
Meeker, CO 81641
(303) 878-4039

Eagle Ranger District
125 W. 5th St., P.O. Box 720
Eagle, CO 81631
(303) 328-6388

Holy Cross Ranger District
401 Main, P.O. Box 190
Minturn, CO 81645
(303) 827-5715

Rifle Ranger District
0094 County Road 244
Rifle, CO 81650
(303) 625-2371

Sopris Ranger District
620 Main, P.O. Box 309
Carbondale, CO 81623-0309
(303) 963-2266

National Park Service

Rocky Mountain Regional Office
12795 W. Alameda Pkwy.
P.O. Box 25287
Denver, CO 80225-0287
(303) 969-2000

Bent's Fort
35101 Highway 194 East
La Junta, CO 81050

Black Canyon of the Gunnison
  National Monument
P.O. Box 1648
Montrose, CO 81401

Colorado National Monument
Fruita, CO 81521

Curecanti National Recreation Area
P.O. Box 1040
Gunnison, CO 81230

Dinosaur National Monument
P.O. Box 210
Dinosaur, CO 81610

Florissant National Monument
P.O. Box 185
Florissant, CO 80816

Mesa Verde National Park
Mesa Verde National Park, CO 81330

Great Sand Dunes National
  Monument
Mosca, CO 81146

Rocky Mountain National Park
Estes Park, CO 80517

National Wildlife Refuges in Colorado

Alamosa-Monte Vista National
Wildlife Refuge Complex
Box 1148
Alamosa, CO 81101
(303) 589-4021

Arapaho National Wildlife Refuge
Box 457
Walden, CO 80480
(303) 723-4717

Browns Park National Wildlife Refuge
1318 Highway 381
Maybell, CO 81640

APPENDIX III

State Office and Land Management Agencies

Colorado Geological Survey
1313 Sherman, Room 423
Denver, CO 80203
(303) 866-3567

Department of Natural Resources
1313 Sherman St., Room 718
Denver, CO 80203
(303) 866-3311

Division of Parks and Recreation
1313 Sherman Street, Room 618
Denver, CO 80203
(303) 866-3437

State Historical Society
1300 Broadway
Denver, CO 80203
(303) 866-3682

Governor's Office
136 State Capitol Building
Denver, CO 80203
(303) 866-2471

Division of Wildlife
6060 Broadway
Denver, CO 80216
(303) 297-1192

State Climatologist, National Weather
Service
2520 Galena Street
Denver, CO 80010
(303) 837-3788

State Office of Tourism
986 State Capitol Building
Denver, CO 80203
(303) 866-2205

APPENDIX IV

Information Sources

Books

We've listed the following books because they offer added information on hiking safety and backcountry ethics, as well as giving you that in-depth look at the various regions of the state we spoke of in the introduction. Not listed below because of their sheer numbers are many interesting books available on Colorado history and natural history. Better bookstores carry them, as well as many Denver area libraries.

A Climbing Guide to Colorado's Fourteeners by W.R. Borneman and Lyndon J. Lampert. Pruett.

Aspen Snowmass Trails: A Hiking Trail Guide by Warren Olrich. W.H. Olrich.

Backwoods Ethics: Environmental Concerns for Hikers & Campers by Laura and Guy Waterman. Stone Wall Press.

Canyon Hiking Guide to the Colorado Plateau by Michael R. Kelsey. Kelsey.

Colorado's Continental Divide: A Hiking and Backpacking Guide by Ron Ruhoff. Cordillera.

Colorado Hot Springs Guide by Rick Cahill. Pruett.

Colorado's High Thirteeners: A Climbing and Hiking Guide by Mike Garratt and Bob Martin. Cordillera.

Colorado's Indian Peaks Wilderness Area: Classic Hikes and Climbs by Gerry Roach. Fulcrum.

Colorado Mountain Hikes for Everyone: Routes and Maps to 105 Named Summits by Dave Muller. Quality Press.

Colorado's Other Mountains: A Climbing Guide to Selected Peaks Under 14,000 Feet by Walter R. Borneman. Cordillera.

50 Front Range Hiking Trails: Including Rocky Mountain National Park by Richard DuMais. High Peak Pub.

80 Northern Colorado Hiking Trails by Don and Roberta Lowe. The Touchstone Press.

50 West Central Colorado Hiking Trails by Don and Roberta Lowe. The Touchstone Press.

First Aid for Backpackers & Campers by Lowell J. Thomas and Joy L. Sanderson. HR&W.

Foothills to Mount Evans: A Trail Guide by Linda Rathbun & Linda Ringrose. Wordsmiths.

Guide to the Continental Divide Trail by James R. Wolf. Mountain Press.

Hiking Trails of Central Colorado by Bob Martin. Pruett.

Hiking Trails of Northern Colorado by Mary Hagen. Pruett.

Hiking Trails of Southwestern Colorado by Paul Pixler. Pruett.

Hiking Trails of the Boulder Mountain Area by Vici DeHaan. Pruett.

Rocky Mountain Park Trails by Erik Nilsson. Anderson World Books, Inc.

Rocky Mountain Trails. Pruett.

The Colorado Trail: The Official Guide Book by Randy Jacobs. The Freesolo Press.

The Fourteeners: Colorado's Great Mountains by Perry Eberhart and Philip Schmuck. The Swallow Press Inc.

The San Juan Mountains: A Climbing and Hiking Guide by Robert F. Rosebrough. Cordillera.

The South San Juan Wilderness Area by John A. Murray. Pruett.

The Summit Hiker by Mary Ellen Gilliland. Alpenrose Press.

The Vail Hiker and Ski Touring Guide: 40 Historic Hiking and Ski Trails in Eagle County, the Holy Cross and Gore Range Wilderness by Mary Ellen Gilliland. Alpenrose.

The Wilderness Handbook by Paul Petzoldt. Norton.

Trails in Eagle County, the Holy Cross and Gore Range Wilderness by Mary Ellen Gilliland. Alpenrose.

Trails of the Front Range by Louis Kenofer. Pruett.

Walks with Nature in Rocky Mountain National Park by Kent and Donna Dannen. East Woods.

Front Range Resources

The following resources offer a variety of information to add to your enjoyment of Colorado's hiking trails. Though located in Front Range cities, they are valuable resources for people in all regions of Colorado—and to visiting hikers.

Boulder Mountain Parks
P.O. Box 791
Boulder, CO 80306
(303) 442-3408

Boulder Open Space Department
P.O. Box 791
Boulder, CO 80306
(303) 494-0436

Colorado Heritage Center
Colorado Historical Society
1300 Broadway
Denver, CO 80203
(303) 866-3682

Colorado School of Mines
 Geological Museum
16th & Maple Sts.
Golden, CO 80401
(303) 273-3823

Colorado Springs Parks and Recreation
 Department
1401 Recreation Way
Colorado Springs, CO 80905
(719) 578-6640

Denver Mountain Parks
City and County of Denver
Department of Parks and Recreation
945 S. Huron
Denver, CO 80223
(303) 698-4900

Denver Museum of Natural History
2000 Colorado Blvd.
Denver, CO 80206
(303) 370-6363

Denver Public Library
(Energy and Environmental
 Information Center, Western
 History Division, and Map
 Information Center, etc.)
1357 Broadway
Denver, CO 80203
(303) 571-2000

Fort Collins Parks and Recreation
 Department
145 E. Mountain
Fort Collins, CO 80521
(303) 484-4220

Henderson Museum
University of Colorado
Boulder, CO 80309
(303) 492-6165

Historic Denver, Inc.
Market Center
1330 17th St.
Denver, CO 80202
(303) 534-1858

Jefferson County Open Space Department
18301 W. 10th Ave.,
Suite 100
Golden, CO 80401
(303) 278-5925

Pueblo Department of Parks and Recreation
800 Goodnight Ave.
Pueblo, CO. 81005
(303) 566-1745

APPENDIX V

Finding Maps

Maps published by the United States Geological Survey (USGS), Trails Illustrated, the Bureau of Land Management (BLM) and the National Forest Service are recommended as supplements to those in this guide.

The USGS maps are detailed 7.5 and 15 minutes quads and are available from many outlets throughout the state. (See the list at the end of this section.) These topographic maps are the most detailed maps available and are recommended for more difficult hikes, particularly if you are hiking in a little-used area or off-trail.

Trails Illustrated maps are based on USGS topo maps modified by Trails Illustrated in conjunction with Forest Service and BLM personnel and other experts. These maps are printed on a 100% plastic material which is waterproof and tear resistant, which makes them easier to carry and use than USGS maps.

The Forest Service publishes maps for each of the eleven national forests and two national grasslands in Colorado. The Bureau of Land Management publishes maps, as well. They provide a general view of the area in which you'll be hiking and also show most well-marked hiking trails. These maps are available at national forest and ranger districts, BLM offices, and at many of the outlets selling USGS maps.

The National Park Service publishes maps—generally as part of a brochure—for each of the parks. Stop in at a ranger station on the way to the trailhead or call or write the regional office (see Federal Land Management Agencies, Appendix II).

The Colorado Division of Parks and Outdoor Recreation offers brochures—and sometimes maps within them—on each of the state parks (see State Offices and Land Management Agencies, Appendix III).

Many Front Range cities offer maps of their trail systems along with other information on their parks and recreation resources (see Front Range Resources Section, Appendix IV).

Trails Illustrated maps should be available at many of these outlets and may be purchased directly from the publisher. For a catalog write:

Trails Illustrated
P.O. Box 3610
Evergreen, CO 80439-3425

In addition, you may obtain a USGS map catalog and all topographic maps for the state over the counter or by mail order from:

Western Distribution Branch
US Geological Survey
Box 25286, Federal Center, Bldg. 41
Denver, CO 80225

The following are outlets through Colorado for topographic maps:

Alamosa:
  Alamosa Gems & Minerals
  Alamosa Sporting Goods
  Narrow Gauge Newsstand
  Spencer Sporting Goods

Antonito:
  Fox Creek Store

Aspen:
  Aspen Sports
  Carl's Pharmacy
  Fothergill's Outdoor Sportsman
  Timberline Book & Poster
  Ute Mountaineer
  Sport Stalker

Bailey:
  Knotty Pine Sports Center

Basalt:
  Colorado Country
  Harry's Sporting Goods

Bayfield:
  Ponderosa Shopping Center

Boulder:
  Boulder Army Store
  Boulder Bookstore
  Boulder Map Gallery
  The Boulder Mountaineer
  Colorado Book Store
  Dick's Bicycle Center
  McGuckin Hardware
  Mountain Mend
  Mountain Sports
  Neptune Mountaineering
  University Book Center

Breckenridge:
  The Knorr House
  Mountain Pride Books
  The Paper Place
  Recreation Sports
  Weber's Books & Drawings

Broomfield:
  Timely Discount Topos

Buena Vista:
  Coast to Coast Store
  The Hi-Rocky Store
  Sportsman Center
  The Trailhead
  Valley View Conoco

Canon City:
  The Book Corral
  Clarr's Photo & Ski Shop

Carbondale:
  Carbondale Drug
  High Country Sports
  Life Cycle

Castle Rock:
  Business Supplies & Services

Central City:
  The Gypsum Rose

Clark:
  The Clark Store
  Country Cupboard

Colorado Springs:
  Bear Creek Nature Center
  The Book Home
  The Chinook Bookshop
  Grand West Outfitters
  Mountain Chalet
  The Ski Haus

Conifer:
  Conifer Village Hardware

Copper Mountain:
  Christy Sports

Cortez:
  Quality Bookstore

Cotopaxi:
  Cotopaxi Store

Craig:
  Glenn's Archery Shop
  Johnson's Archery Shop
  Sportsman's Information Center

Creede:
  Ramble House
  San Juan Sports

Crested Butte:
  The Alpiner
  Flatiron Sports

Cripple Creek:
  Cripple Creek District Museum
  Golden Leaves

Del Norte:
  Kimball's Sporting Goods

Denver:
  The Colorado Mountain Club
  Colorado Outdoor Sports
  Eddie Bauer
  Gart Brothers
  Sports International
  Tattered Cover Bookstore
  Telemark Ski & Mountaineering

Dillon:
  Green Mountain Inn
  Wilderness Sports

Dolores:
  The Outfitter Sporting Goods

Durango:
  Avalanche Bookstore
  Durango Alpine Sports
  Hassle Free Sports
  Maria's Bookshop
  Outdoorsman
  Pine Needle Mountaineering

Eagle:
  Eagle Pharmacy
  Game & Fish Depot

Englewood:
  Mountain Miser
  The Prospector's Cache

Estes Park:
  Colorado Wilderness Sports
  Estes Park Hardware
  Rocky Mountain Nature Association
  Scot's Sporting Goods
  The Sport Shop
  Western Brands Outdoor World

Evergreen:
  Paragon Sports
  The Sport Mine

Fairplay:
  Crossroads
  Park County Historical Society

Fort Collins:
  Adventure Outfitters
  Al's Newsstand
  B. Dalton Bookseller
  Bighorn Sporting Goods

Fort Collins (cont.):
  The Book Train
  City News Stand
  Jax Surplus
  The Mountain Shop
  The Outpost Trading Co.
  Sports Outfitters
  Woody Newsstand

Fraser:
  Fraser Valley Ace Hardware

Frisco:
  Antlers Trading Post

Fruita:
  Colorado National Monument

Glenwood Springs:
  Army Surplus
  Eagle Eye Graphics
  Summit Canyon Mountaineering

Golden:
  Jeffco Blueprint & School Supply
  Vistabooks

Georgetown:
  Buckskin Leathers
  Museum Shop

Granby:
  Country Hardware
  Fletcher's Sporting Goods
  Rocky Mountain Outfitters

Grand Lake:
  Grand Country Sports
  Never Summer Mountain Products

Grand Junction:
  Beaver Creek Sports
  Grand River Sports
  Readmor Bookstore
  Timberline Sporting Goods
  Wapati Wilderness

Greeley:
  Aims College Bookstore
  Alpine Haus

Gunnison:
  The Book Worm
  Elmer's Sporting Goods
  Gunnison Country Times
  Berfield's Stage Stop

Howard:
 J.M. Sporting Goods

Idaho Springs:
 Area Sports

Ignacio:
 Wisemen True Value Hardware

Kremmling:
 Fishing Hole Sporting Goods
 Gambles

Lake City:
 The General Store
 The Sportsman
 Silver Spur
 The Timberline Craftsman

Lakewood:
 Christy Sports
 Map Express

La Veta
 Adobe Arch Trading Post

Leadville:
 Bill's Sport Shop
 Cass's
 Leadville Surplus
 Mountain Sports
 The Rock Hut
 Ye Olde Book & Card Shoppe

Longmont:
 City Newstand
 Sport Chalet

Loveland:
 Footnote Books
 Loveland Sport Center
 Outdoor Shop

Manitou Springs:
 Sage Mercantile

Mead:
 The Shootin' Shop

Monte Vista:
 Monte's Book Store

Montezuma:
 Inn Montezuma

Montrose:
 Adams Office Supply
 Black Canyon Center
 Jeans Westerner
 Montrose Sporting Goods

Monument:
 The Neighborhood Bookie

Nederland:
 Nederland Pit Stop

Ouray:
 Benham's Bear Creek Store
 Big Horn Mercantile
 Cabin Fever Shop
 Ouray Cottage Motel

Pagosa Springs:
 Pagosa Hardware
 Pagosa Ski Rental
 Pagosa Sports
 Pagosa Springs Trading Post
 Rocky Mountain Gifts
 Ski & Bow Rack
 Ponderosa True Value Home Center

Paonia:
 Mountain Spirit Sports
 The North Fork Times
 Rubincon Sports

Pueblo:
 Great Divide Ski, Bike & Hike
 Johnson's Sport & Ski
 Pueblo Sporting Goods

Red Feather Lakes:
 Red Feather Trading Post

Rifle:
 Buckhorn Sporting Goods
 Timberline Sporting Goods

Salida:
 Monarch Crest
 Tuttle's Trading Post

Silver Plume:
 Charring Cross Station

Silverton:
 The Prospect Hole

South Fork:
  Four Seasons Sporting Goods
  Rainbow Lodge & Grocery

Steamboat Springs:
  The Grand Tradition
  Mountain Craft
  Ski Haus International
  Straightline Products
  Steamboat Springs Sporting Goods
  Werner's Storm Hut

Tabernash:
  Nelson Fly & Tackle Shop

Telluride:
  Olympic Sports
  Telluride Sports

Vail:
  Christy Sports
  John Gault Mountaineering
  Vail Mountaineering
  West Slope Surplus

Walden:
  Sportsman's Supply

Westcliffe:
  Alpine Lodge
  Colorado Adventuring
  Valley Hardware

Winter Park:
  Enchanted Forest Bookstore
  Vasquez Sports

Yampa:
  Montgomery's General Merchandise
  The Yampa Western Store

APPENDIX VI

The Hiker's Checklist

Always make and check your own checklist!

If you've ever hiked into the backcountry and discovered that you've forgotten an "essential," you know that it's a good idea to make a checklist and check the items off as you pack so that you won't forget the things you want and need. Here are some ideas:

Clothing

_____ Dependable rain parka
_____ Rain pants
_____ Windbreaker
_____ Thermal underwear
_____ Shorts
_____ Long pants or sweatpants
_____ Wool cap or balaclava
_____ Hat
_____ Wool shirt or sweater
_____ Jacket or parka
_____ Extra socks
_____ Underwear
_____ Lightweight shirts
_____ T-shirts
_____ Bandana(s)
_____ Mittens or gloves
_____ Belt

Footwear

_____ Sturdy, comfortable boots
_____ Lightweight camp shoes

Bedding

_____ Sleeping bag
_____ Foam pad or air mattress
_____ Ground sheet (plastic or nylon)
_____ Dependable tent

Hauling

_____ Backpack and/or day pack

Cooking

_____ One-quart water container (plastic)
_____ One-gallon water container for camp use (collapsible)
_____ Backpack stove and extra fuel
_____ Funnel
_____ Aluminum foil

_____ Cooking pots
_____ Bowls/plates
_____ Utensils (spoons, forks small spatula, knife)
_____ Pot scrubber
_____ Matches in waterproof container

Food and Drink

_____ Cereal
_____ Bread
_____ Crackers
_____ Cheese
_____ Trail Mix
_____ Margarine
_____ Powdered soups
_____ Salt/pepper
_____ Main course meals
_____ Snacks
_____ Hot chocolate
_____ Tea
_____ Powdered milk
_____ Drink mixes

Photography

_____ Camera and film
_____ Filters
_____ Lens brush/paper

Miscellaneous

_____ Sunglasses
_____ Map and a compass
_____ Toilet paper
_____ Pocketknife
_____ Sunscreen
_____ Good insect repellant
_____ Lip balm

_____ Flashlight with good
batteries and a spare bulb

_____ Candle(s)

_____ First-aid kit

_____ (See section on "Backcounty
Safety")

_____ Survival kit

_____ Small garden trowel or shovel

_____ Water filter or purification tablets

_____ Plastic bags (for trash)

_____ Soap

_____ Towel

_____ Toothbrush

_____ Fishing license

_____ Fishing rod, reel, lures,
flies, etc.

_____ Binoculars

_____ Waterproof covering
for pack

_____ Watch

_____ Sewing kit

AFTERWORD *by Kirk Koepsel*

When one thinks of Colorado, it is usually of the majestic Rocky Mountains; in Colorado this range reaches its apex. The snowcapped summits of the Rockies stretch north and south across the state like a string of pearls. They have lured outdoor enthusiasts to Colorado from the time the state was first settled. However, Colorado is more than mountains—much more. The Rockies comprise just the central third of the state.

West of the mountains lie the deserts of the Colorado Plateau, famous for its slick rock canyons and roaring white water rivers.

East of the mountains is a Colorado painted with a more subtle beauty. There you'll find great open expanses of the high plains where the shortgrass prairie once supported huge herds of bison as well as the migratory Indians who followed the herds. Although the bison and Indians are gone, one can still sense the old west by hiking near and around Colorado's isolated buttes and mesas. The plains are also noted for blood-red sunsets along the almost limitless western horizon.

Caryn and Peter Boddie's book is one of the few hiking guides that provides information to the user for areas in all three regions of Colorado. Although most people come to Colorado to enjoy its mountains, the high plains and Colorado Plateau have much to offer. A hike in plains or plateau regions can be particularly rewarding in the spring, winter, and fall when the high country is snowed in.

Coloradans take great pride in the state's natural beauty. We have dedicated substantial effort and resources protecting this beauty. Two and a half million acres of land has been designated wilderness, and over a half a million acres are located in national parks and monuments throughout the state.

We have other reasons apart from the beauty of our wildlands for protecting them. Wilderness is a sort of reservoir for the diversity of the natural world, it provides clean air basins, and watershed protection, and—in Colorado—it contributes mightily to a healthy economy. Our wildlands are a major attraction, which draw people to explore the state's natural wonders and to spend over $6 billion per year in Colorado.

However, much has yet to be done to diversify our protected areas. Coloradans have tended to direct their energy at protecting the state's high country. Most of Colorado's wilderness is located in the Rocky Mountains and protects the snowcapped peaks. Little of the high plains or Colorado Plateau have been protected.

Over the past few years, we have taken an increasing interest in these regions of the state. Conservationists are currently preparing a proposal to designate 1.5 million acres of wilderness in the deserts of the Colorado Plateau. Many of the areas being considered for wilderness designation are described in this book, including the natural arches of the Black Ridge and the limestone gorge cut by the Yampa River through Cross Mountain.

Conservationists have also been busy determining what can be done to protect the high plains. We have recommended that wilderness areas be designated in the Pawnee National Grasslands. We have also been working with the Forest Service to better protect the spectacular Pawnee Buttes, the heart of those grasslands.

In the southern part of the state, our efforts have been geared toward the expansion of the Comanche National Grasslands. We hope to soon see the Purgatoire River Canyon added to the Grasslands. The canyon contains outstanding scenery, great wildlife habitat and incredible recreational opportunities. In addition, the adobe ruins of a spanish town and dinosaur tracks can also be found in the canyon.

Colorado is truly a remarkable state offering incredible diversity in landscape and year-round outdoor activities. *The Hiker's Guide to Colorado* introduces you to many facets of Colorado's natural environment. If you enjoy the areas in this book and want to make sure that people in the future have the same opportunities to enjoy them, become involved!

1. Join a grass-roots conservation organization and participate in it.
2. Become knowledgeable about the need for wilderness protection.
3. Write to your legislators. (Wilderness areas are designated by acts of Congress.)

About the Authors

Caryn and Peter Boddie live in Littleton, Colorado with their children Crystal and Robin. Peter is an hydrologist. Caryn is a writer. They are avid outdoorspeople.

The authors hiking in Scotland.